THEY FELL FROM THE SKY™

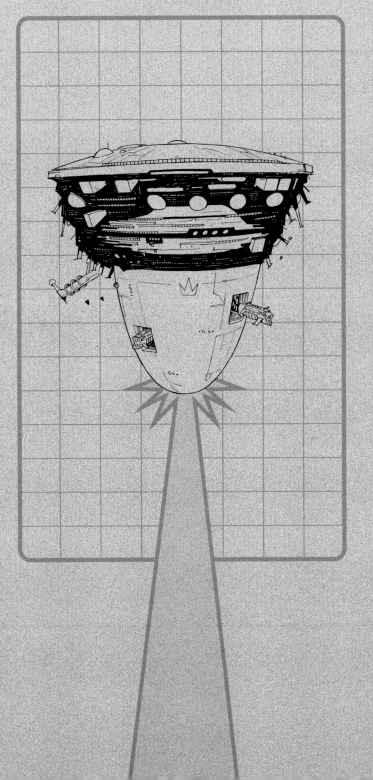

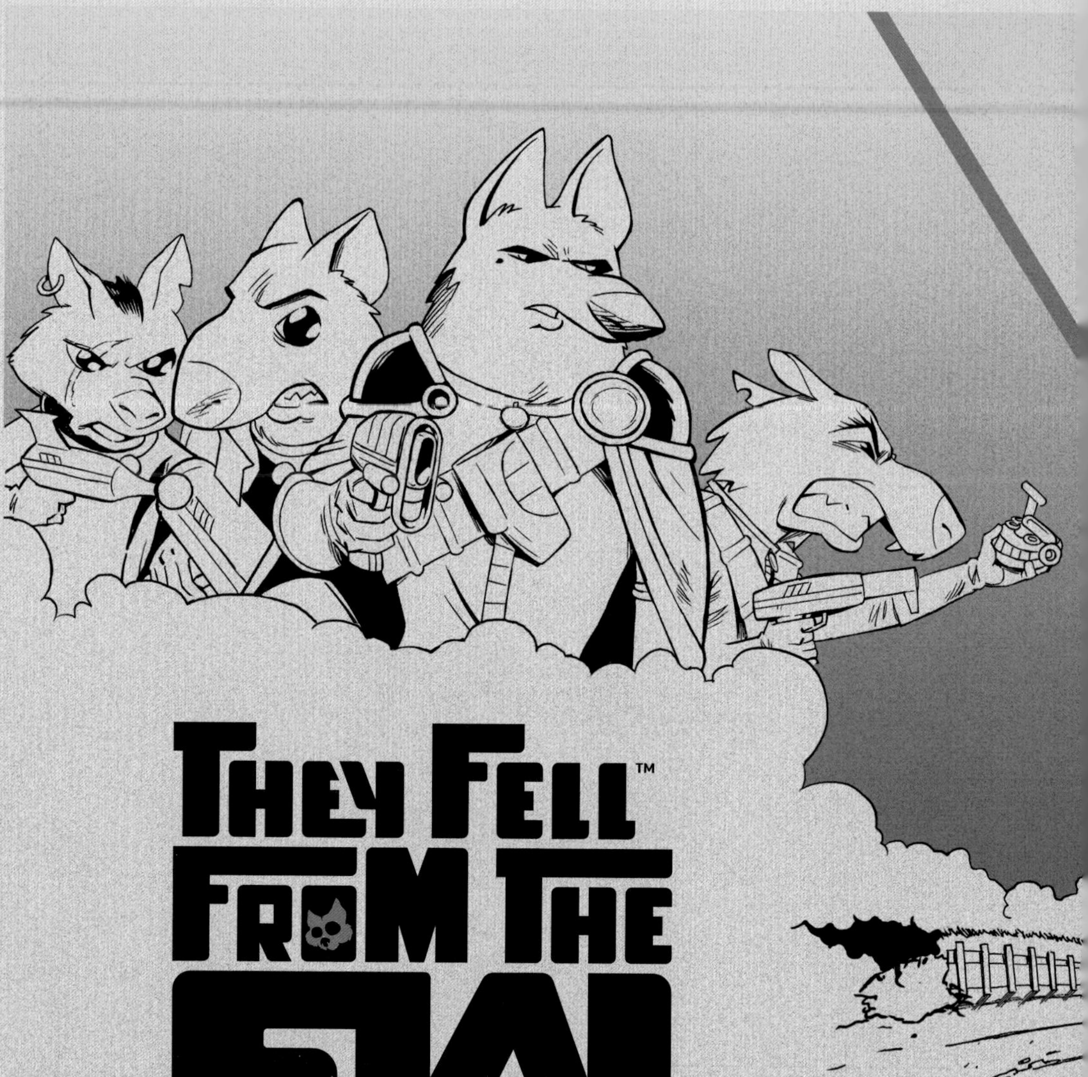

THEY FELL FROM THE SKY™

LIEZL BUENAVENTURA
WRITER

XAVIER TÁRREGA
ARTIST

BARRY HALL
COLOR ASSISTANT

CHRIS SANCHEZ
EDITOR

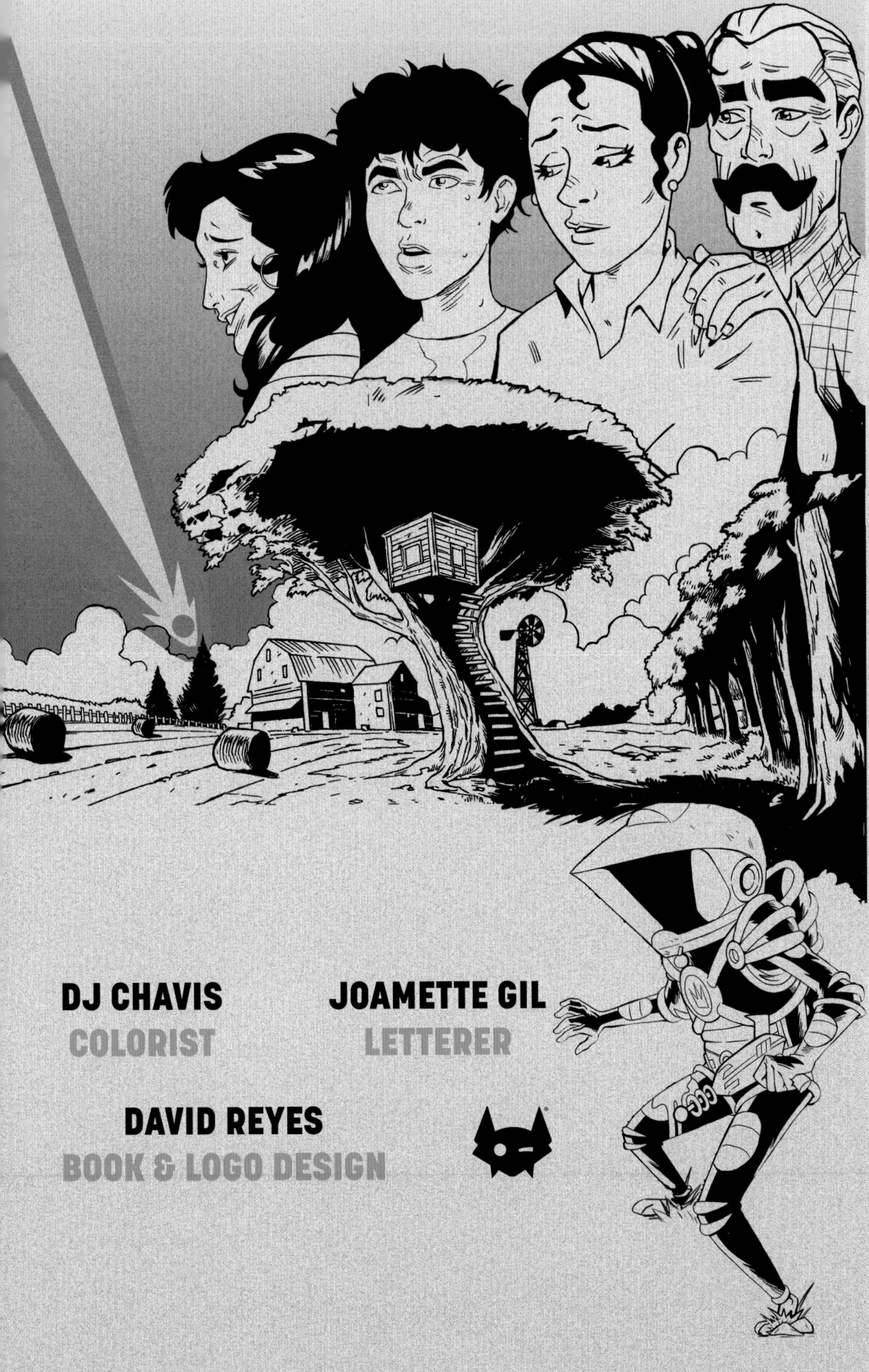

DJ CHAVIS
COLORIST

JOAMETTE GIL
LETTERER

DAVID REYES
BOOK & LOGO DESIGN

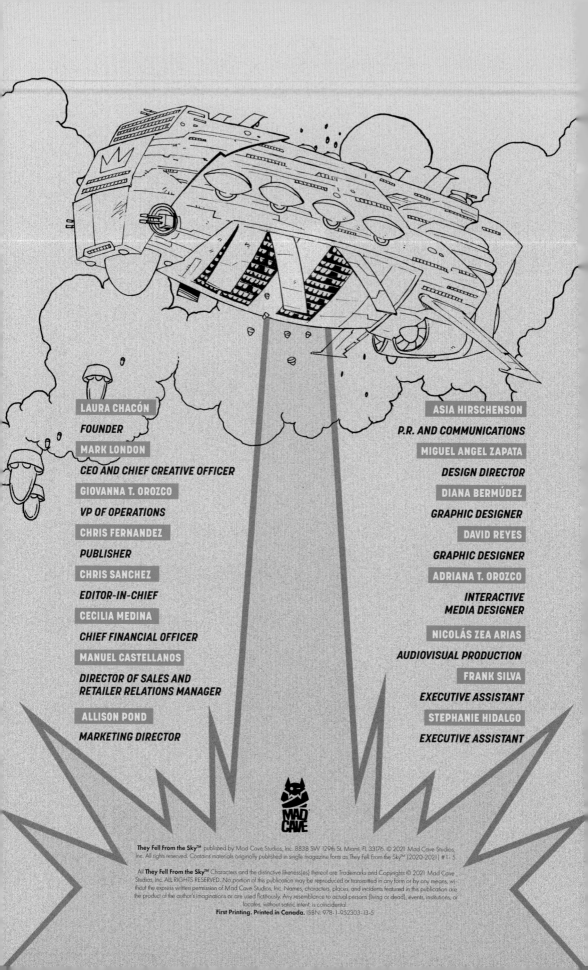

They Fell From the Sky™ published by Mad Cave Studios, Inc. 8838 SW 129th St. Miami, FL 33176. © 2021 Mad Cave Studios, Inc. All rights reserved. Contains materials originally published in single magazine form as They Fell From the Sky™ (2020-2021) #1- 5.

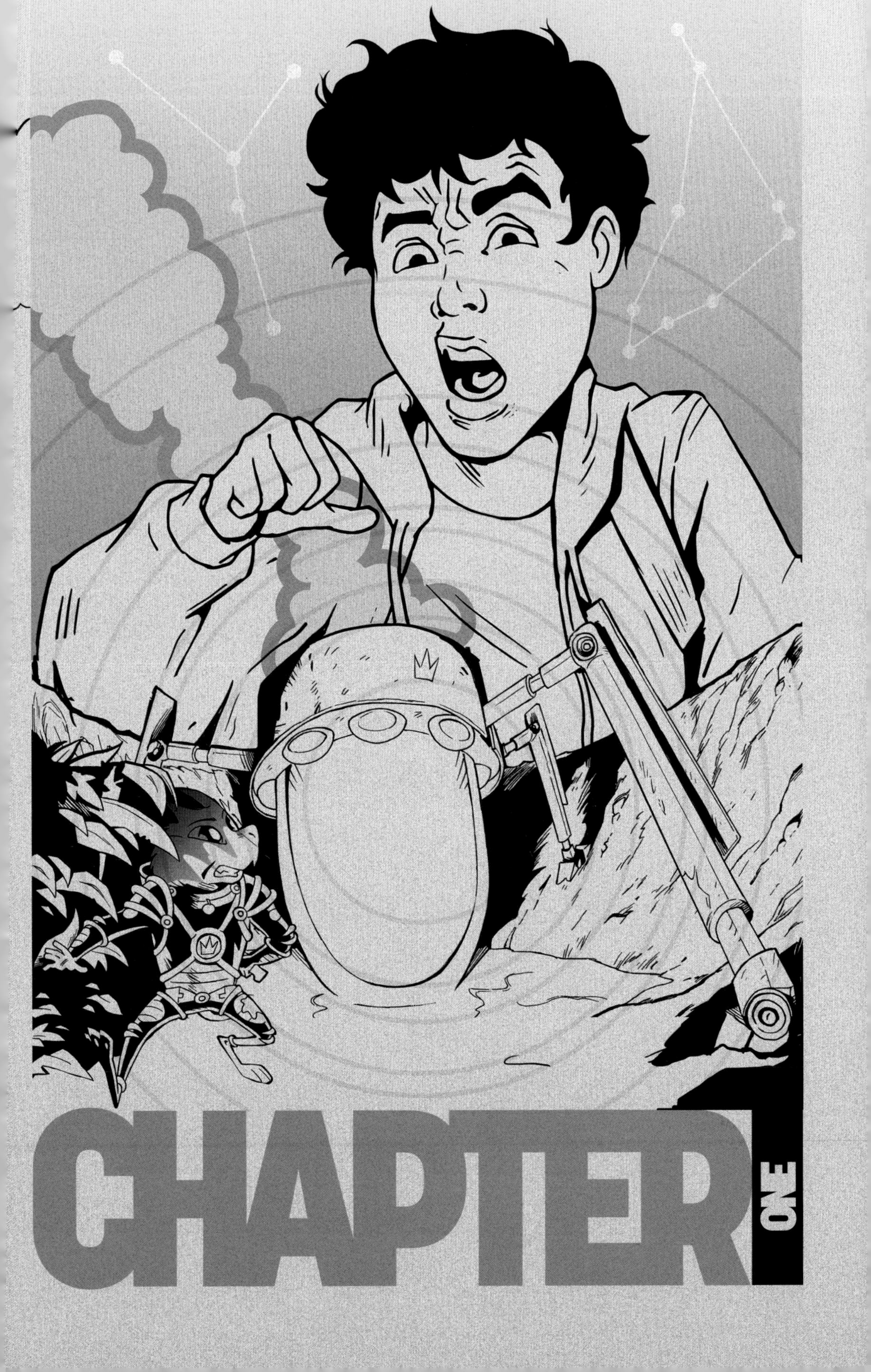

CHAPTER ONE

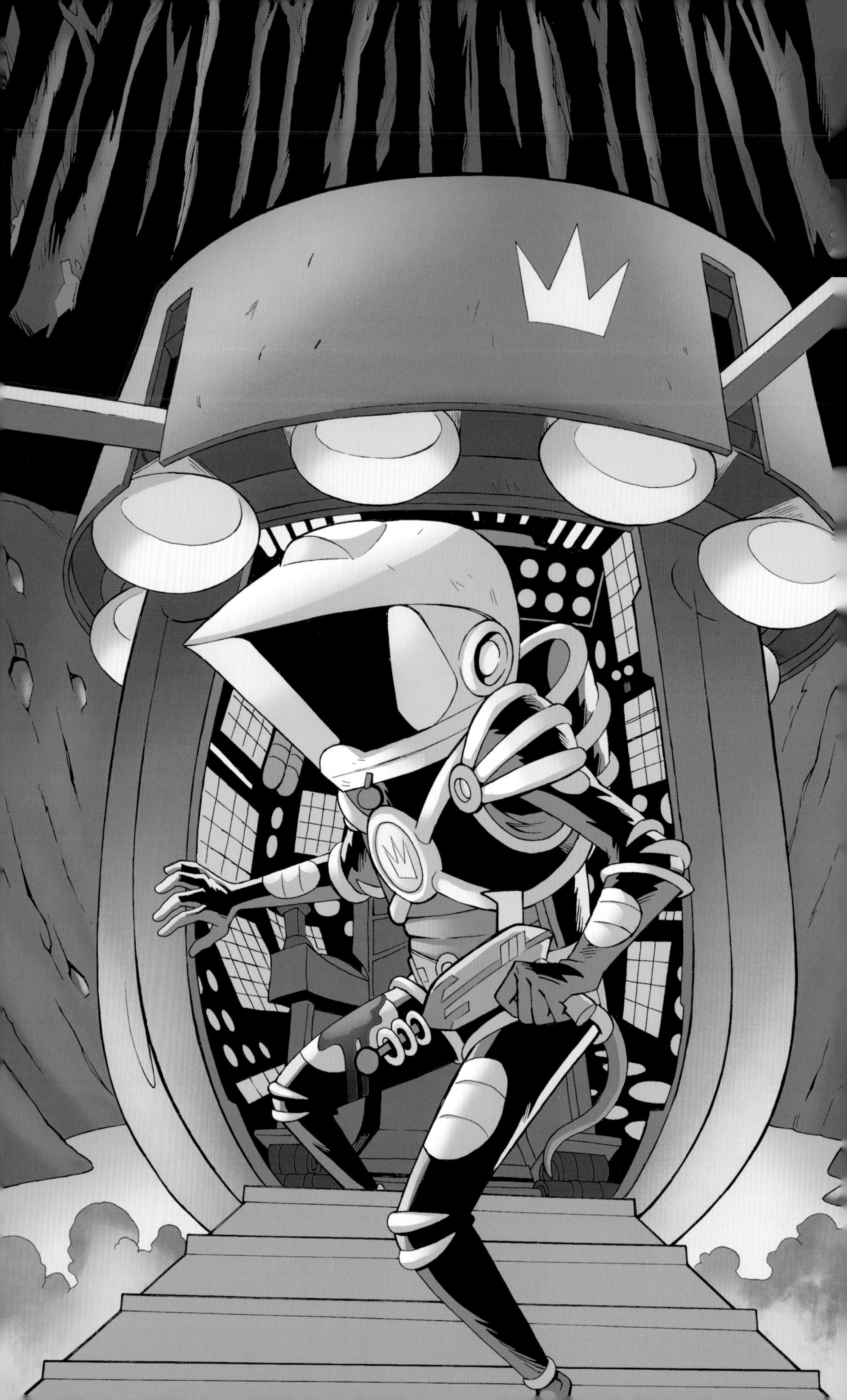

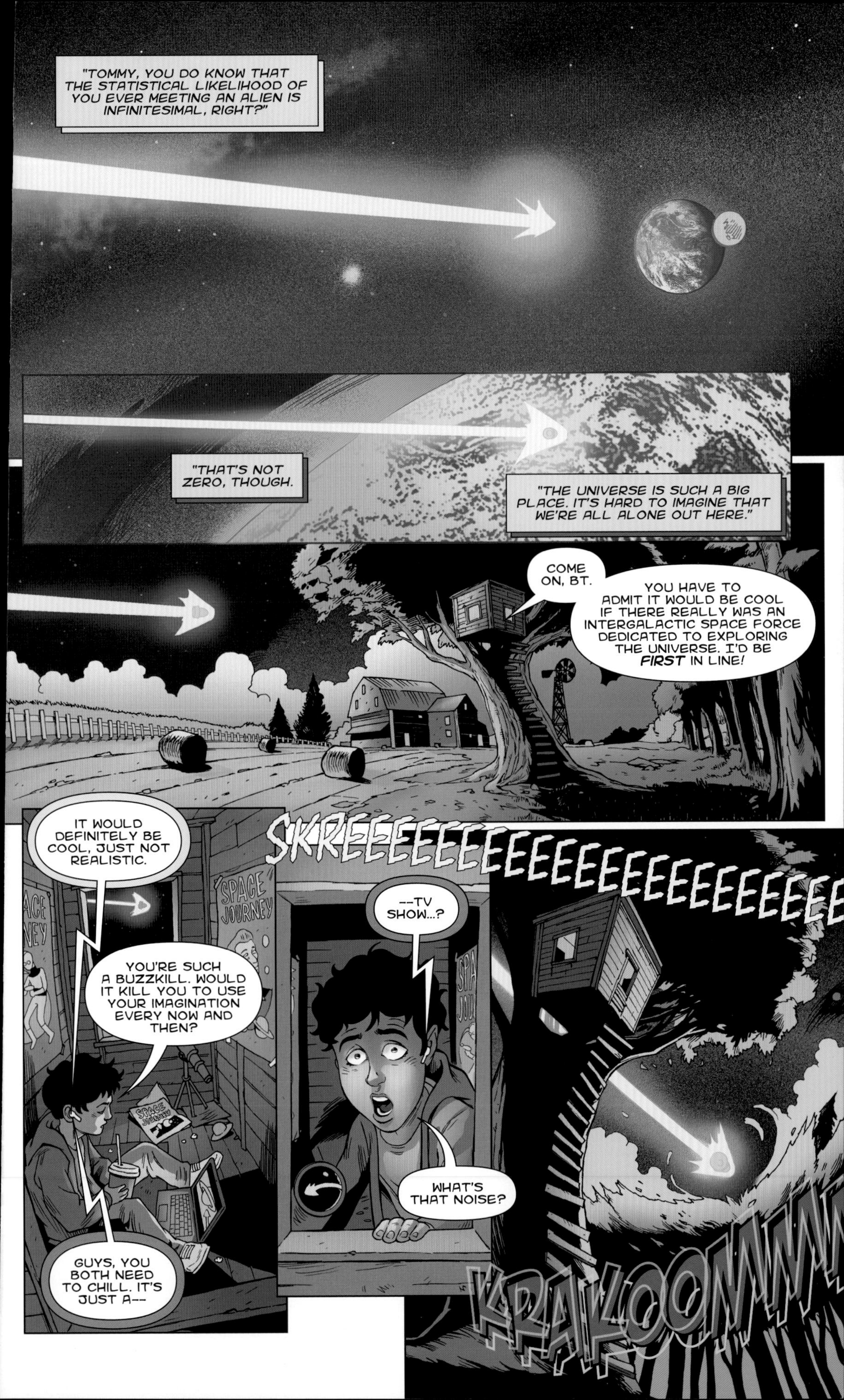

"TOMMY, YOU DO KNOW THAT THE STATISTICAL LIKELIHOOD OF YOU EVER MEETING AN ALIEN IS INFINITESIMAL, RIGHT?"
"THAT'S NOT ZERO, THOUGH.
"THE UNIVERSE IS SUCH A BIG PLACE. IT'S HARD TO IMAGINE THAT WE'RE ALL ALONE OUT HERE."
COME ON, BT.
YOU HAVE TO ADMIT IT WOULD BE COOL IF THERE REALLY WAS AN INTERGALACTIC SPACE FORCE DEDICATED TO EXPLORING THE UNIVERSE. I'D BE *FIRST* IN LINE!
IT WOULD DEFINITELY BE COOL, JUST NOT REALISTIC.
SPACE JOURNEY
YOU'RE SUCH A BUZZKILL. WOULD IT KILL YOU TO USE YOUR IMAGINATION EVERY NOW AND THEN?
SPACE JOURNEY
GUYS, YOU BOTH NEED TO CHILL. IT'S JUST A--
SKREEEEEEEEEEEEEEEEEEEEEEE
--TV SHOW...?
WHAT'S THAT NOISE?
KRAKOOMMM

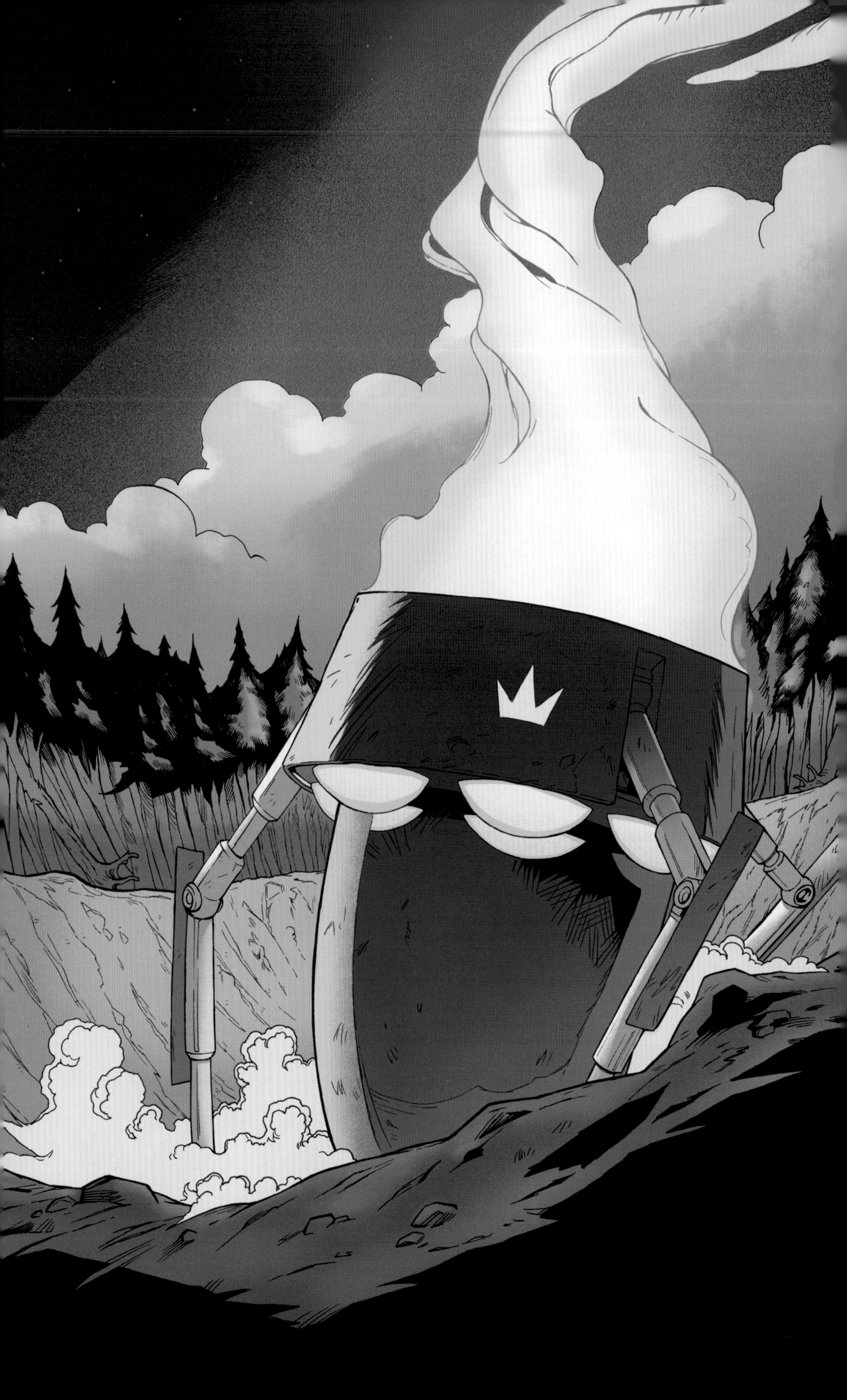

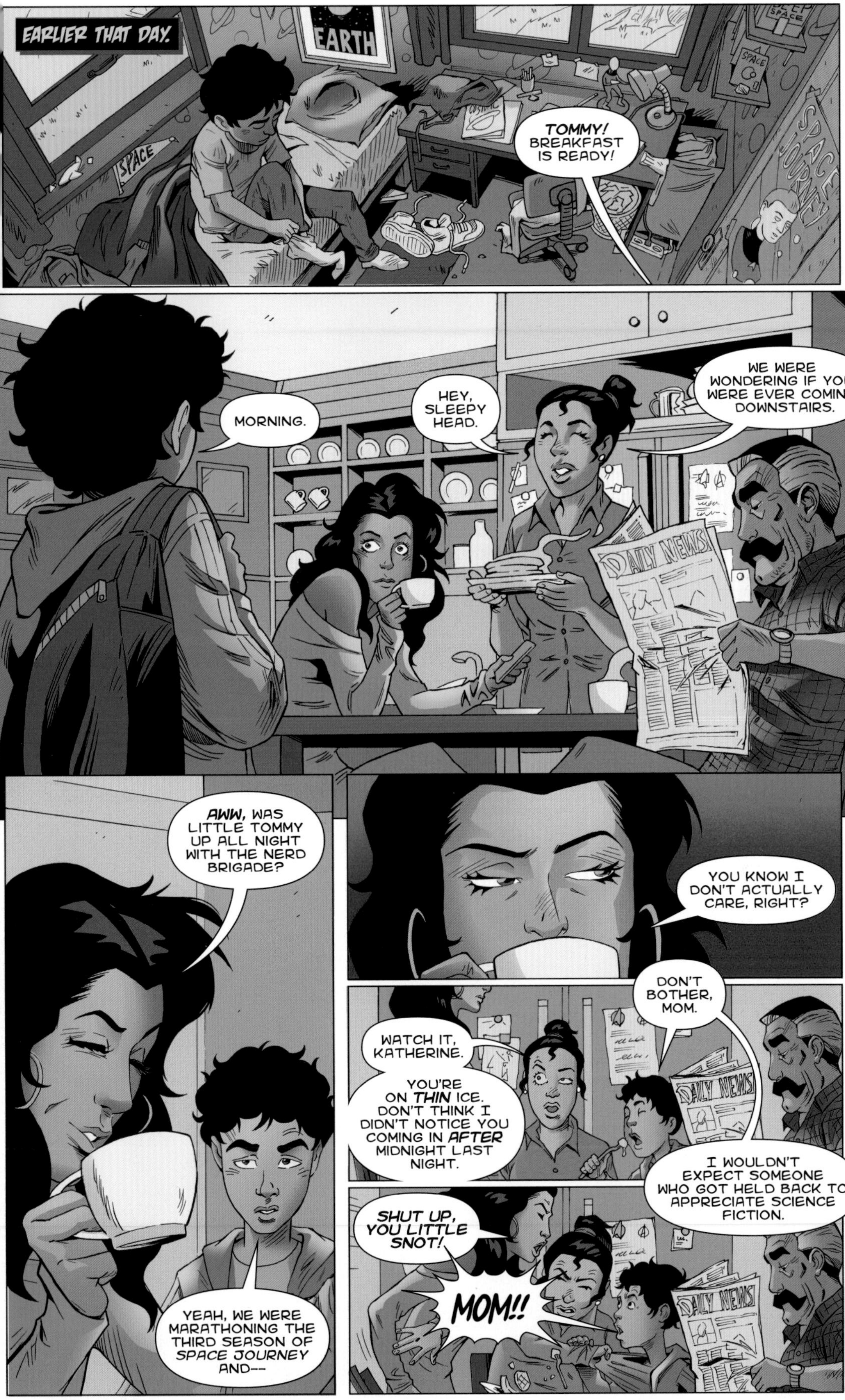
EARLIER THAT DAY.
TOMMY! BREAKFAST IS READY!
MORNING.
HEY, SLEEPY HEAD.
WE WERE WONDERING IF YOU WERE EVER COMING DOWNSTAIRS.
AWW, WAS LITTLE TOMMY UP ALL NIGHT WITH THE NERD BRIGADE?
YEAH, WE WERE MARATHONING THE THIRD SEASON OF *SPACE JOURNEY* AND--
YOU KNOW I DON'T ACTUALLY CARE, RIGHT?
WATCH IT, KATHERINE.
YOU'RE ON *THIN* ICE. DON'T THINK I DIDN'T NOTICE YOU COMING IN *AFTER* MIDNIGHT LAST NIGHT.
DON'T BOTHER, MOM.
I WOULDN'T EXPECT SOMEONE WHO GOT HELD BACK TO APPRECIATE SCIENCE FICTION.
SHUT UP, YOU LITTLE SNOT!
MOM!!

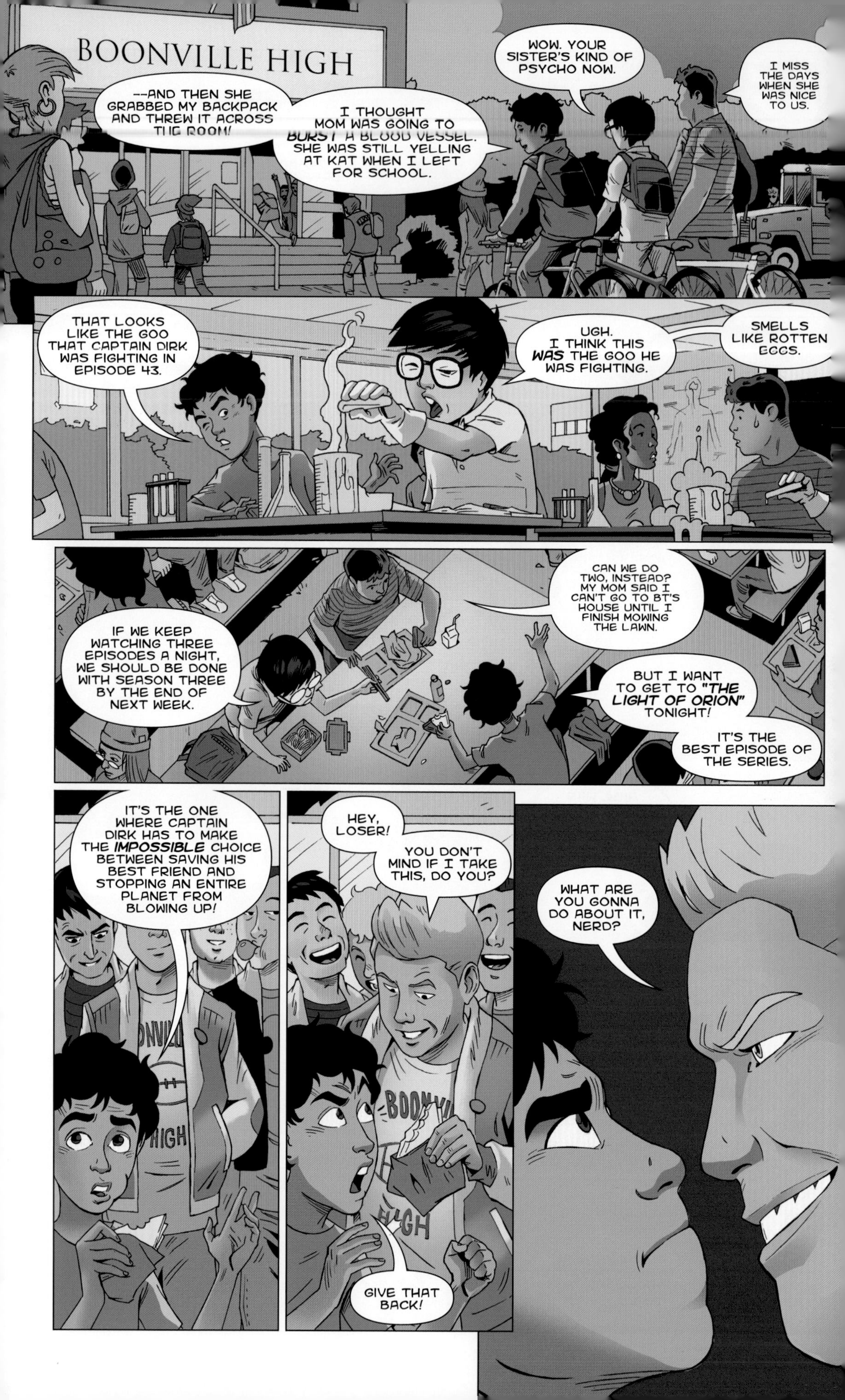
BOONVILLE HIGH
--AND THEN SHE GRABBED MY BACKPACK AND THREW IT ACROSS THE ROOM!
I THOUGHT MOM WAS GOING TO *BURST* A BLOOD VESSEL. SHE WAS STILL YELLING AT KAT WHEN I LEFT FOR SCHOOL.
WOW. YOUR SISTER'S KIND OF PSYCHO NOW.
I MISS THE DAYS WHEN SHE WAS NICE TO US.
THAT LOOKS LIKE THE GOO THAT CAPTAIN DIRK WAS FIGHTING IN EPISODE 43.
UGH. I THINK THIS **WAS** THE GOO HE WAS FIGHTING.
SMELLS LIKE ROTTEN EGGS.
IF WE KEEP WATCHING THREE EPISODES A NIGHT, WE SHOULD BE DONE WITH SEASON THREE BY THE END OF NEXT WEEK.
CAN WE DO TWO, INSTEAD? MY MOM SAID I CAN'T GO TO BT'S HOUSE UNTIL I FINISH MOWING THE LAWN.
BUT I WANT TO GET TO ***"THE LIGHT OF ORION"*** TONIGHT!
IT'S THE BEST EPISODE OF THE SERIES.
IT'S THE ONE WHERE CAPTAIN DIRK HAS TO MAKE THE ***IMPOSSIBLE*** CHOICE BETWEEN SAVING HIS BEST FRIEND AND STOPPING AN ENTIRE PLANET FROM BLOWING UP!
HEY, LOSER!
YOU DON'T MIND IF I TAKE THIS, DO YOU?
GIVE THAT BACK!
WHAT ARE YOU GONNA DO ABOUT IT, NERD?

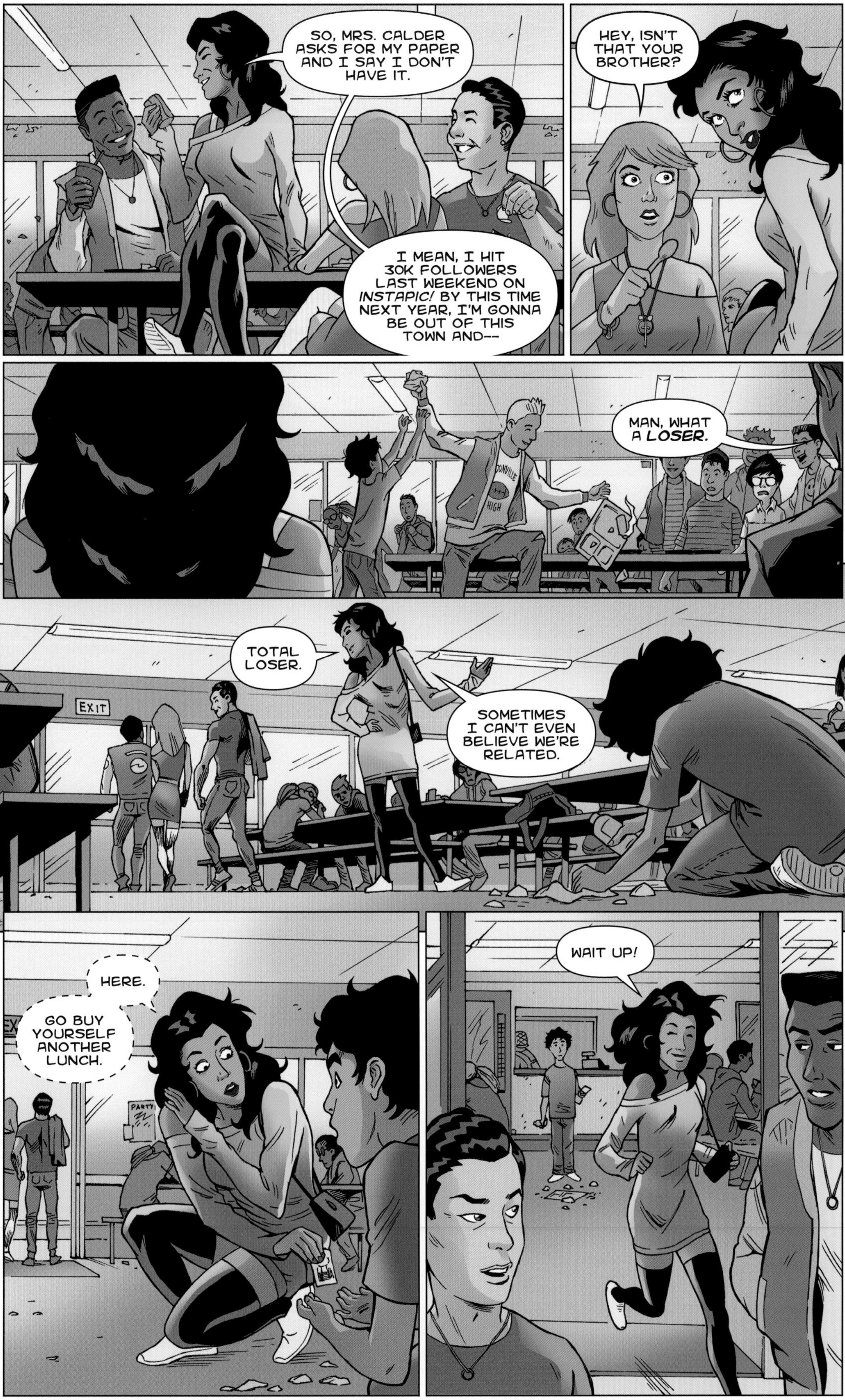
SO, MRS. CALDER ASKS FOR MY PAPER AND I SAY I DON'T HAVE IT.
I MEAN, I HIT 30K FOLLOWERS LAST WEEKEND ON *INSTAPIC!* BY THIS TIME NEXT YEAR, I'M GONNA BE OUT OF THIS TOWN AND--
HEY, ISN'T THAT YOUR BROTHER?
MAN, WHAT A **LOSER.**
TOTAL LOSER.
SOMETIMES I CAN'T EVEN BELIEVE WE'RE RELATED.
EXIT
HERE.
GO BUY YOURSELF ANOTHER LUNCH.
WAIT UP!

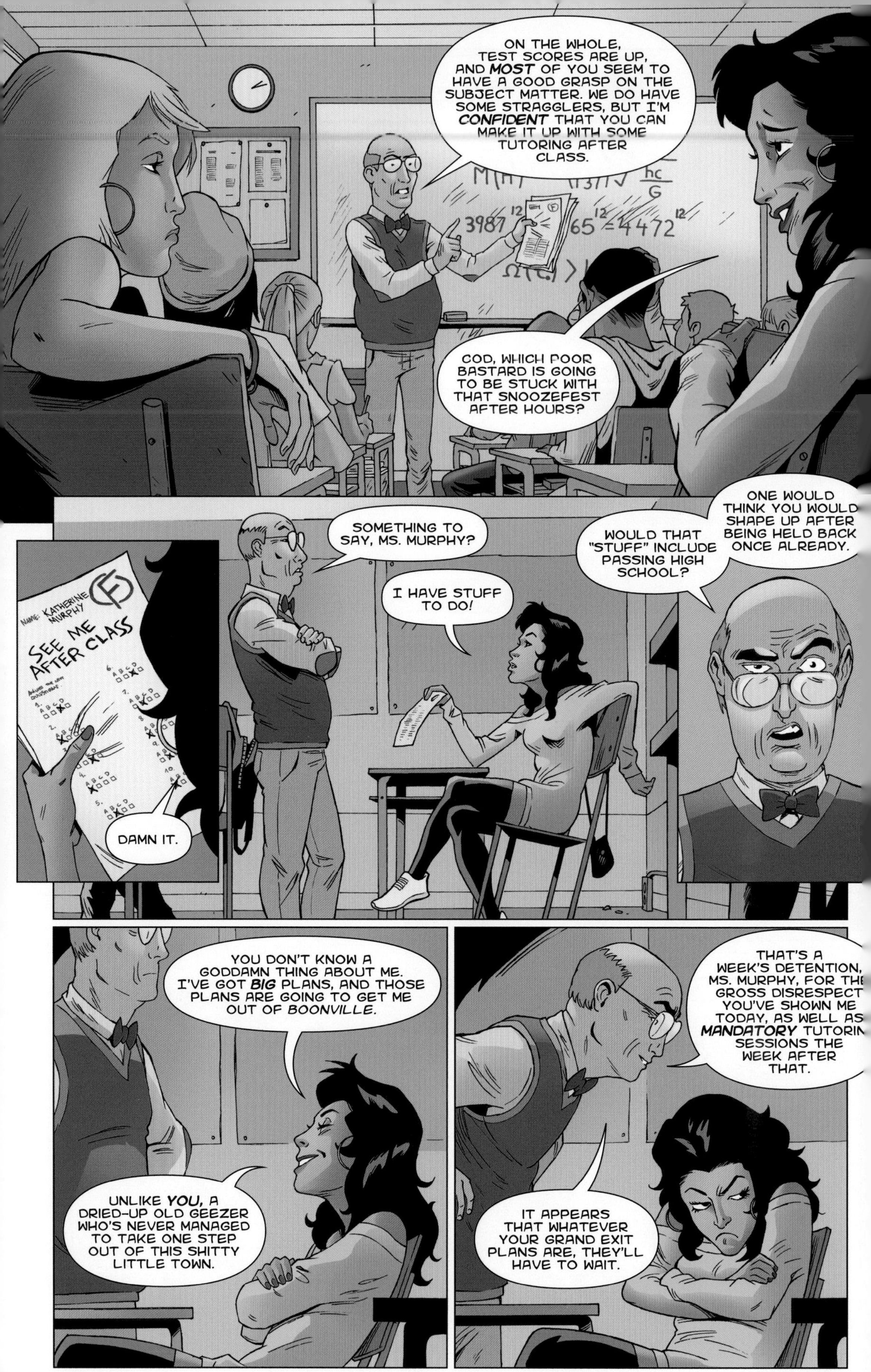
ON THE WHOLE, TEST SCORES ARE UP, AND *MOST* OF YOU SEEM TO HAVE A GOOD GRASP ON THE SUBJECT MATTER. WE DO HAVE SOME STRAGGLERS, BUT I'M *CONFIDENT* THAT YOU CAN MAKE IT UP WITH SOME TUTORING AFTER CLASS.
GOD, WHICH POOR BASTARD IS GOING TO BE STUCK WITH THAT SNOOZEFEST AFTER HOURS?
NAME: KATHERINE MURPHY
F
SEE ME AFTER CLASS
DAMN IT.
SOMETHING TO SAY, MS. MURPHY?
I HAVE STUFF TO DO!
WOULD THAT "STUFF" INCLUDE PASSING HIGH SCHOOL?
ONE WOULD THINK YOU WOULD SHAPE UP AFTER BEING HELD BACK ONCE ALREADY.
YOU DON'T KNOW A GODDAMN THING ABOUT ME. I'VE GOT *BIG* PLANS, AND THOSE PLANS ARE GOING TO GET ME OUT OF *BOONVILLE*.
UNLIKE *YOU,* A DRIED-UP OLD GEEZER WHO'S NEVER MANAGED TO TAKE ONE STEP OUT OF THIS SHITTY LITTLE TOWN.
THAT'S A WEEK'S DETENTION, MS. MURPHY, FOR THE GROSS DISRESPECT YOU'VE SHOWN ME TODAY, AS WELL AS *MANDATORY* TUTORING SESSIONS THE WEEK AFTER THAT.
IT APPEARS THAT WHATEVER YOUR GRAND EXIT PLANS ARE, THEY'LL HAVE TO WAIT.

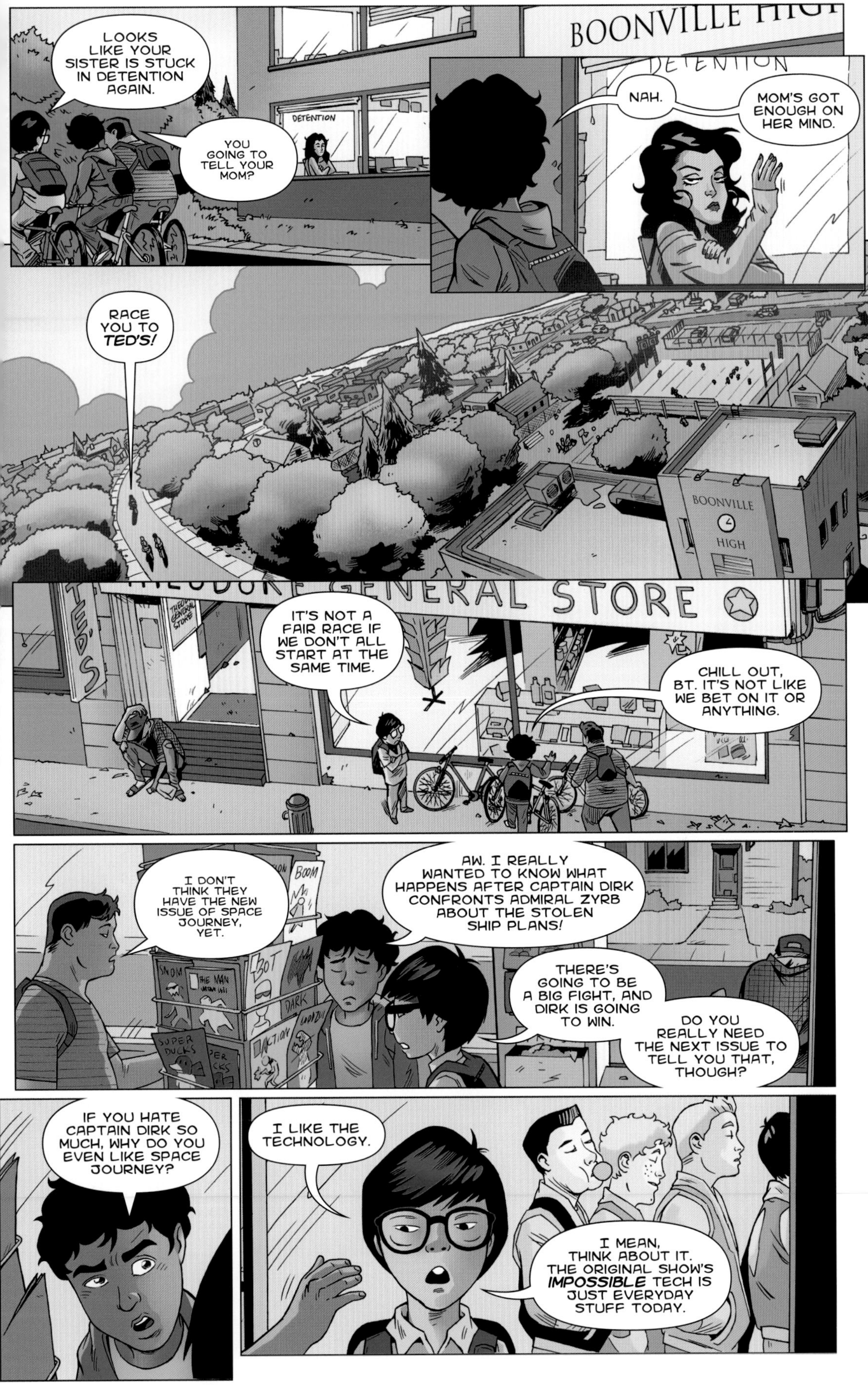
BOONVILLE HIGH
LOOKS LIKE YOUR SISTER IS STUCK IN DETENTION AGAIN.
DETENTION
YOU GOING TO TELL YOUR MOM?
DETENTION
NAH.
MOM'S GOT ENOUGH ON HER MIND.
RACE YOU TO ***TED'S!***
BOONVILLE HIGH
THEODORE GENERAL STORE
TED'S
IT'S NOT A FAIR RACE IF WE DON'T ALL START AT THE SAME TIME.
CHILL OUT, BT. IT'S NOT LIKE WE BET ON IT OR ANYTHING.
I DON'T THINK THEY HAVE THE NEW ISSUE OF SPACE JOURNEY, YET.
AW. I REALLY WANTED TO KNOW WHAT HAPPENS AFTER CAPTAIN DIRK CONFRONTS ADMIRAL ZYRB ABOUT THE STOLEN SHIP PLANS!
THERE'S GOING TO BE A BIG FIGHT, AND DIRK IS GOING TO WIN.
DO YOU REALLY NEED THE NEXT ISSUE TO TELL YOU THAT, THOUGH?
IF YOU HATE CAPTAIN DIRK SO MUCH, WHY DO YOU EVEN LIKE SPACE JOURNEY?
I LIKE THE TECHNOLOGY.
I MEAN, THINK ABOUT IT. THE ORIGINAL SHOW'S ***IMPOSSIBLE*** TECH IS JUST EVERYDAY STUFF TODAY.

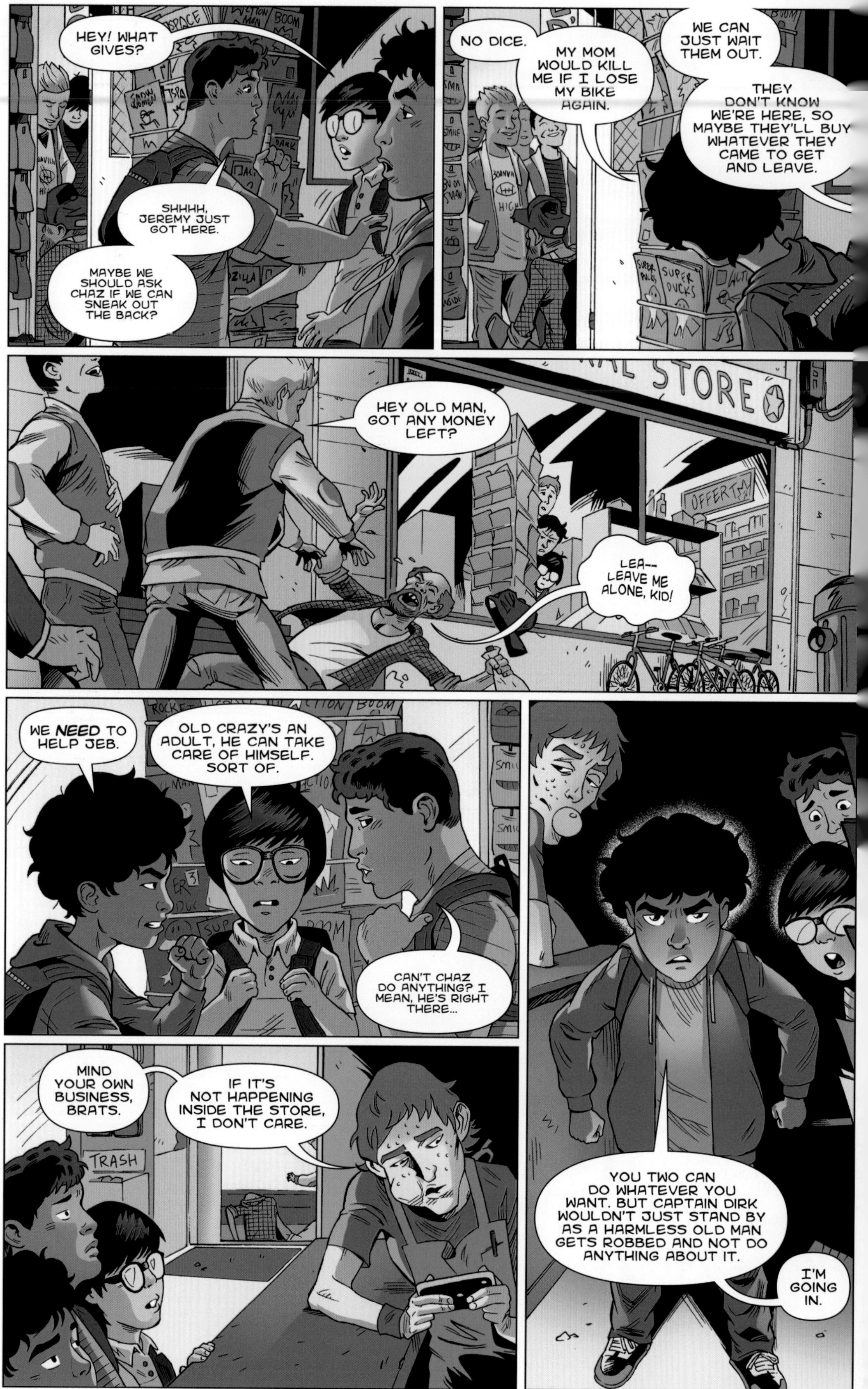
HEY! WHAT GIVES?
SHHHH, JEREMY JUST GOT HERE.
MAYBE WE SHOULD ASK CHAZ IF WE CAN SNEAK OUT THE BACK?
NO DICE.
MY MOM WOULD KILL ME IF I LOSE MY BIKE AGAIN.
WE CAN JUST WAIT THEM OUT.
THEY DON'T KNOW WE'RE HERE, SO MAYBE THEY'LL BUY WHATEVER THEY CAME TO GET AND LEAVE.
HEY OLD MAN, GOT ANY MONEY LEFT?
LEA-- LEAVE ME ALONE, KID!
WE ***NEED*** TO HELP JEB.
OLD CRAZY'S AN ADULT, HE CAN TAKE CARE OF HIMSELF. SORT OF.
CAN'T CHAZ DO ANYTHING? I MEAN, HE'S RIGHT THERE...
MIND YOUR OWN BUSINESS, BRATS.
IF IT'S NOT HAPPENING INSIDE THE STORE, I DON'T CARE.
TRASH
YOU TWO CAN DO WHATEVER YOU WANT. BUT CAPTAIN DIRK WOULDN'T JUST STAND BY AS A HARMLESS OLD MAN GETS ROBBED AND NOT DO ANYTHING ABOUT IT.
I'M GOING IN.

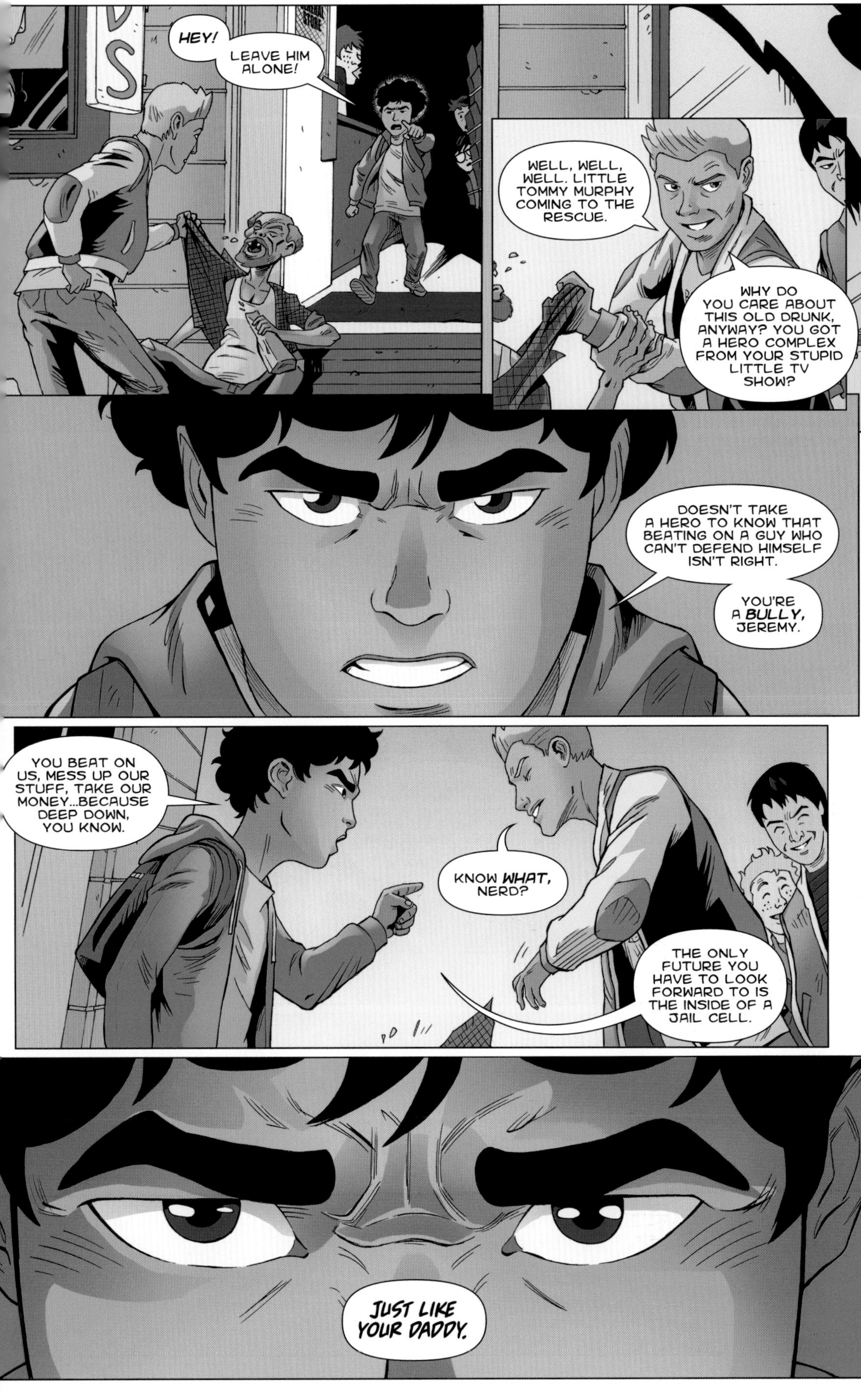
HEY!
LEAVE HIM ALONE!
GENERAL STORE
WELL, WELL, WELL. LITTLE TOMMY MURPHY COMING TO THE RESCUE.
WHY DO YOU CARE ABOUT THIS OLD DRUNK, ANYWAY? YOU GOT A HERO COMPLEX FROM YOUR STUPID LITTLE TV SHOW?
DOESN'T TAKE A HERO TO KNOW THAT BEATING ON A GUY WHO CAN'T DEFEND HIMSELF ISN'T RIGHT.
YOU'RE A **BULLY,** JEREMY.
YOU BEAT ON US, MESS UP OUR STUFF, TAKE OUR MONEY...BECAUSE DEEP DOWN, YOU KNOW.
KNOW **WHAT,** NERD?
THE ONLY FUTURE YOU HAVE TO LOOK FORWARD TO IS THE INSIDE OF A JAIL CELL.
JUST LIKE YOUR DADDY.

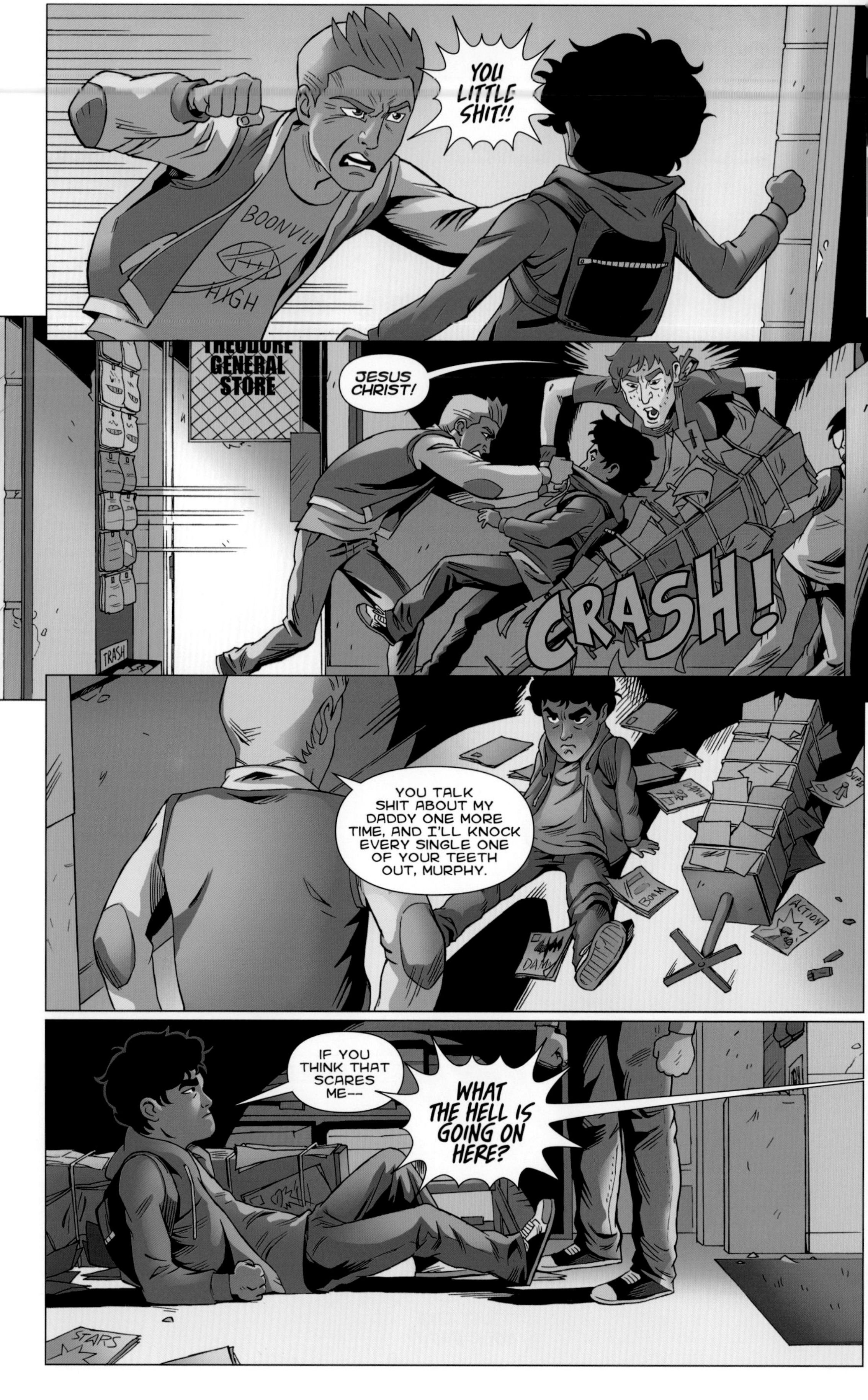
YOU LITTLE SHIT!!
BOONVILL
HIGH
THEODORE GENERAL STORE
JESUS CHRIST!
TRASH
CRASH!
YOU TALK SHIT ABOUT MY DADDY ONE MORE TIME, AND I'LL KNOCK EVERY SINGLE ONE OF YOUR TEETH OUT, MURPHY.
ACTION
IF YOU THINK THAT SCARES ME--
WHAT THE HELL IS GOING ON HERE?
STARS

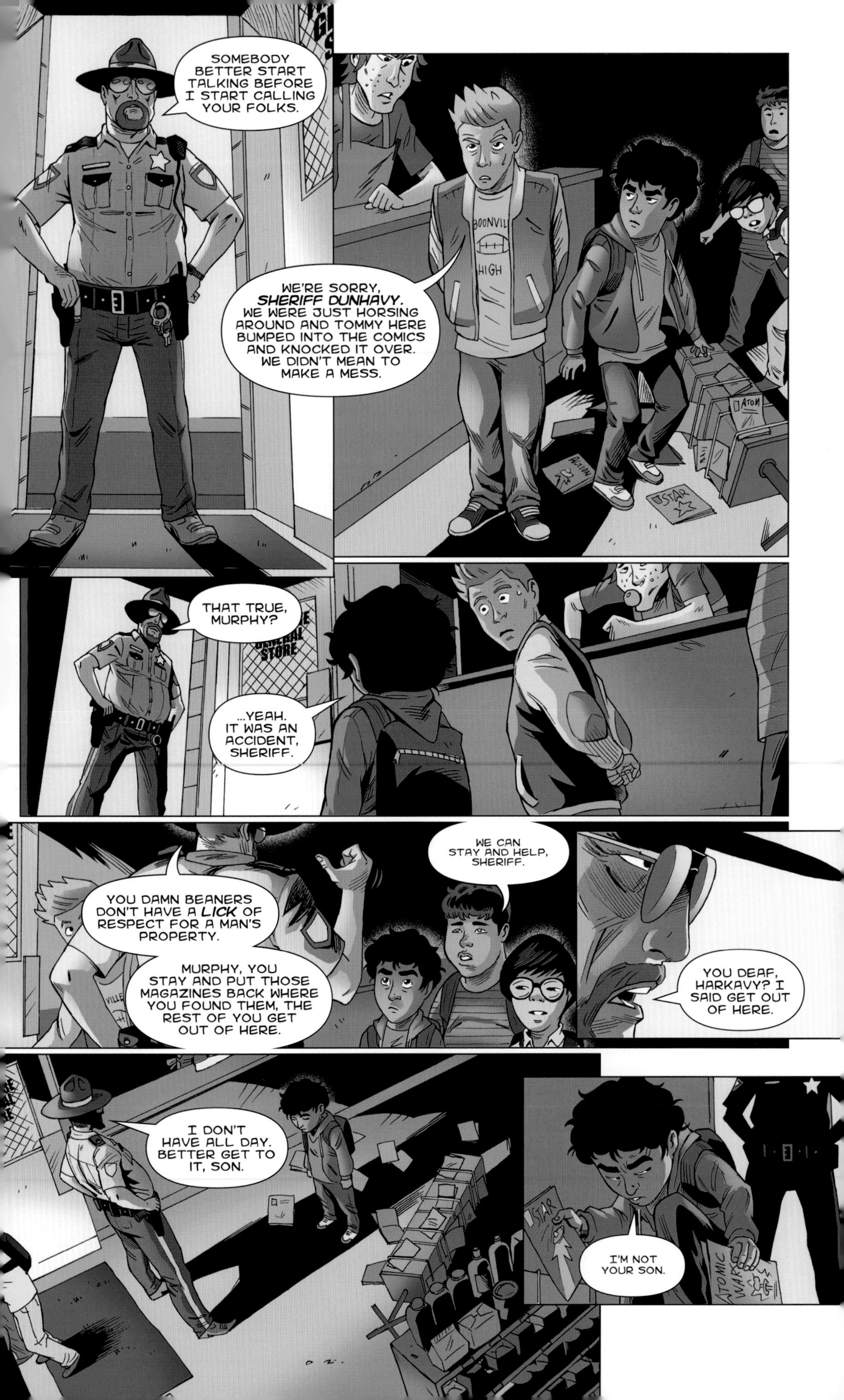
SOMEBODY BETTER START TALKING BEFORE I START CALLING YOUR FOLKS.
WE'RE SORRY, *SHERIFF DUNHAVY.* WE WERE JUST HORSING AROUND AND TOMMY HERE BUMPED INTO THE COMICS AND KNOCKED IT OVER. WE DIDN'T MEAN TO MAKE A MESS.
THAT TRUE, MURPHY?
...YEAH. IT WAS AN ACCIDENT, SHERIFF.
YOU DAMN BEANERS DON'T HAVE A *LICK* OF RESPECT FOR A MAN'S PROPERTY.
MURPHY, YOU STAY AND PUT THOSE MAGAZINES BACK WHERE YOU FOUND THEM, THE REST OF YOU GET OUT OF HERE.
WE CAN STAY AND HELP, SHERIFF.
YOU DEAF, HARKAVY? I SAID GET OUT OF HERE.
I DON'T HAVE ALL DAY. BETTER GET TO IT, SON.
I'M NOT YOUR SON.

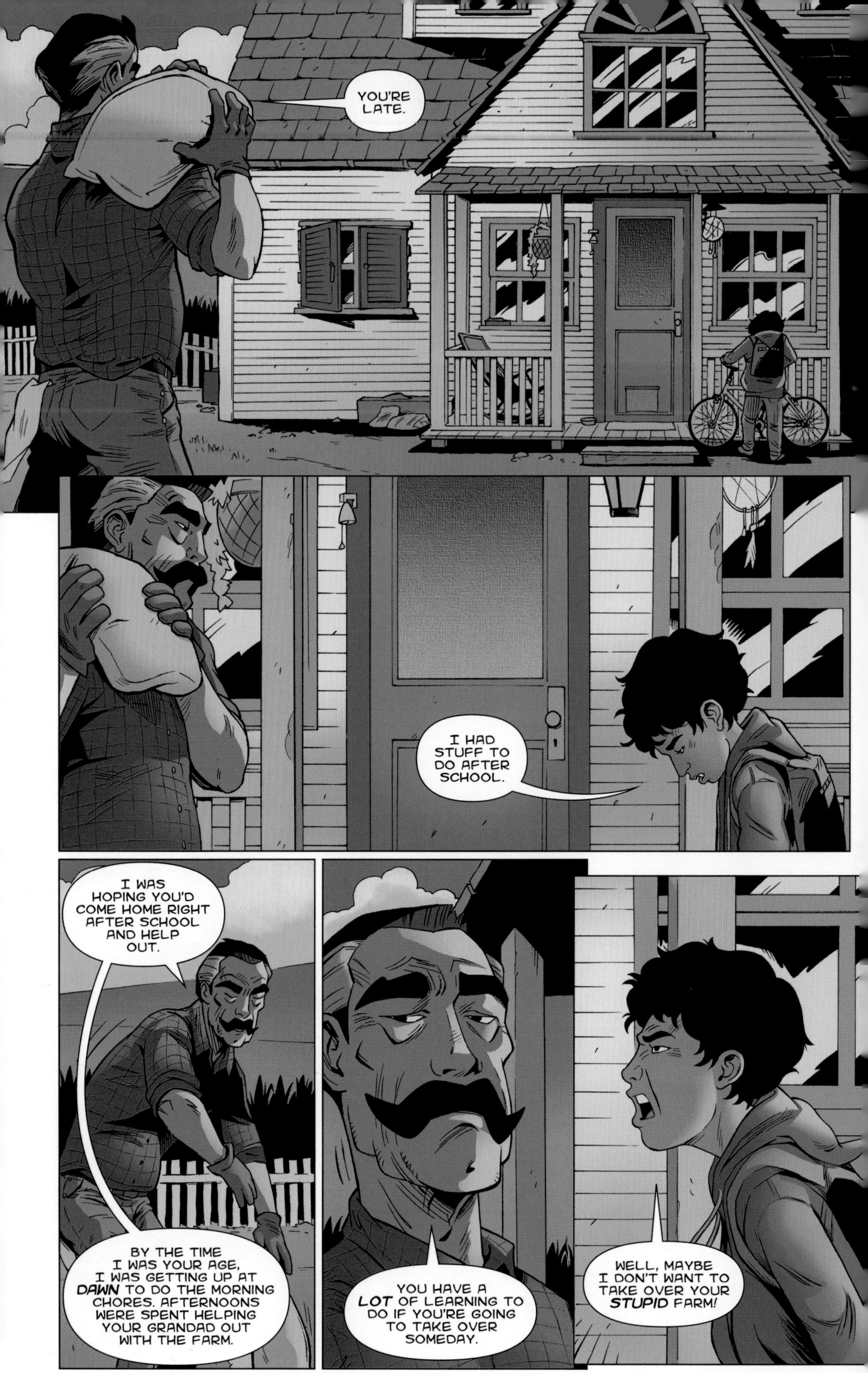
YOU'RE LATE.
I HAD STUFF TO DO AFTER SCHOOL.
I WAS HOPING YOU'D COME HOME RIGHT AFTER SCHOOL AND HELP OUT.
BY THE TIME I WAS YOUR AGE, I WAS GETTING UP AT DAWN TO DO THE MORNING CHORES. AFTERNOONS WERE SPENT HELPING YOUR GRANDAD OUT WITH THE FARM.
YOU HAVE A LOT OF LEARNING TO DO IF YOU'RE GOING TO TAKE OVER SOMEDAY.
WELL, MAYBE I DON'T WANT TO TAKE OVER YOUR STUPID FARM!

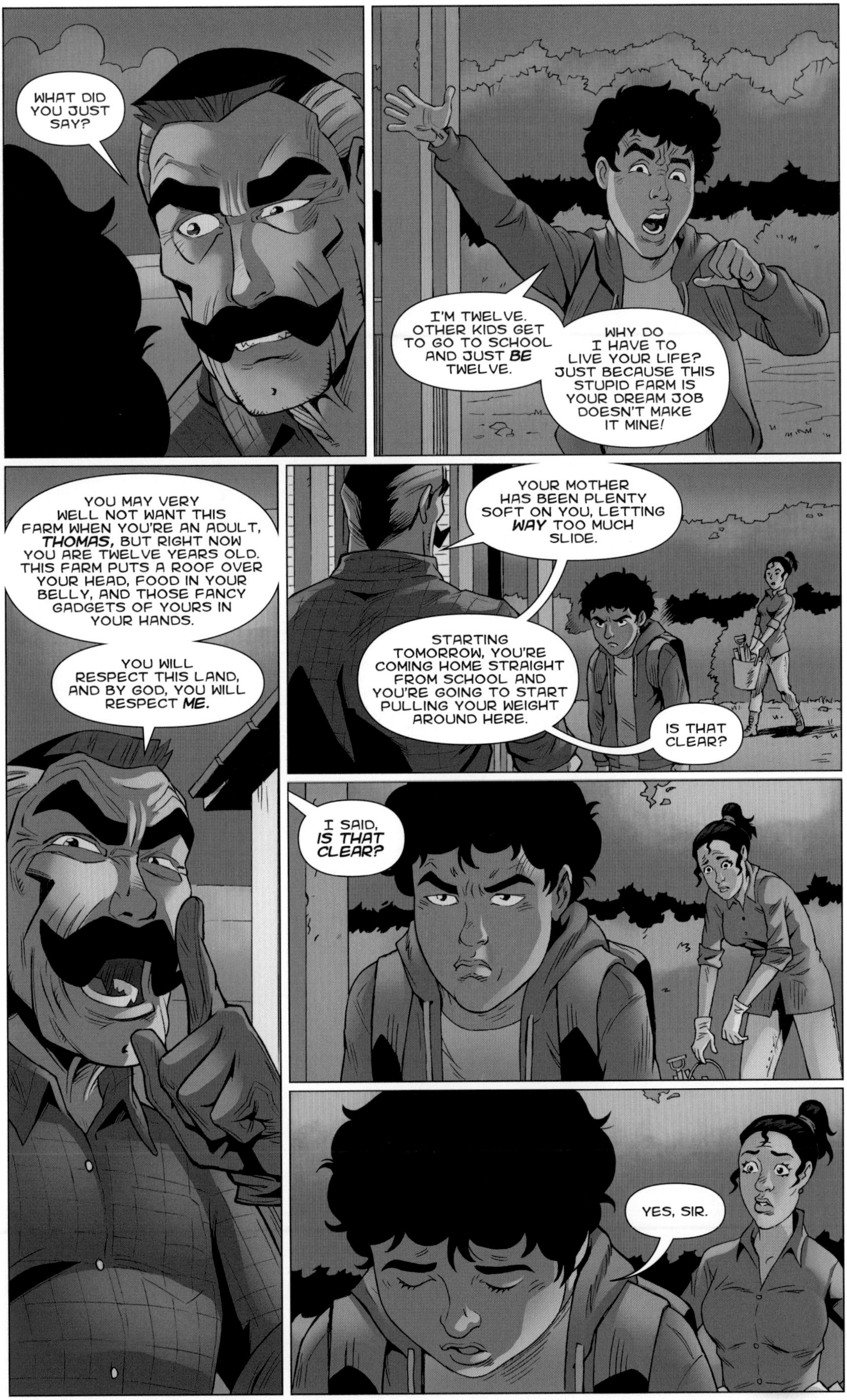
WHAT DID YOU JUST SAY?
I'M TWELVE. OTHER KIDS GET TO GO TO SCHOOL AND JUST **BE** TWELVE.
WHY DO I HAVE TO LIVE YOUR LIFE? JUST BECAUSE THIS STUPID FARM IS YOUR DREAM JOB DOESN'T MAKE IT MINE!
YOU MAY VERY WELL NOT WANT THIS FARM WHEN YOU'RE AN ADULT, ***THOMAS,*** BUT RIGHT NOW YOU ARE TWELVE YEARS OLD. THIS FARM PUTS A ROOF OVER YOUR HEAD, FOOD IN YOUR BELLY, AND THOSE FANCY GADGETS OF YOURS IN YOUR HANDS.
YOU WILL RESPECT THIS LAND, AND BY GOD, YOU WILL RESPECT ***ME.***
YOUR MOTHER HAS BEEN PLENTY SOFT ON YOU, LETTING ***WAY*** TOO MUCH SLIDE.
STARTING TOMORROW, YOU'RE COMING HOME STRAIGHT FROM SCHOOL AND YOU'RE GOING TO START PULLING YOUR WEIGHT AROUND HERE.
IS THAT CLEAR?
I SAID, ***IS THAT CLEAR?***
YES, SIR.

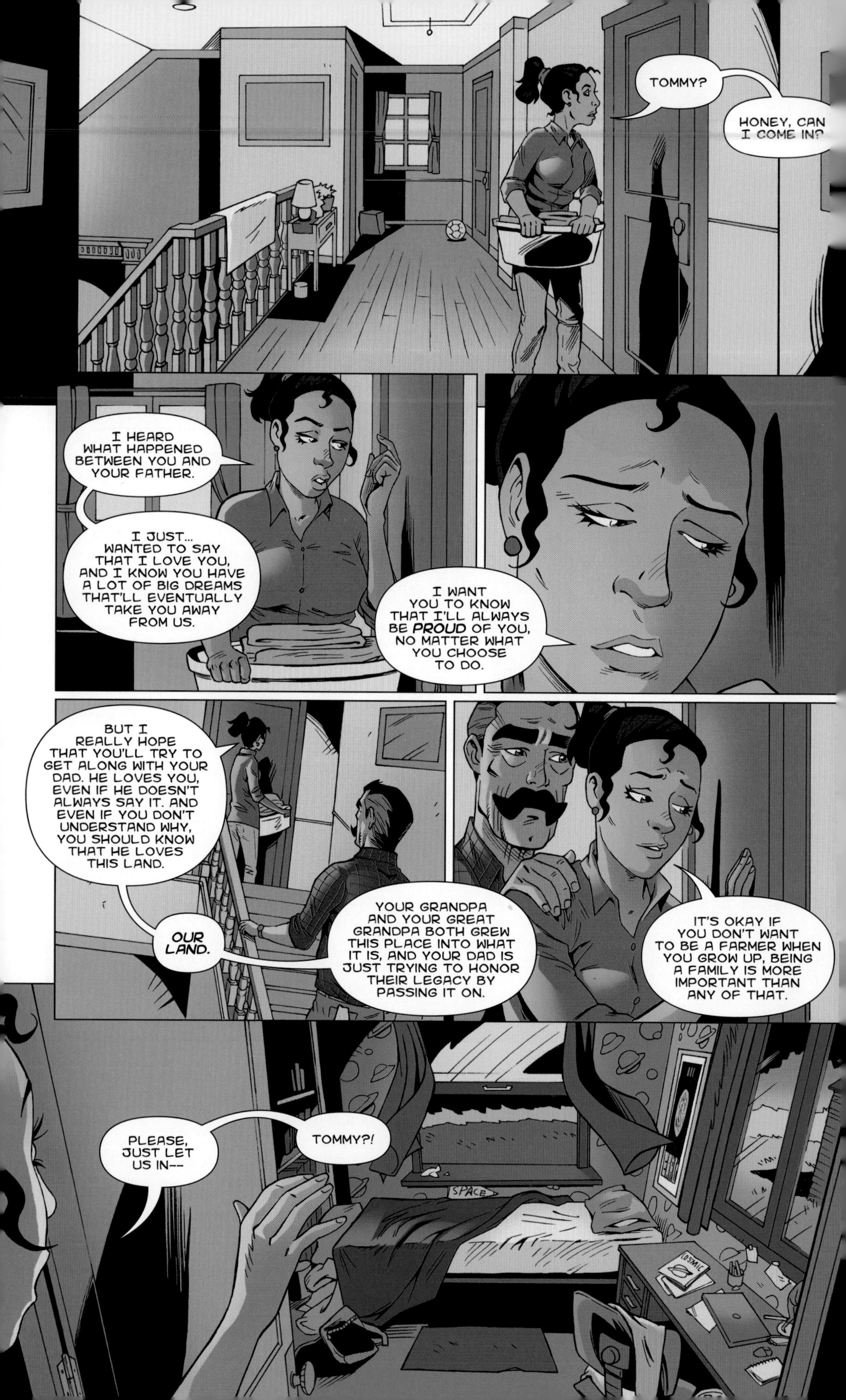
TOMMY?
HONEY, CAN I COME IN?
I HEARD WHAT HAPPENED BETWEEN YOU AND YOUR FATHER.
I JUST... WANTED TO SAY THAT I LOVE YOU, AND I KNOW YOU HAVE A LOT OF BIG DREAMS THAT'LL EVENTUALLY TAKE YOU AWAY FROM US.
I WANT YOU TO KNOW THAT I'LL ALWAYS BE *PROUD* OF YOU, NO MATTER WHAT YOU CHOOSE TO DO.
BUT I REALLY HOPE THAT YOU'LL TRY TO GET ALONG WITH YOUR DAD. HE LOVES YOU, EVEN IF HE DOESN'T ALWAYS SAY IT. AND EVEN IF YOU DON'T UNDERSTAND WHY, YOU SHOULD KNOW THAT HE LOVES THIS LAND.
OUR LAND.
YOUR GRANDPA AND YOUR GREAT GRANDPA BOTH GREW THIS PLACE INTO WHAT IT IS, AND YOUR DAD IS JUST TRYING TO HONOR THEIR LEGACY BY PASSING IT ON.
IT'S OKAY IF YOU DON'T WANT TO BE A FARMER WHEN YOU GROW UP, BEING A FAMILY IS MORE IMPORTANT THAN ANY OF THAT.
PLEASE, JUST LET US IN--
TOMMY?!
SPACE
COSMIC

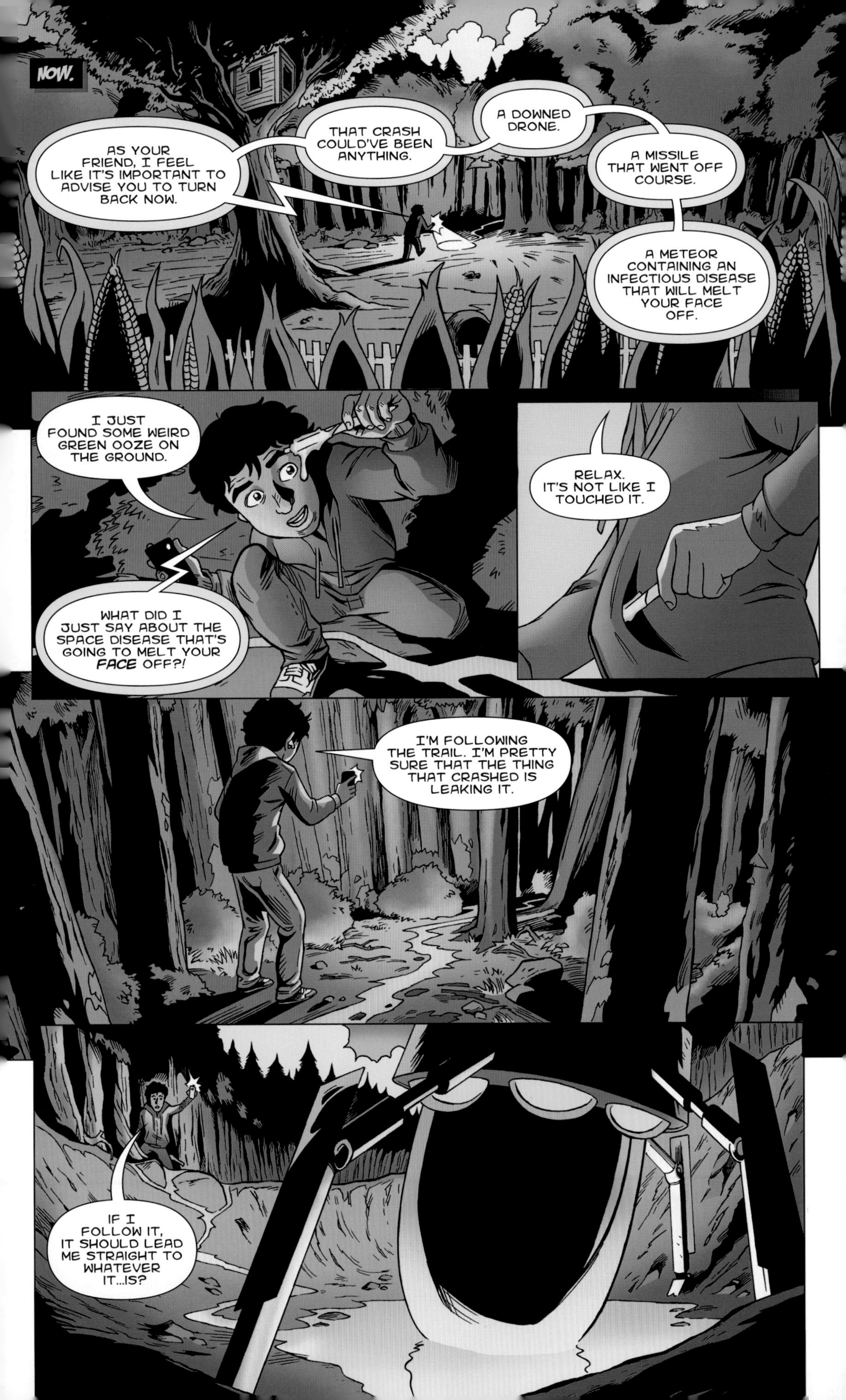
NOW.
AS YOUR FRIEND, I FEEL LIKE IT'S IMPORTANT TO ADVISE YOU TO TURN BACK NOW.
THAT CRASH COULD'VE BEEN ANYTHING.
A DOWNED DRONE.
A MISSILE THAT WENT OFF COURSE.
A METEOR CONTAINING AN INFECTIOUS DISEASE THAT WILL MELT YOUR FACE OFF.
I JUST FOUND SOME WEIRD GREEN OOZE ON THE GROUND.
WHAT DID I JUST SAY ABOUT THE SPACE DISEASE THAT'S GOING TO MELT YOUR *FACE* OFF?!
RELAX. IT'S NOT LIKE I TOUCHED IT.
I'M FOLLOWING THE TRAIL. I'M PRETTY SURE THAT THE THING THAT CRASHED IS LEAKING IT.
IF I FOLLOW IT, IT SHOULD LEAD ME STRAIGHT TO WHATEVER IT...IS?

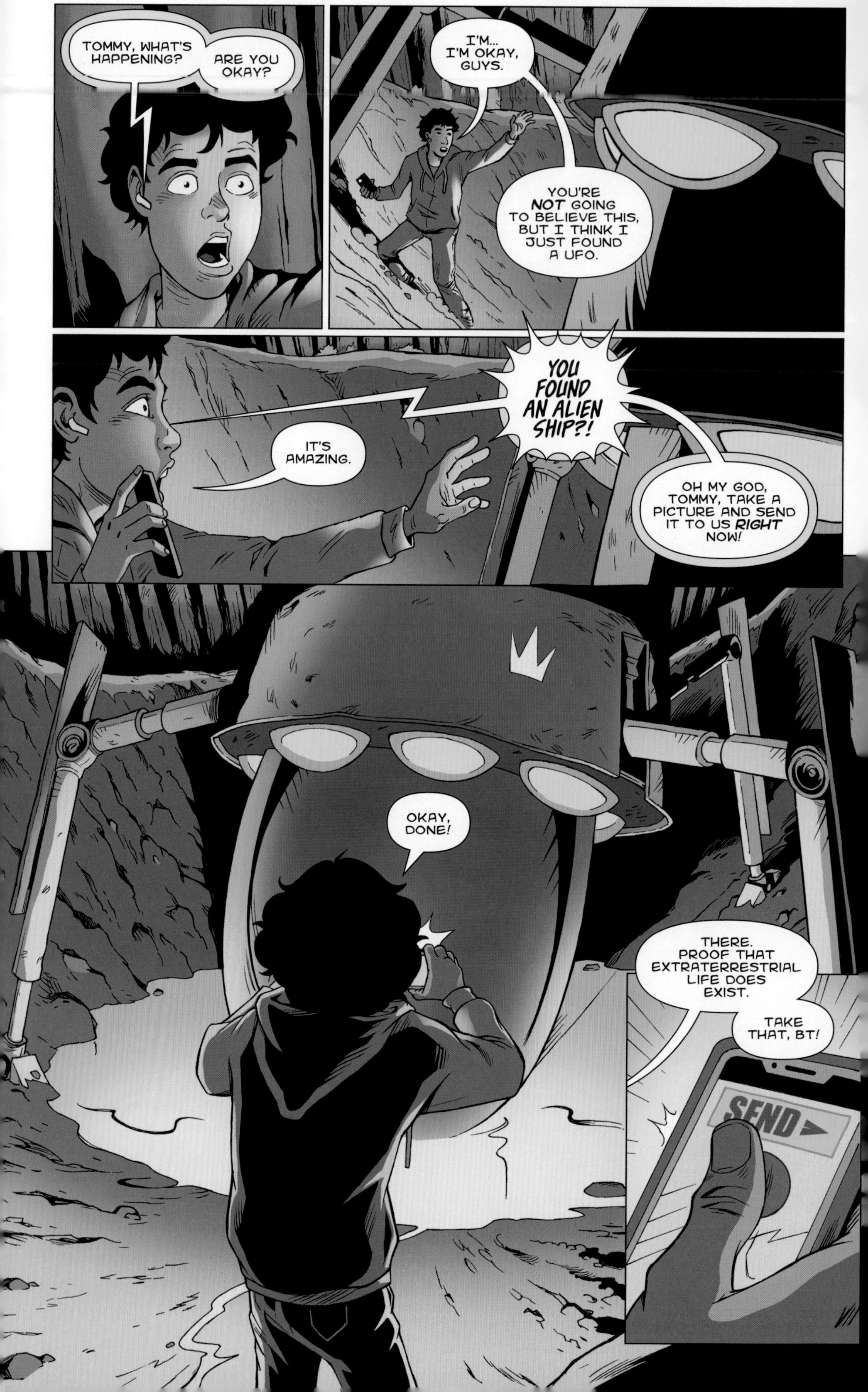
TOMMY, WHAT'S HAPPENING?
ARE YOU OKAY?
I'M... I'M OKAY, GUYS.
YOU'RE **NOT** GOING TO BELIEVE THIS, BUT I THINK I JUST FOUND A UFO.
YOU FOUND AN ALIEN SHIP?!
IT'S AMAZING.
OH MY GOD, TOMMY, TAKE A PICTURE AND SEND IT TO US **RIGHT** NOW!
OKAY, DONE!
THERE. PROOF THAT EXTRATERRESTRIAL LIFE DOES EXIST.
TAKE THAT, BT!
SEND

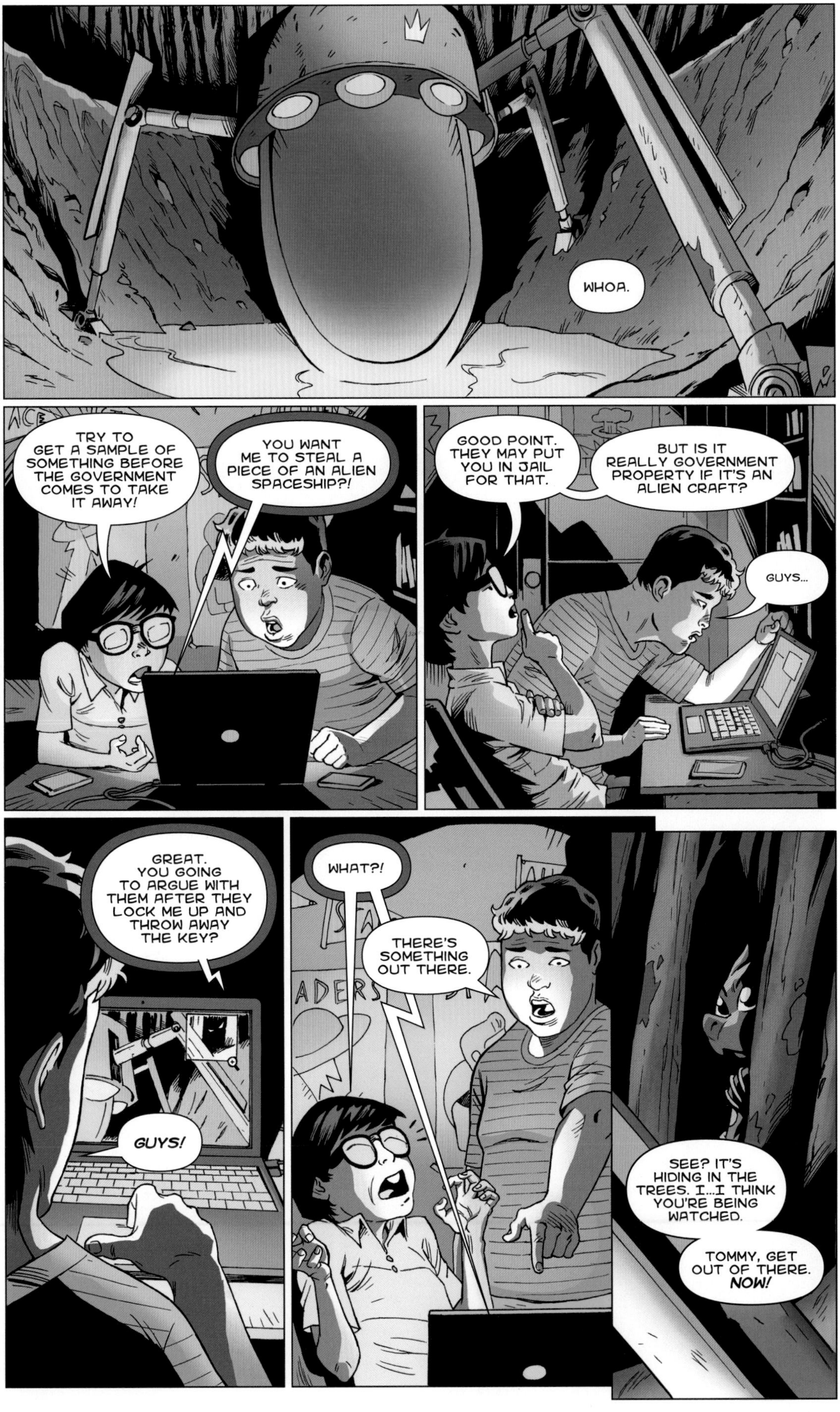
WHOA.
TRY TO GET A SAMPLE OF SOMETHING BEFORE THE GOVERNMENT COMES TO TAKE IT AWAY!
YOU WANT ME TO STEAL A PIECE OF AN ALIEN SPACESHIP?!
GOOD POINT. THEY MAY PUT YOU IN JAIL FOR THAT.
BUT IS IT REALLY GOVERNMENT PROPERTY IF IT'S AN ALIEN CRAFT?
GUYS...
GREAT. YOU GOING TO ARGUE WITH THEM AFTER THEY LOCK ME UP AND THROW AWAY THE KEY?
GUYS!
WHAT?!
THERE'S SOMETHING OUT THERE.
SEE? IT'S HIDING IN THE TREES. I...I THINK YOU'RE BEING WATCHED.
TOMMY, GET OUT OF THERE. NOW!

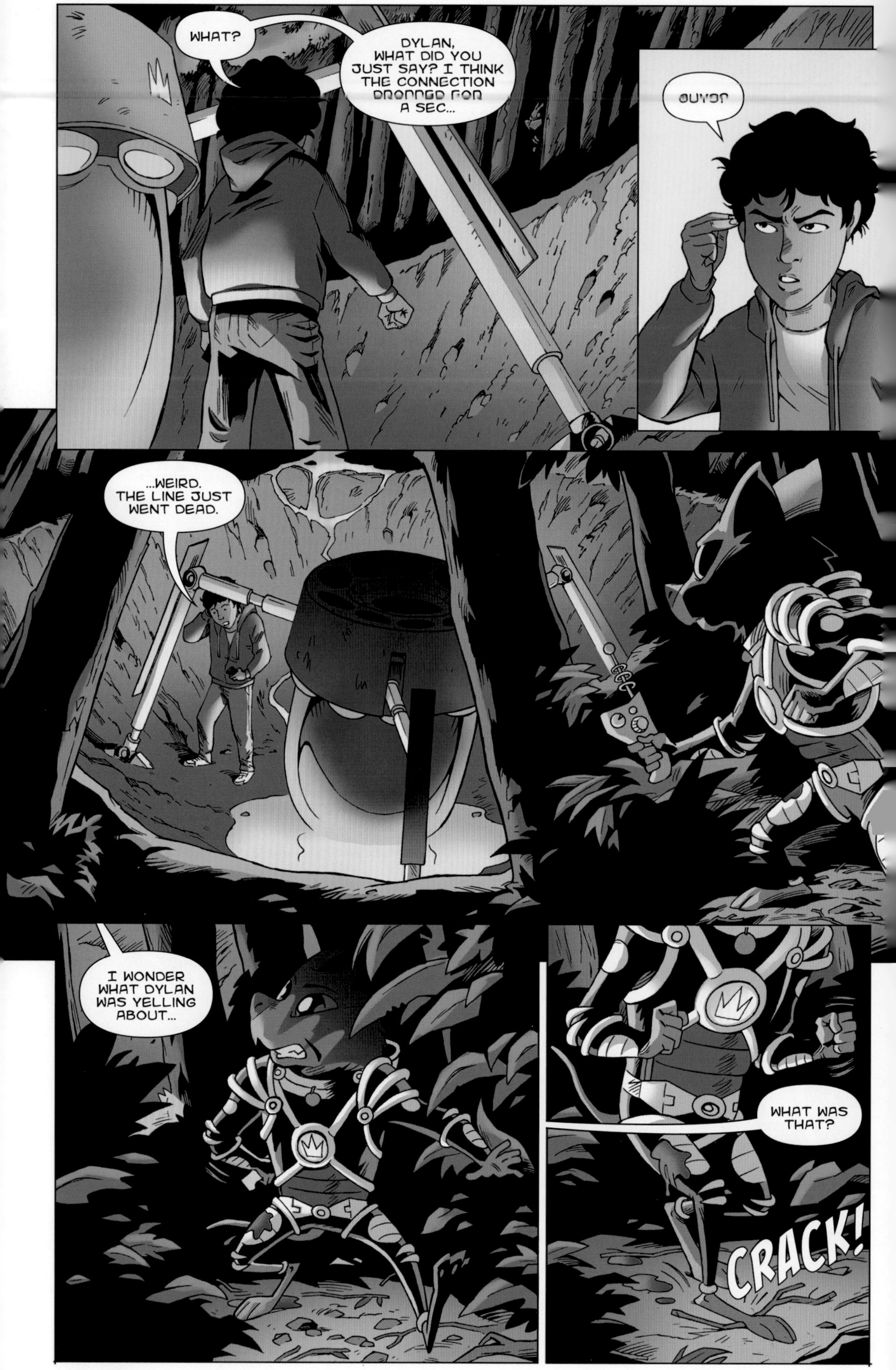
WHAT?
DYLAN, WHAT DID YOU JUST SAY? I THINK THE CONNECTION DROPPED FOR A SEC...
...WEIRD. THE LINE JUST WENT DEAD.
I WONDER WHAT DYLAN WAS YELLING ABOUT...
WHAT WAS THAT?
CRACK!

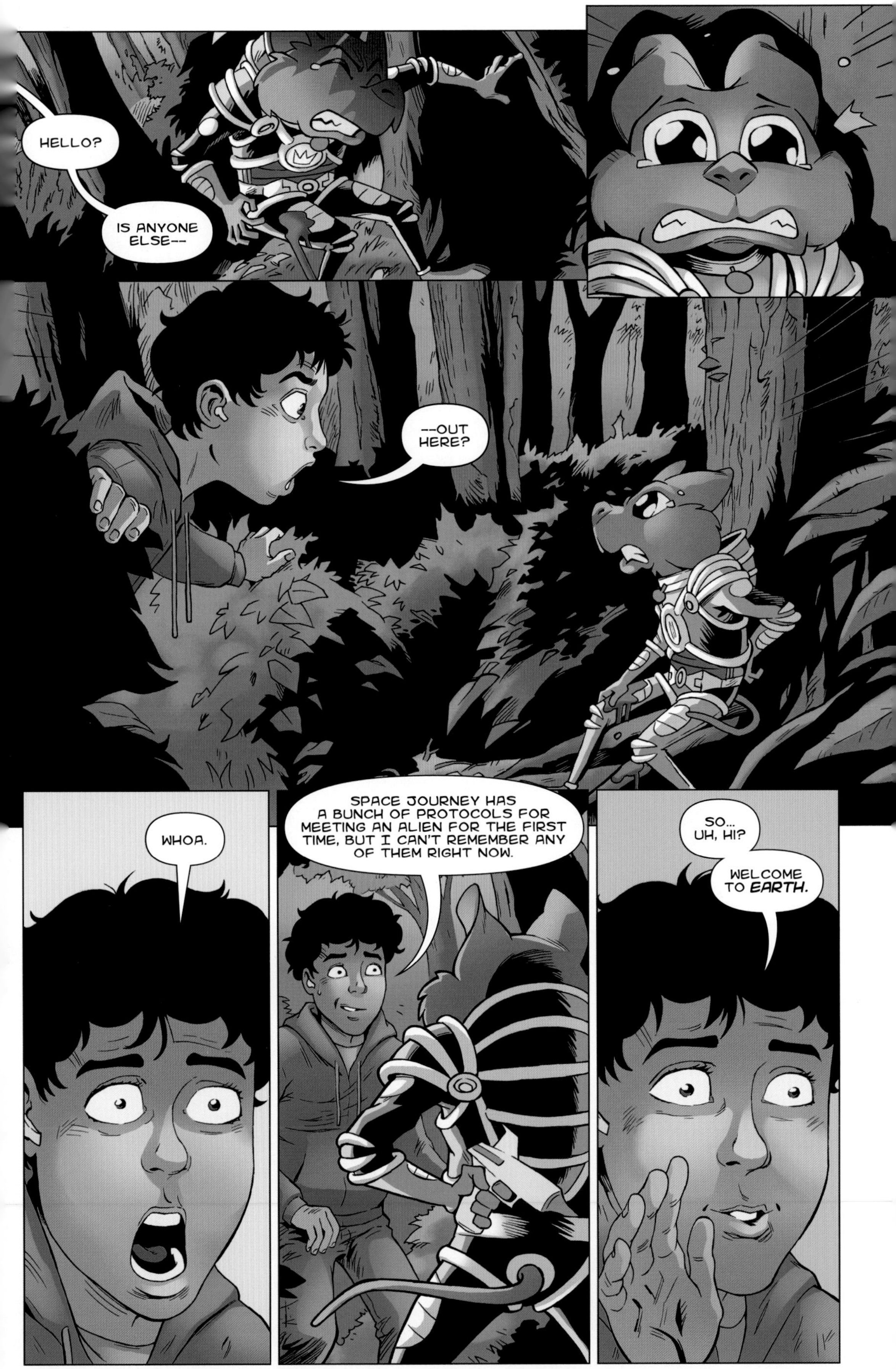
HELLO?
IS ANYONE ELSE--
--OUT HERE?
WHOA.
SPACE JOURNEY HAS A BUNCH OF PROTOCOLS FOR MEETING AN ALIEN FOR THE FIRST TIME, BUT I CAN'T REMEMBER ANY OF THEM RIGHT NOW.
SO... UH, HI?
WELCOME TO **EARTH.**

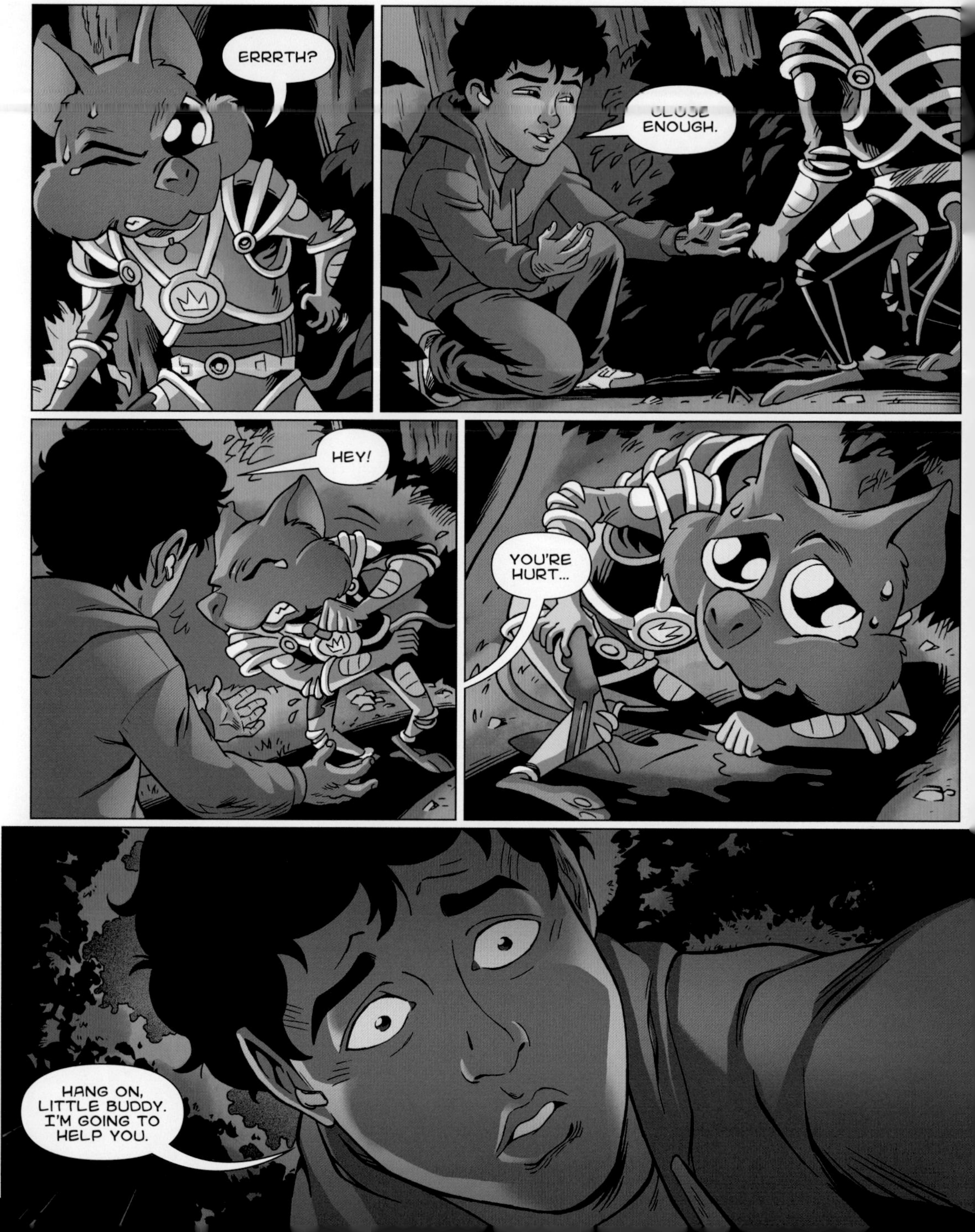
ERRRTH?
CLOSE ENOUGH.
HEY!
YOU'RE HURT...
HANG ON, LITTLE BUDDY. I'M GOING TO HELP YOU.

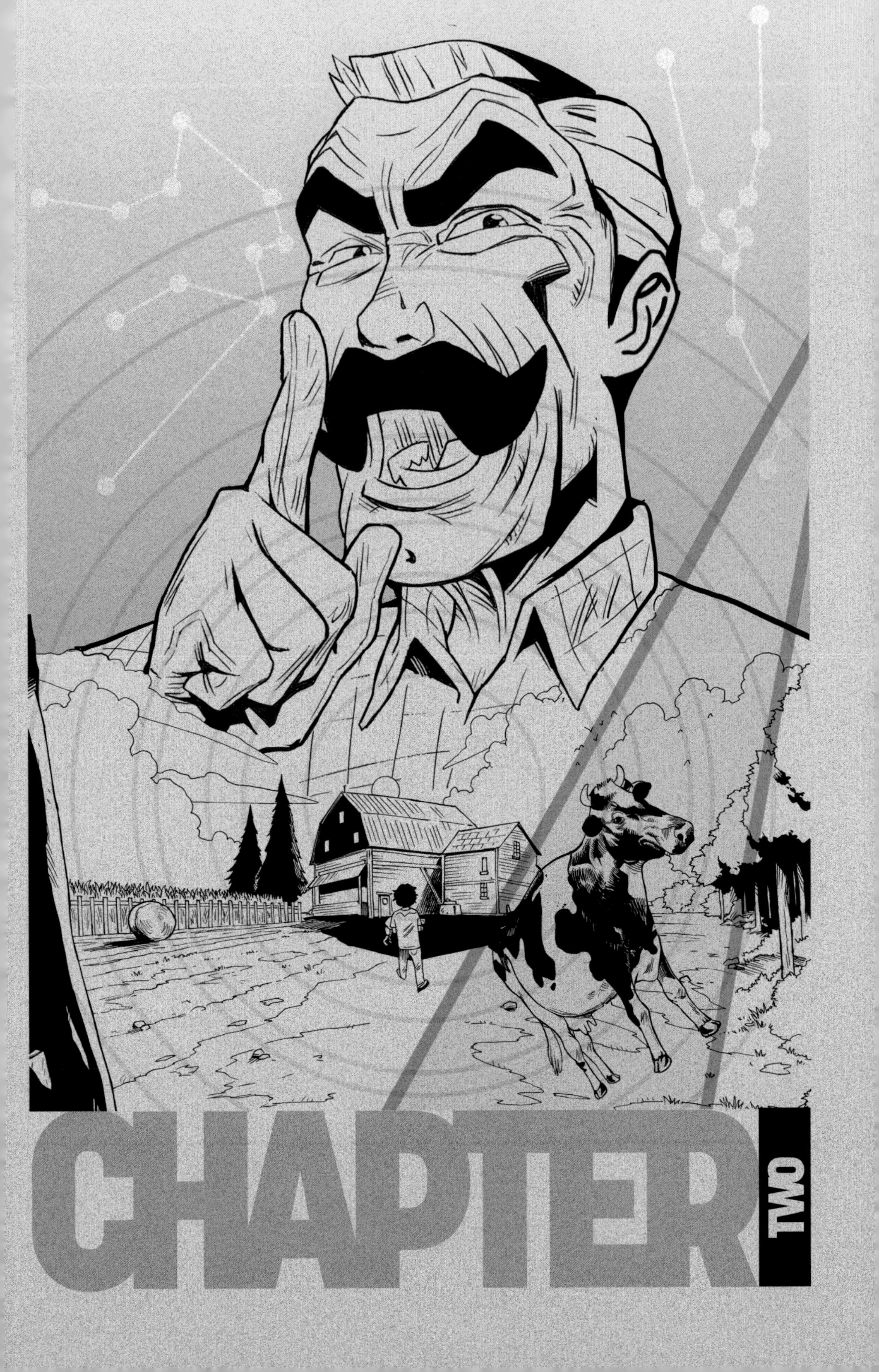

CHAPTER TWO

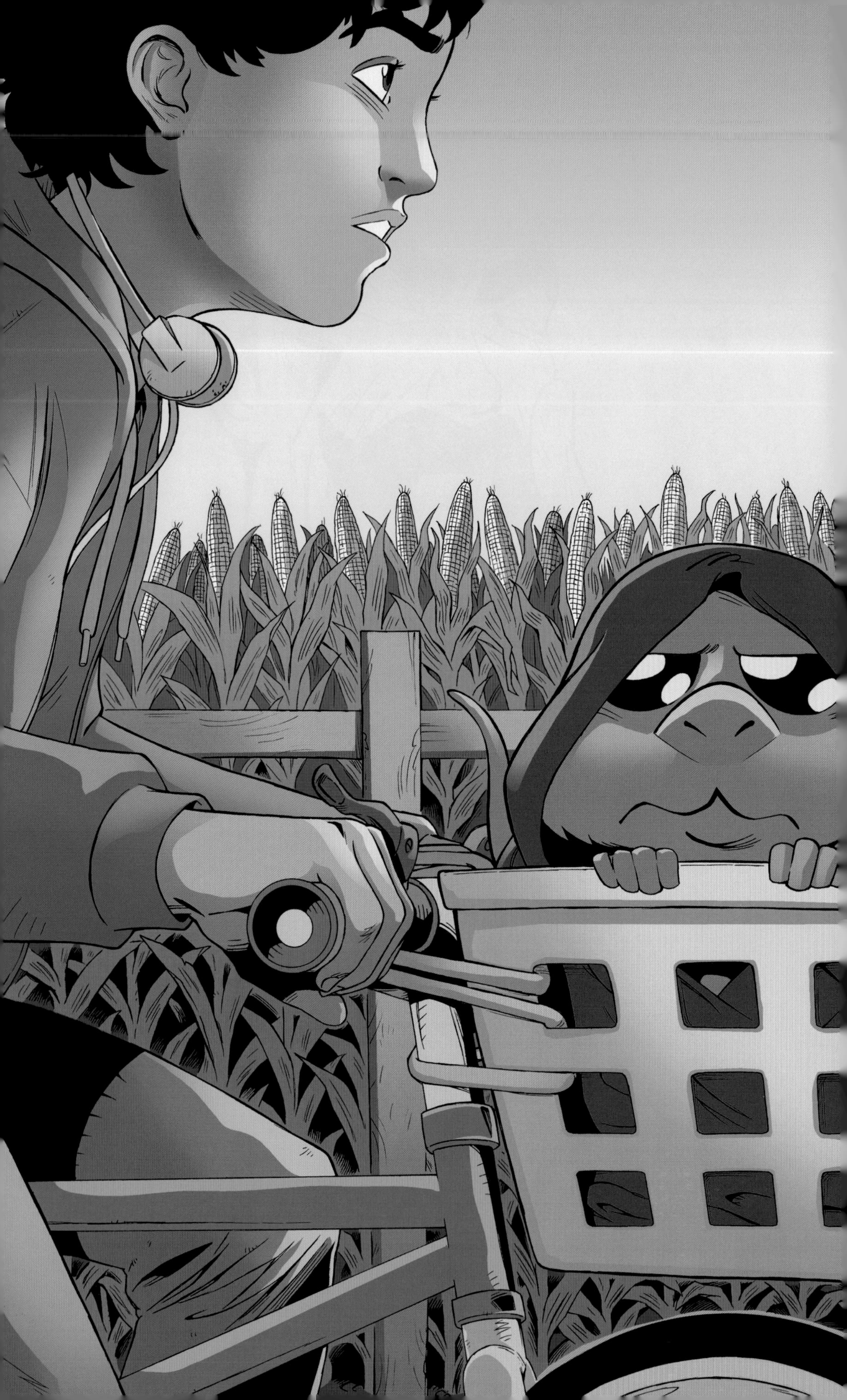

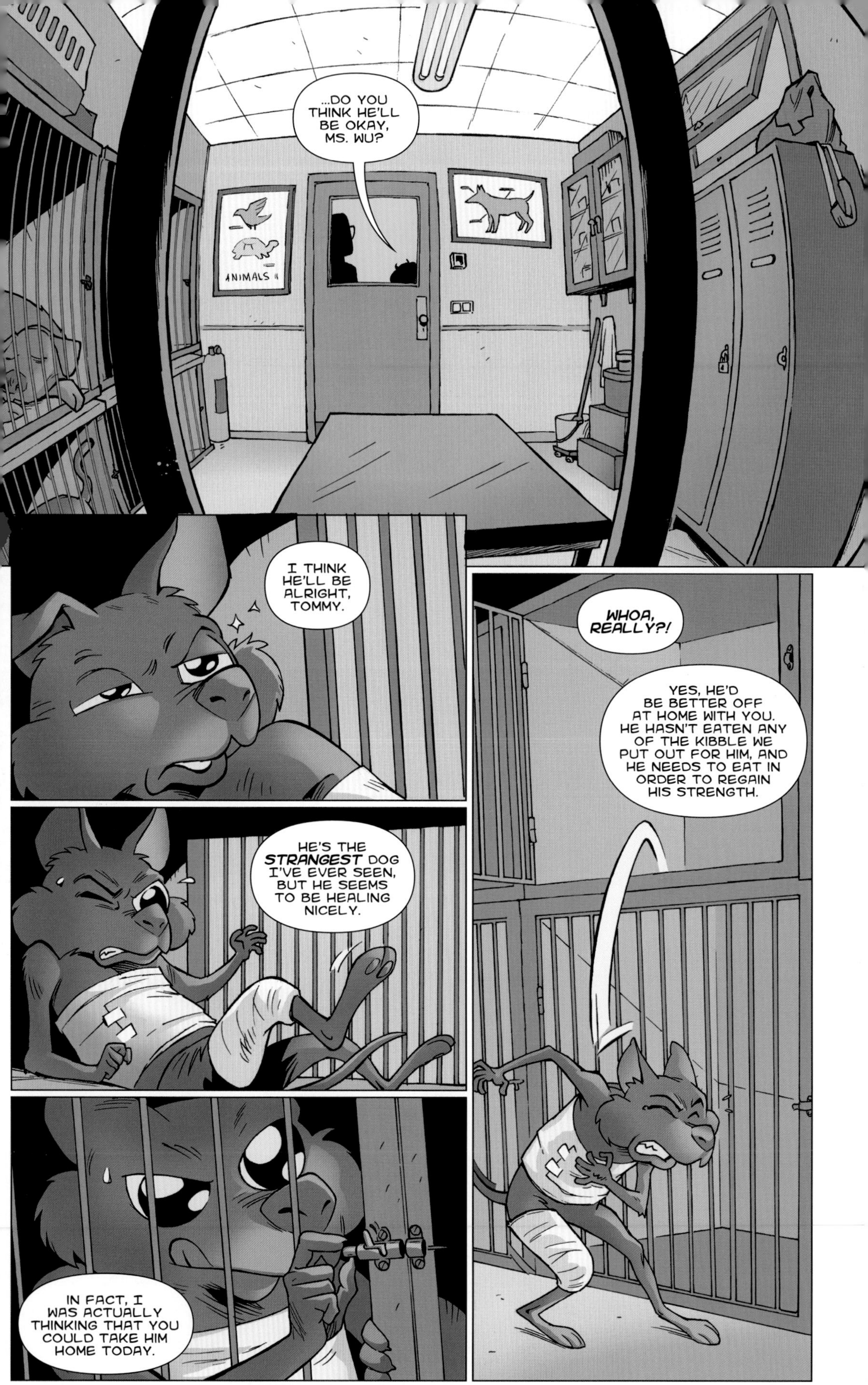
...DO YOU THINK HE'LL BE OKAY, MS. WU?
ANIMALS
I THINK HE'LL BE ALRIGHT, TOMMY.
HE'S THE STRANGEST DOG I'VE EVER SEEN, BUT HE SEEMS TO BE HEALING NICELY.
IN FACT, I WAS ACTUALLY THINKING THAT YOU COULD TAKE HIM HOME TODAY.
WHOA, REALLY?!
YES, HE'D BE BETTER OFF AT HOME WITH YOU. HE HASN'T EATEN ANY OF THE KIBBLE WE PUT OUT FOR HIM, AND HE NEEDS TO EAT IN ORDER TO REGAIN HIS STRENGTH.

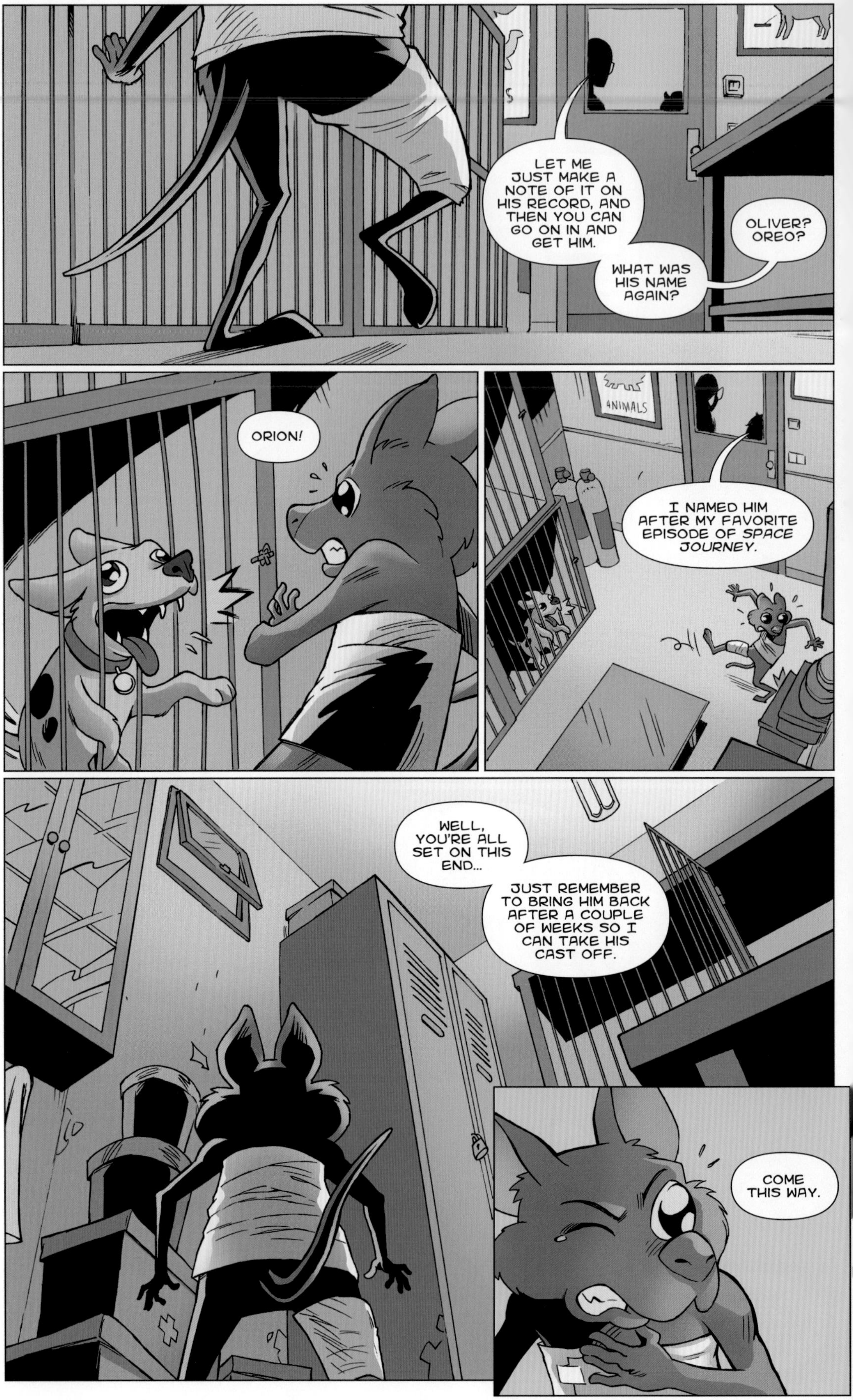
LET ME JUST MAKE A NOTE OF IT ON HIS RECORD, AND THEN YOU CAN GO ON IN AND GET HIM.
WHAT WAS HIS NAME AGAIN?
OLIVER? OREO?
ORION!
ANIMALS
I NAMED HIM AFTER MY FAVORITE EPISODE OF *SPACE JOURNEY*.
WELL, YOU'RE ALL SET ON THIS END...
JUST REMEMBER TO BRING HIM BACK AFTER A COUPLE OF WEEKS SO I CAN TAKE HIS CAST OFF.
COME THIS WAY.

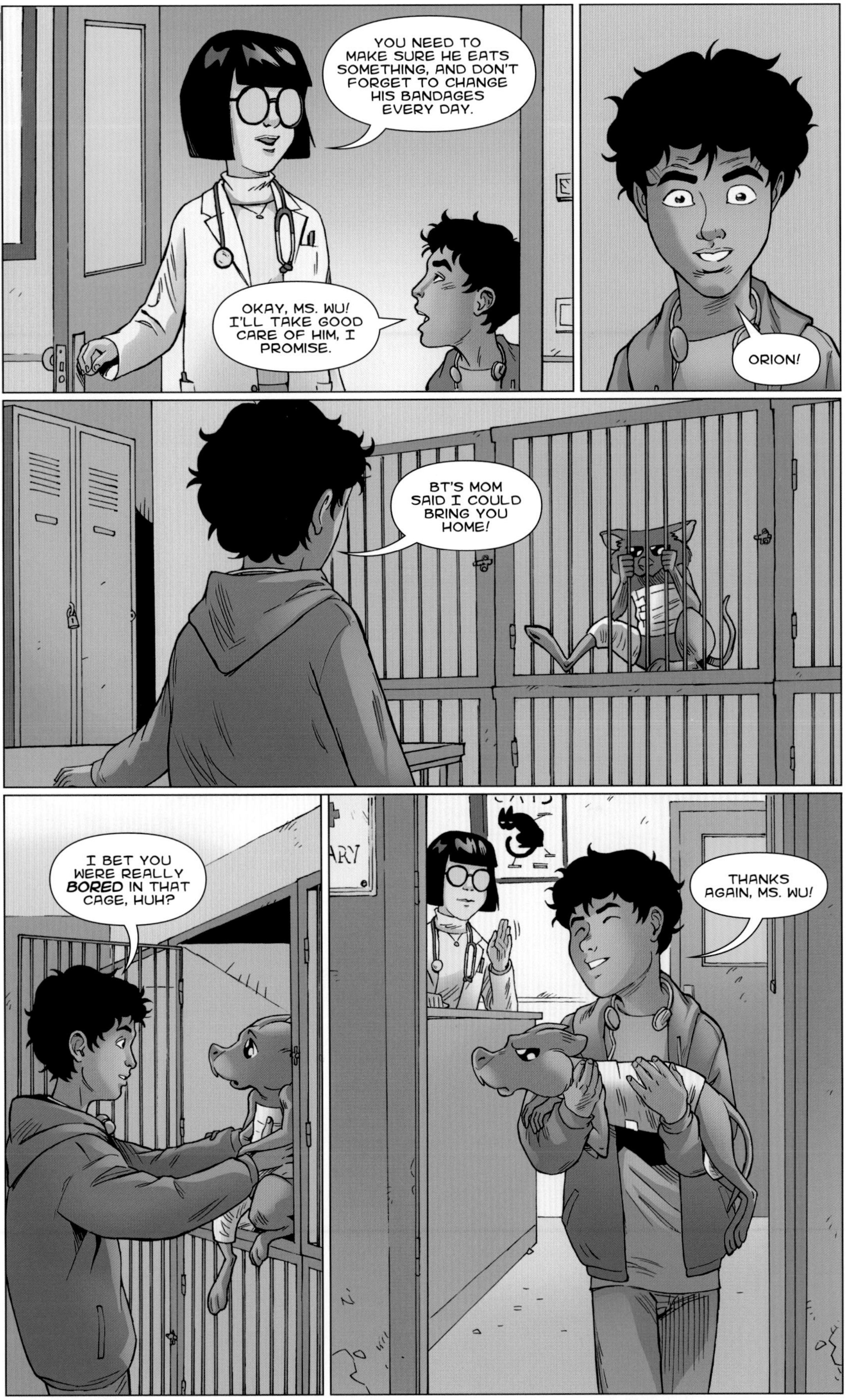
YOU NEED TO MAKE SURE HE EATS SOMETHING, AND DON'T FORGET TO CHANGE HIS BANDAGES EVERY DAY.
OKAY, MS. WU! I'LL TAKE GOOD CARE OF HIM, I PROMISE.
ORION!
BT'S MOM SAID I COULD BRING YOU HOME!
I BET YOU WERE REALLY *BORED* IN THAT CAGE, HUH?
THANKS AGAIN, MS. WU!

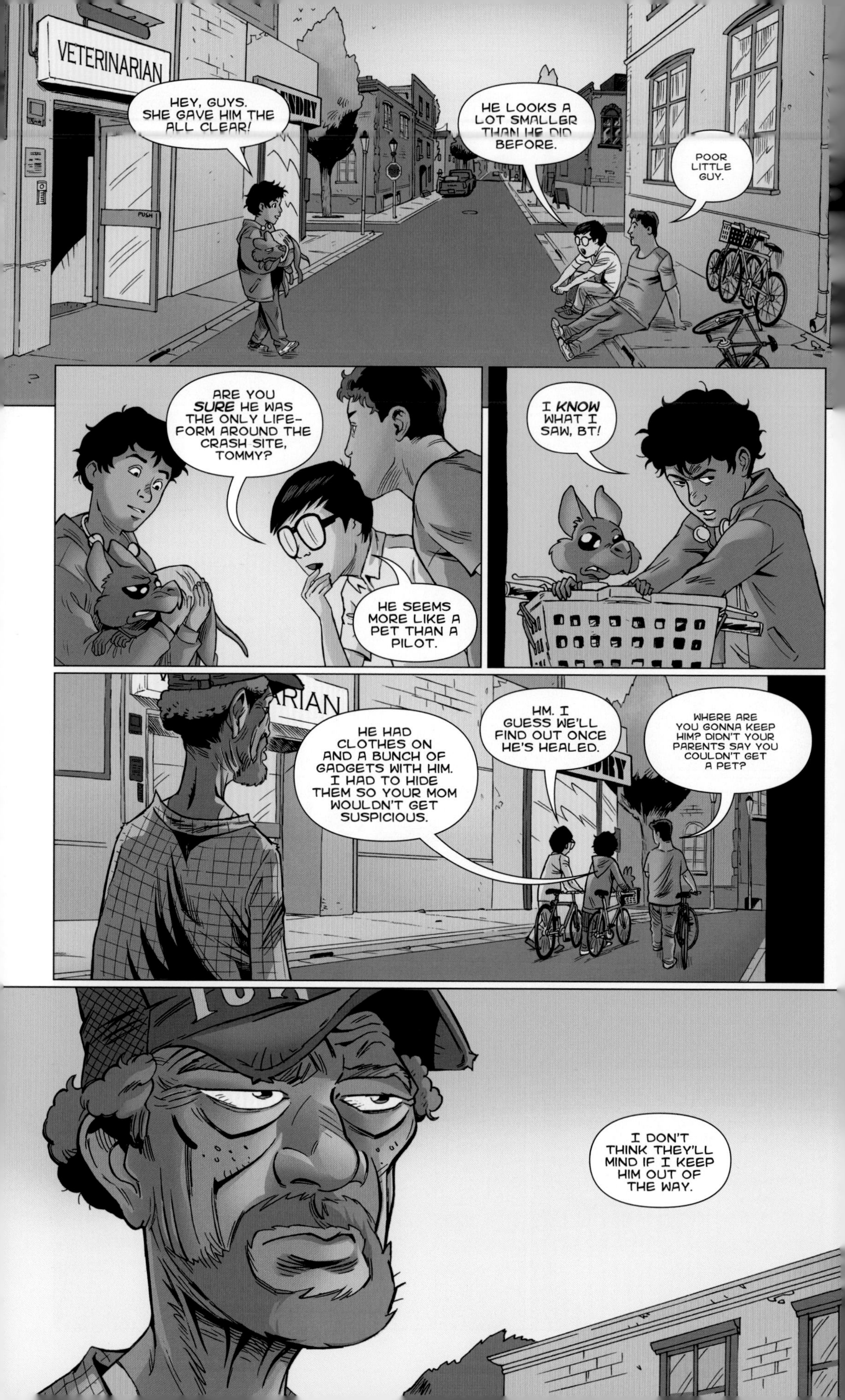
VETERINARIAN
HEY, GUYS. SHE GAVE HIM THE ALL CLEAR!
HE LOOKS A LOT SMALLER THAN HE DID BEFORE.
POOR LITTLE GUY.
ARE YOU SURE HE WAS THE ONLY LIFE-FORM AROUND THE CRASH SITE, TOMMY?
HE SEEMS MORE LIKE A PET THAN A PILOT.
I KNOW WHAT I SAW, BT!
HE HAD CLOTHES ON AND A BUNCH OF GADGETS WITH HIM. I HAD TO HIDE THEM SO YOUR MOM WOULDN'T GET SUSPICIOUS.
HM. I GUESS WE'LL FIND OUT ONCE HE'S HEALED.
WHERE ARE YOU GONNA KEEP HIM? DIDN'T YOUR PARENTS SAY YOU COULDN'T GET A PET?
I DON'T THINK THEY'LL MIND IF I KEEP HIM OUT OF THE WAY.

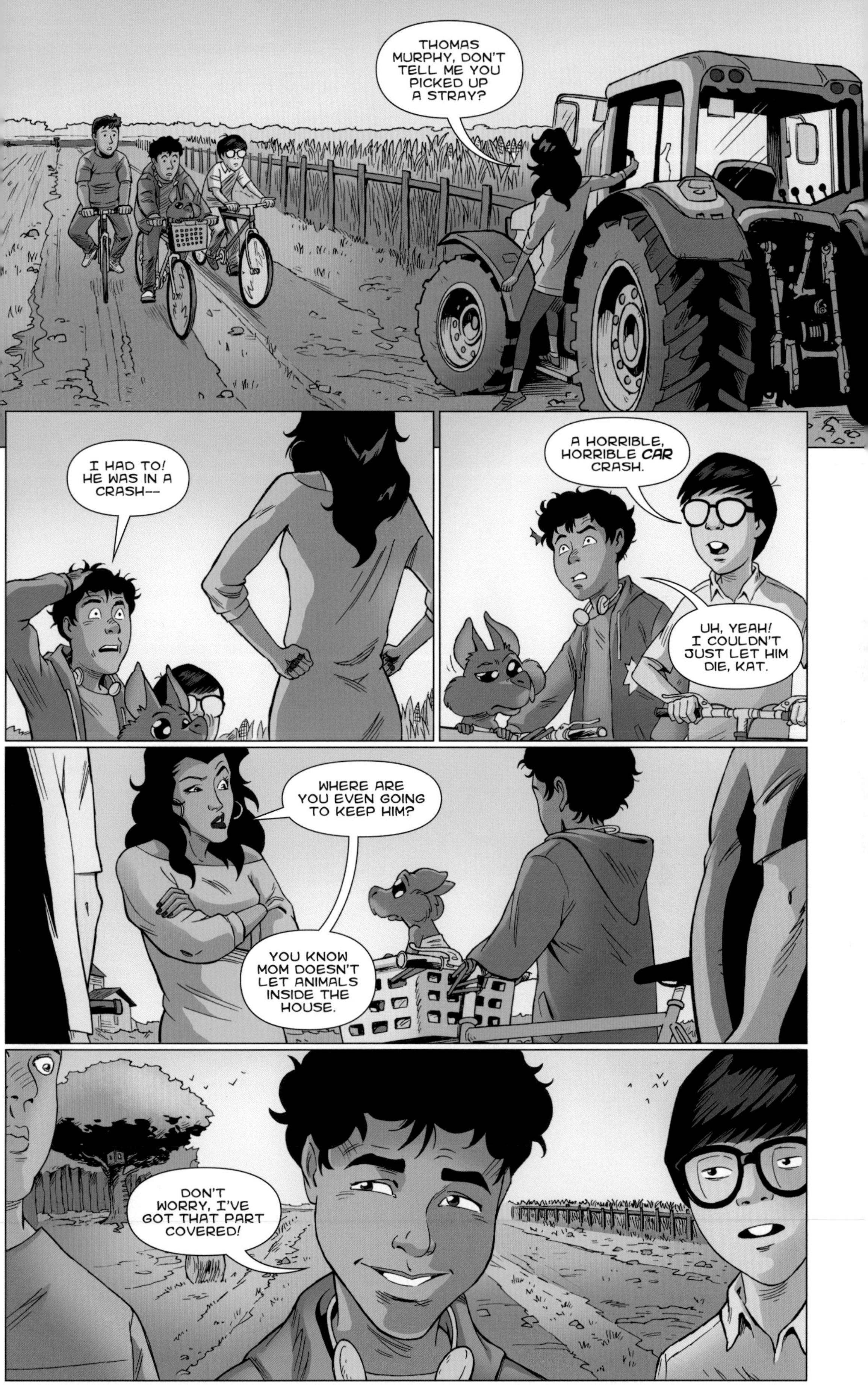
THOMAS MURPHY, DON'T TELL ME YOU PICKED UP A STRAY?
I HAD TO! HE WAS IN A CRASH--
A HORRIBLE, HORRIBLE CAR CRASH.
UH, YEAH! I COULDN'T JUST LET HIM DIE, KAT.
WHERE ARE YOU EVEN GOING TO KEEP HIM?
YOU KNOW MOM DOESN'T LET ANIMALS INSIDE THE HOUSE.
DON'T WORRY, I'VE GOT THAT PART COVERED!

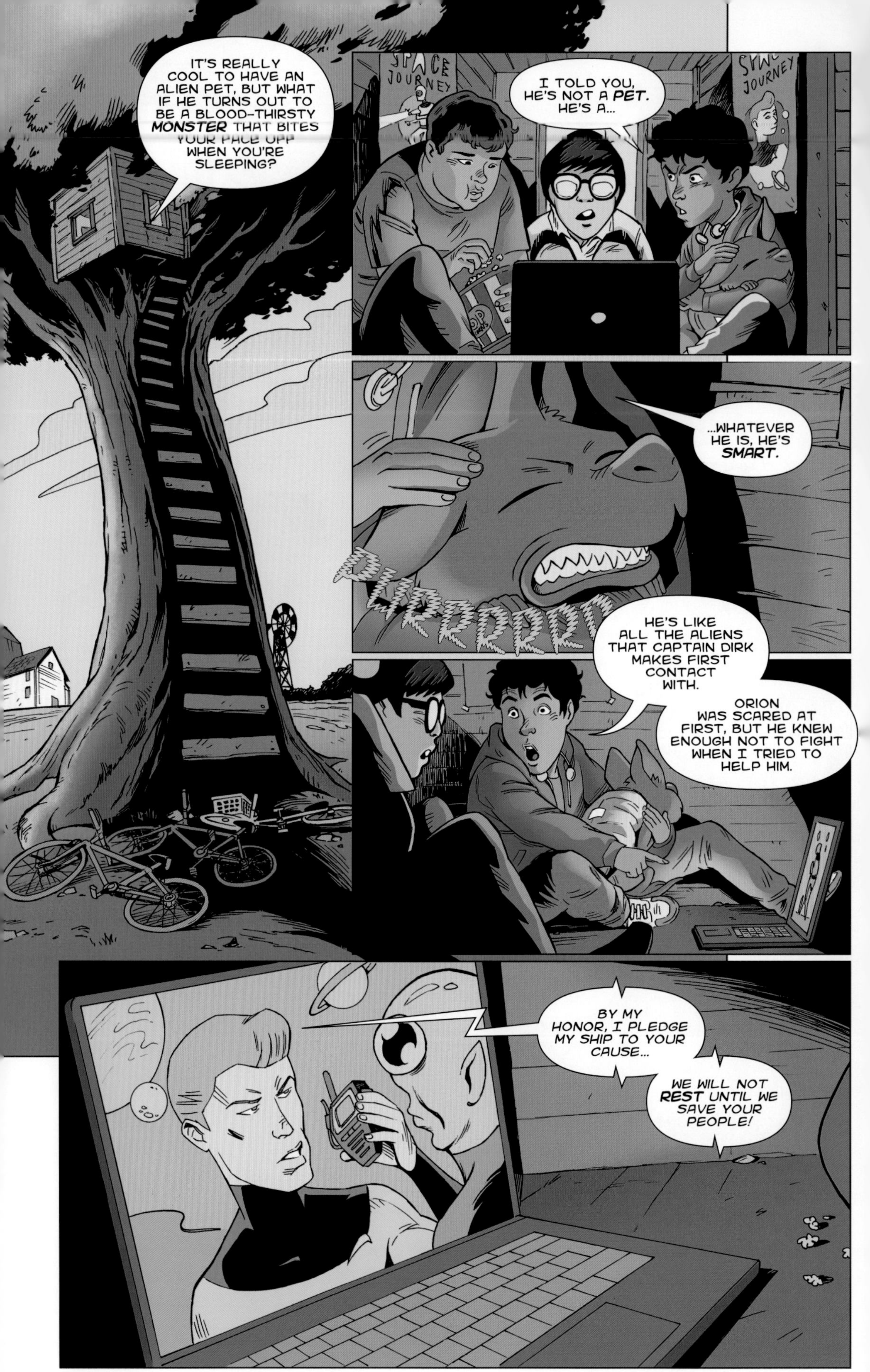
IT'S REALLY COOL TO HAVE AN ALIEN PET, BUT WHAT IF HE TURNS OUT TO BE A BLOOD-THIRSTY **MONSTER** THAT BITES YOUR FACE OFF WHEN YOU'RE SLEEPING?
SPACE JOURNEY
I TOLD YOU, HE'S NOT A ***PET.*** HE'S A...
...WHATEVER HE IS, HE'S ***SMART.***
HE'S LIKE ALL THE ALIENS THAT CAPTAIN DIRK MAKES FIRST CONTACT WITH.
ORION WAS SCARED AT FIRST, BUT HE KNEW ENOUGH NOT TO FIGHT WHEN I TRIED TO HELP HIM.
BY MY HONOR, I PLEDGE MY SHIP TO YOUR CAUSE...
*WE WILL NOT **REST** UNTIL WE SAVE YOUR PEOPLE!*

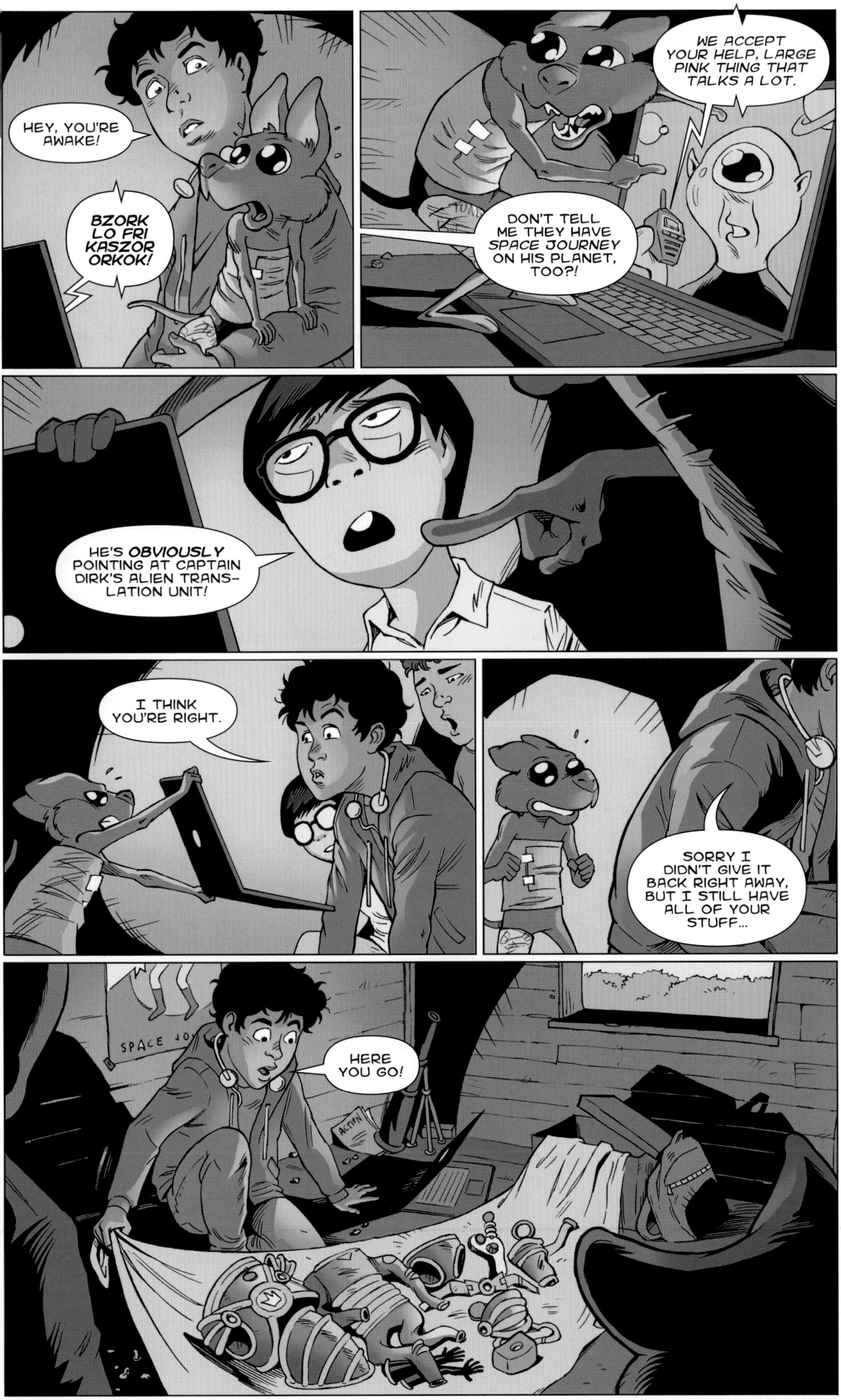
HEY, YOU'RE AWAKE!
BZORK LO FRI KASZOR ORKOK!
WE ACCEPT YOUR HELP, LARGE PINK THING THAT TALKS A LOT.
DON'T TELL ME THEY HAVE SPACE JOURNEY ON HIS PLANET, TOO?!
HE'S OBVIOUSLY POINTING AT CAPTAIN DIRK'S ALIEN TRANS-LATION UNIT!
I THINK YOU'RE RIGHT.
SORRY I DIDN'T GIVE IT BACK RIGHT AWAY, BUT I STILL HAVE ALL OF YOUR STUFF...
SPACE JOU
HERE YOU GO!
ACTION

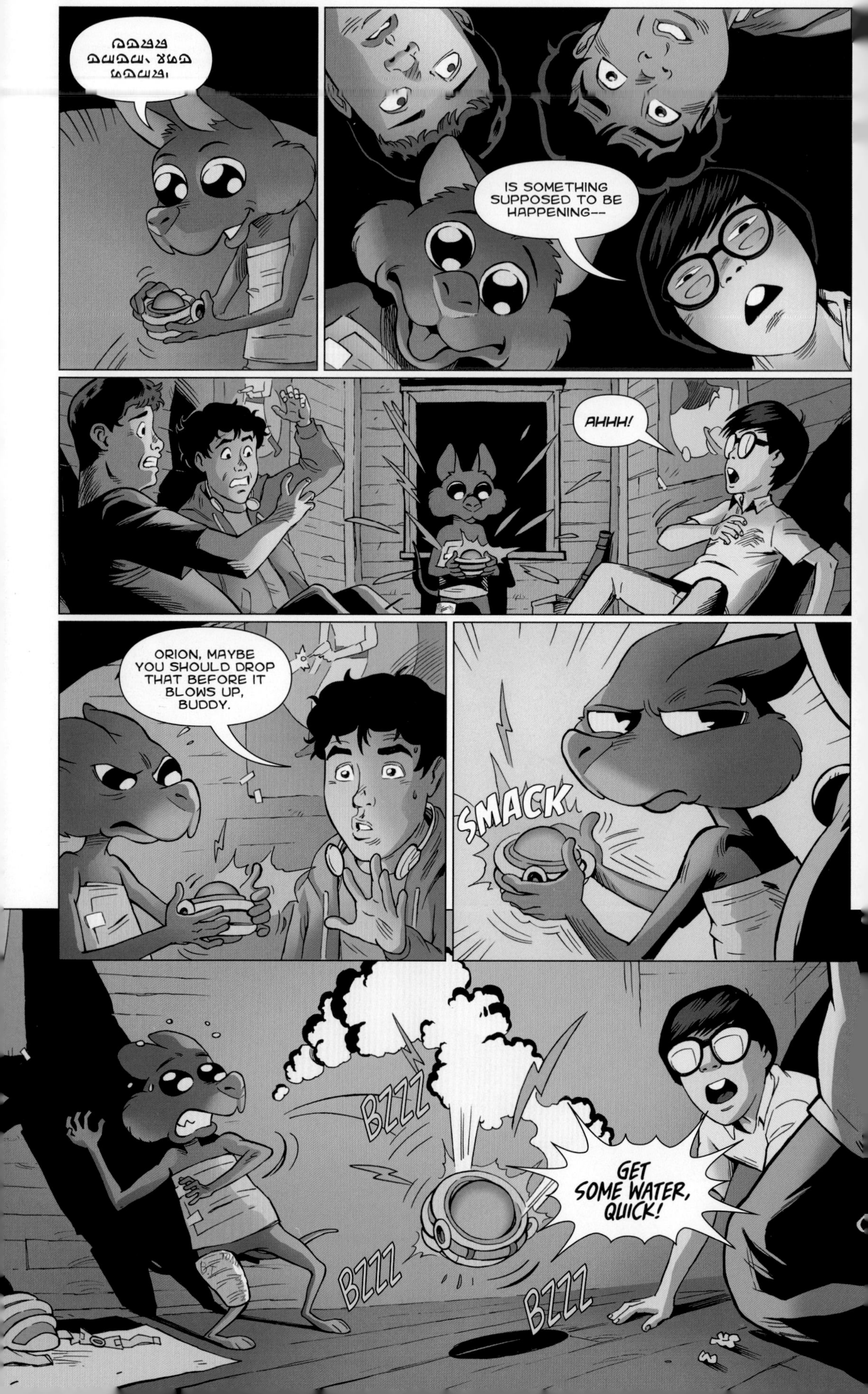
IS SOMETHING SUPPOSED TO BE HAPPENING--
AHHH!
ORION, MAYBE YOU SHOULD DROP THAT BEFORE IT BLOWS UP, BUDDY.
SMACK
BZZZ
GET SOME WATER, QUICK!
BZZZ
BZZZ

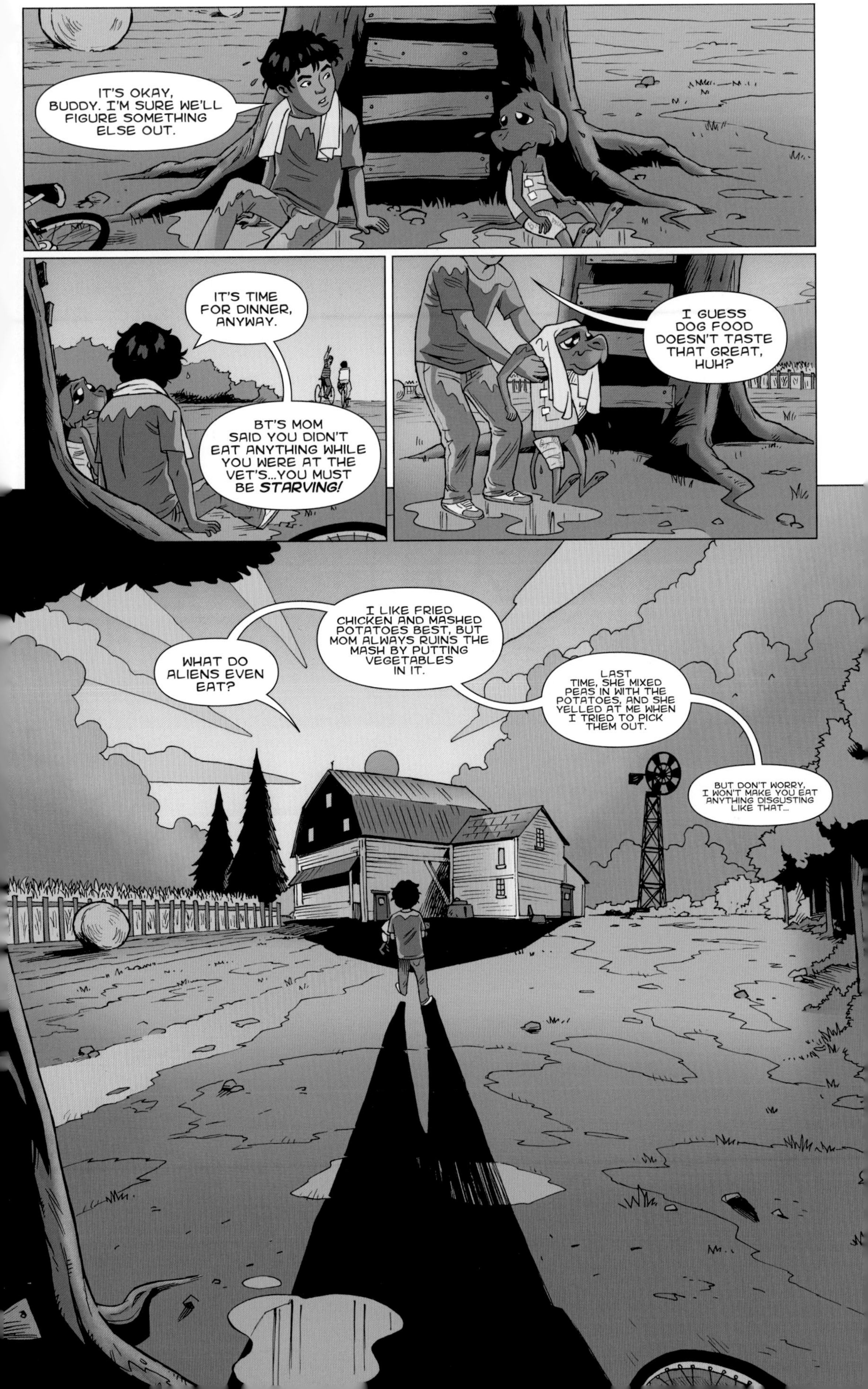
IT'S OKAY, BUDDY. I'M SURE WE'LL FIGURE SOMETHING ELSE OUT.
IT'S TIME FOR DINNER, ANYWAY.
BT'S MOM SAID YOU DIDN'T EAT ANYTHING WHILE YOU WERE AT THE VET'S...YOU MUST BE *STARVING!*
I GUESS DOG FOOD DOESN'T TASTE THAT GREAT, HUH?
WHAT DO ALIENS EVEN EAT?
I LIKE FRIED CHICKEN AND MASHED POTATOES BEST, BUT MOM ALWAYS RUINS THE MASH BY PUTTING VEGETABLES IN IT.
LAST TIME, SHE MIXED PEAS IN WITH THE POTATOES, AND SHE YELLED AT ME WHEN I TRIED TO PICK THEM OUT.
BUT DON'T WORRY, I WON'T MAKE YOU EAT ANYTHING DISGUSTING LIKE THAT...

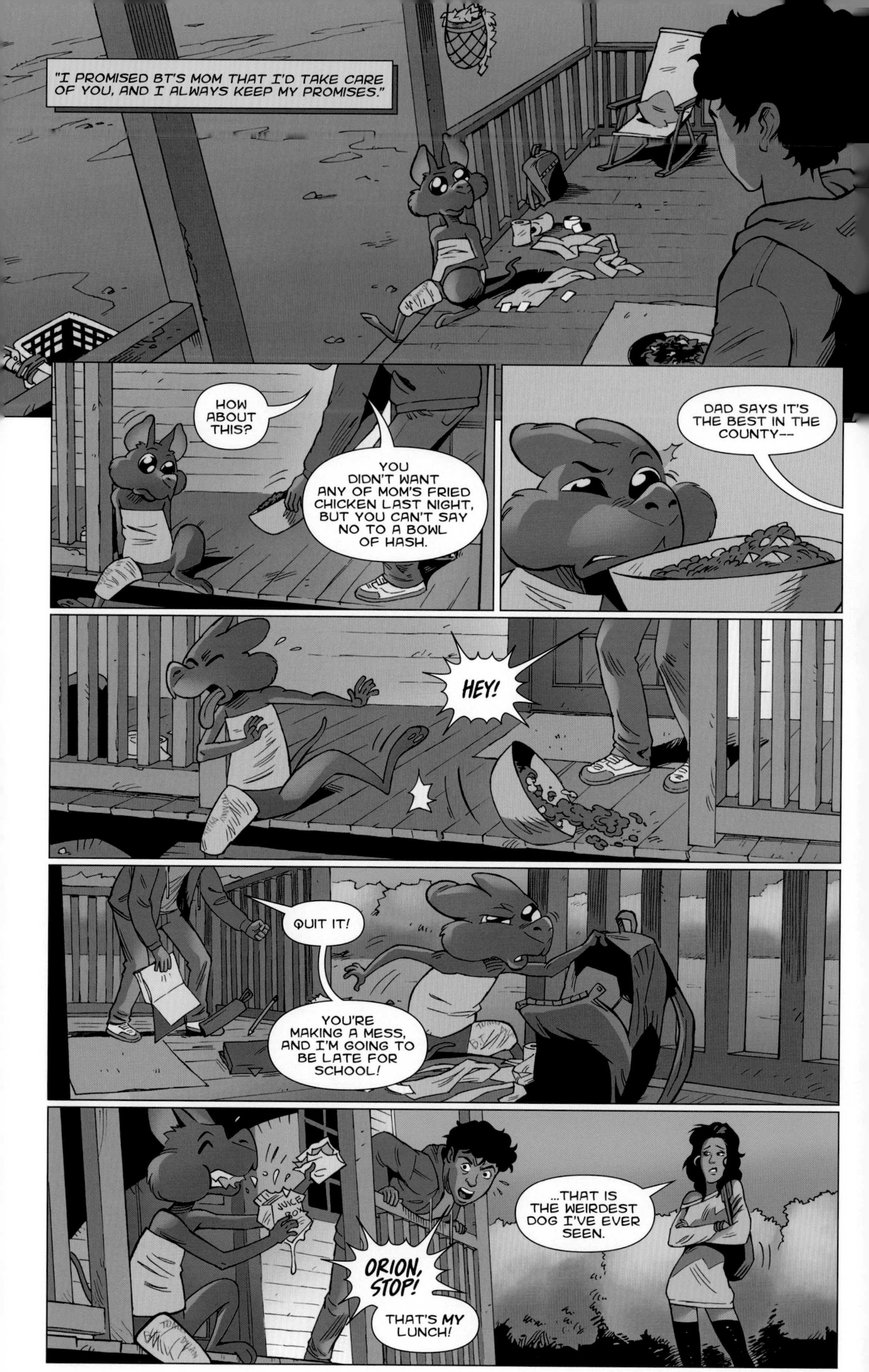
"I PROMISED BT'S MOM THAT I'D TAKE CARE OF YOU, AND I ALWAYS KEEP MY PROMISES."
HOW ABOUT THIS?
YOU DIDN'T WANT ANY OF MOM'S FRIED CHICKEN LAST NIGHT, BUT YOU CAN'T SAY NO TO A BOWL OF HASH.
DAD SAYS IT'S THE BEST IN THE COUNTY--
HEY!
QUIT IT!
YOU'RE MAKING A MESS, AND I'M GOING TO BE LATE FOR SCHOOL!
JUICE BOX
ORION, STOP!
THAT'S MY LUNCH!
...THAT IS THE WEIRDEST DOG I'VE EVER SEEN.

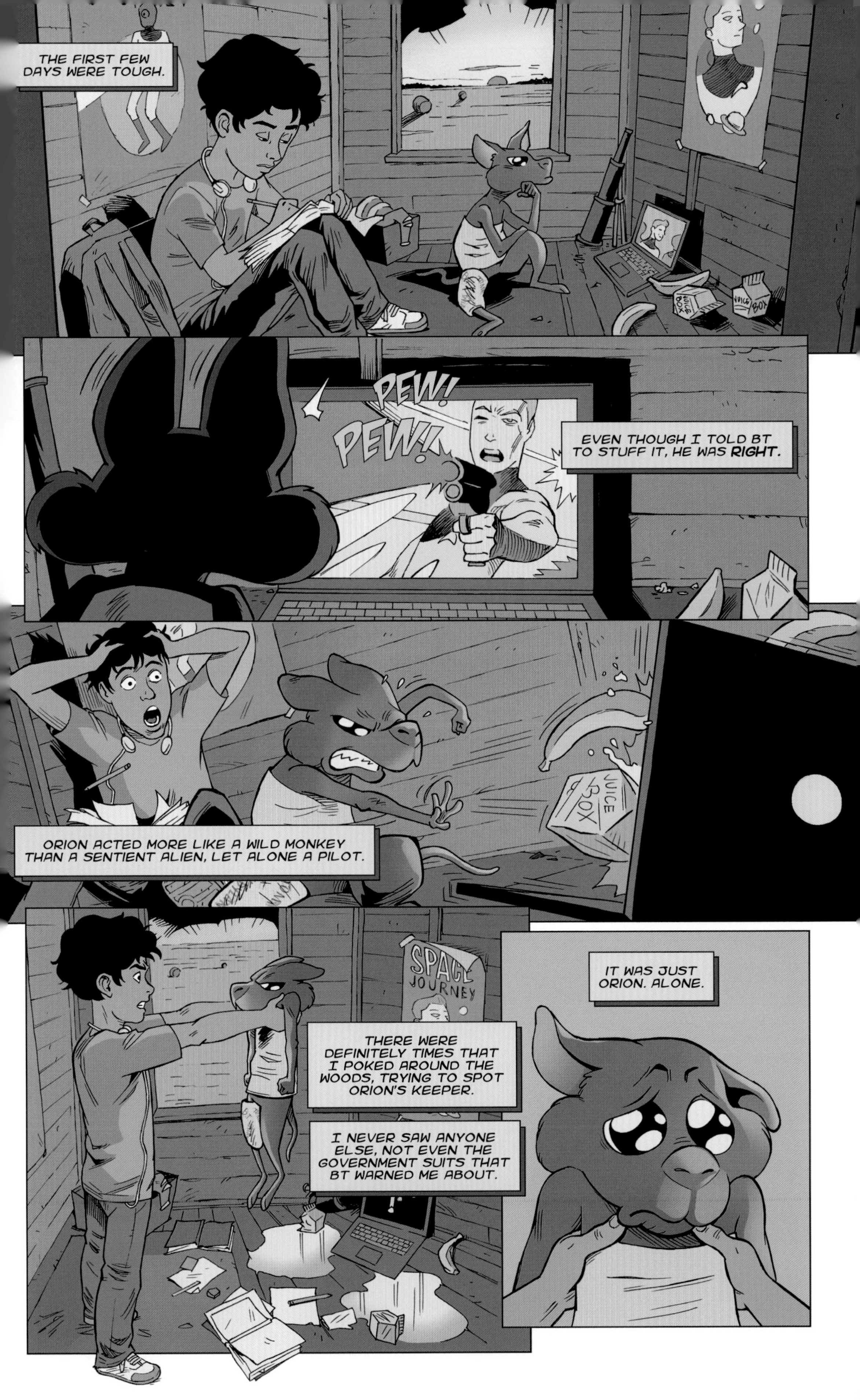
THE FIRST FEW DAYS WERE TOUGH.
JUICE BOX
JUICE BOX
PEW!
PEW!
EVEN THOUGH I TOLD BT TO STUFF IT, HE WAS **RIGHT.**
JUICE BOX
ORION ACTED MORE LIKE A WILD MONKEY THAN A SENTIENT ALIEN, LET ALONE A PILOT.
SPACE JOURNEY
THERE WERE DEFINITELY TIMES THAT I POKED AROUND THE WOODS, TRYING TO SPOT ORION'S KEEPER.
I NEVER SAW ANYONE ELSE, NOT EVEN THE GOVERNMENT SUITS THAT BT WARNED ME ABOUT.
IT WAS JUST ORION. ALONE.

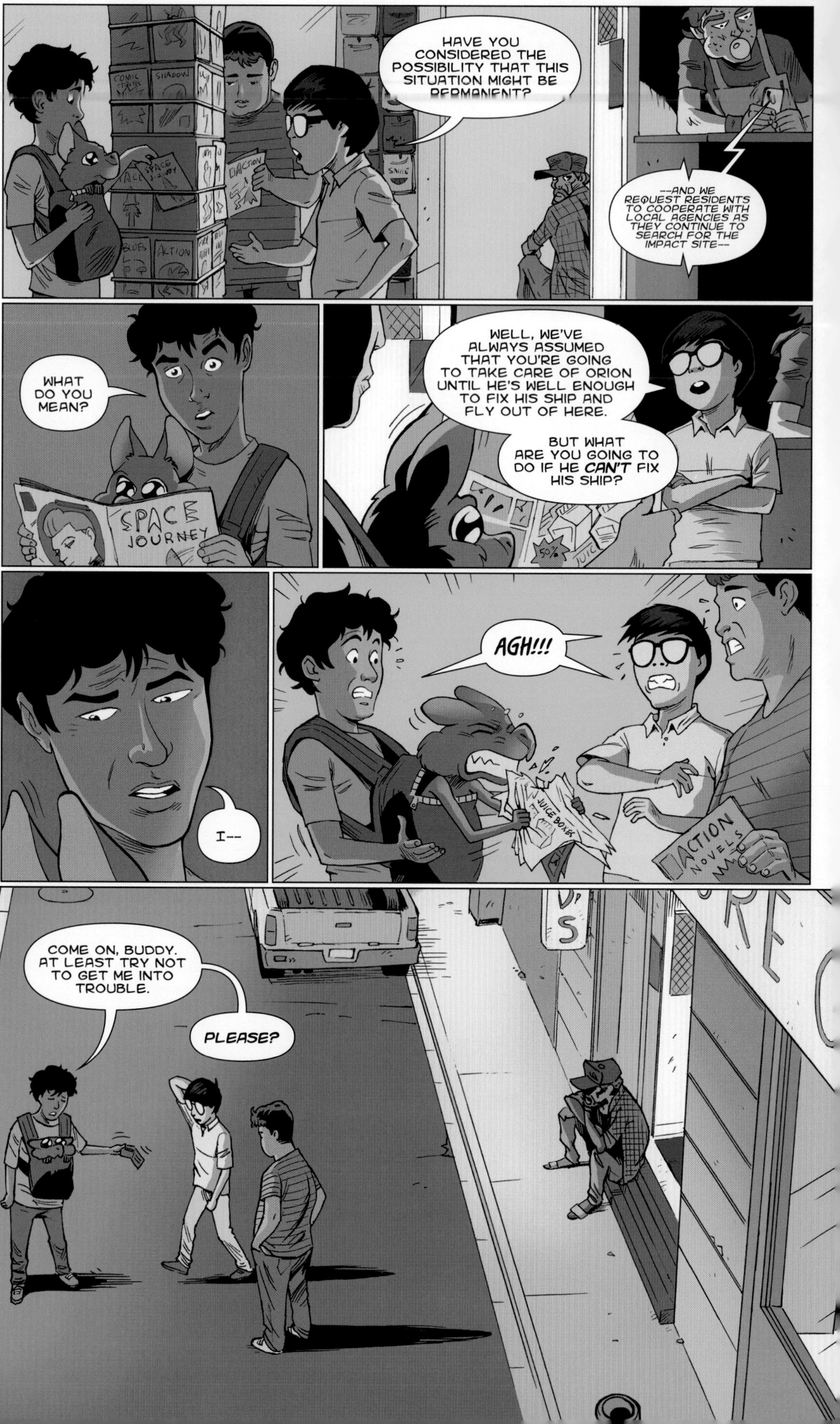

COMIC
SHADOW
SPACE JOURNEY
ACTION
BLUES
ACTION
HAVE YOU CONSIDERED THE POSSIBILITY THAT THIS SITUATION MIGHT BE PERMANENT?
--AND WE REQUEST RESIDENTS TO COOPERATE WITH LOCAL AGENCIES AS THEY CONTINUE TO SEARCH FOR THE IMPACT SITE--
WHAT DO YOU MEAN?
SPACE JOURNEY
WELL, WE'VE ALWAYS ASSUMED THAT YOU'RE GOING TO TAKE CARE OF ORION UNTIL HE'S WELL ENOUGH TO FIX HIS SHIP AND FLY OUT OF HERE.
BUT WHAT ARE YOU GOING TO DO IF HE **CAN'T** FIX HIS SHIP?
50%
I--
AGH!!!
JUICE BOXES
ACTION NOVELS
COME ON, BUDDY. AT LEAST TRY NOT TO GET ME INTO TROUBLE.
PLEASE?

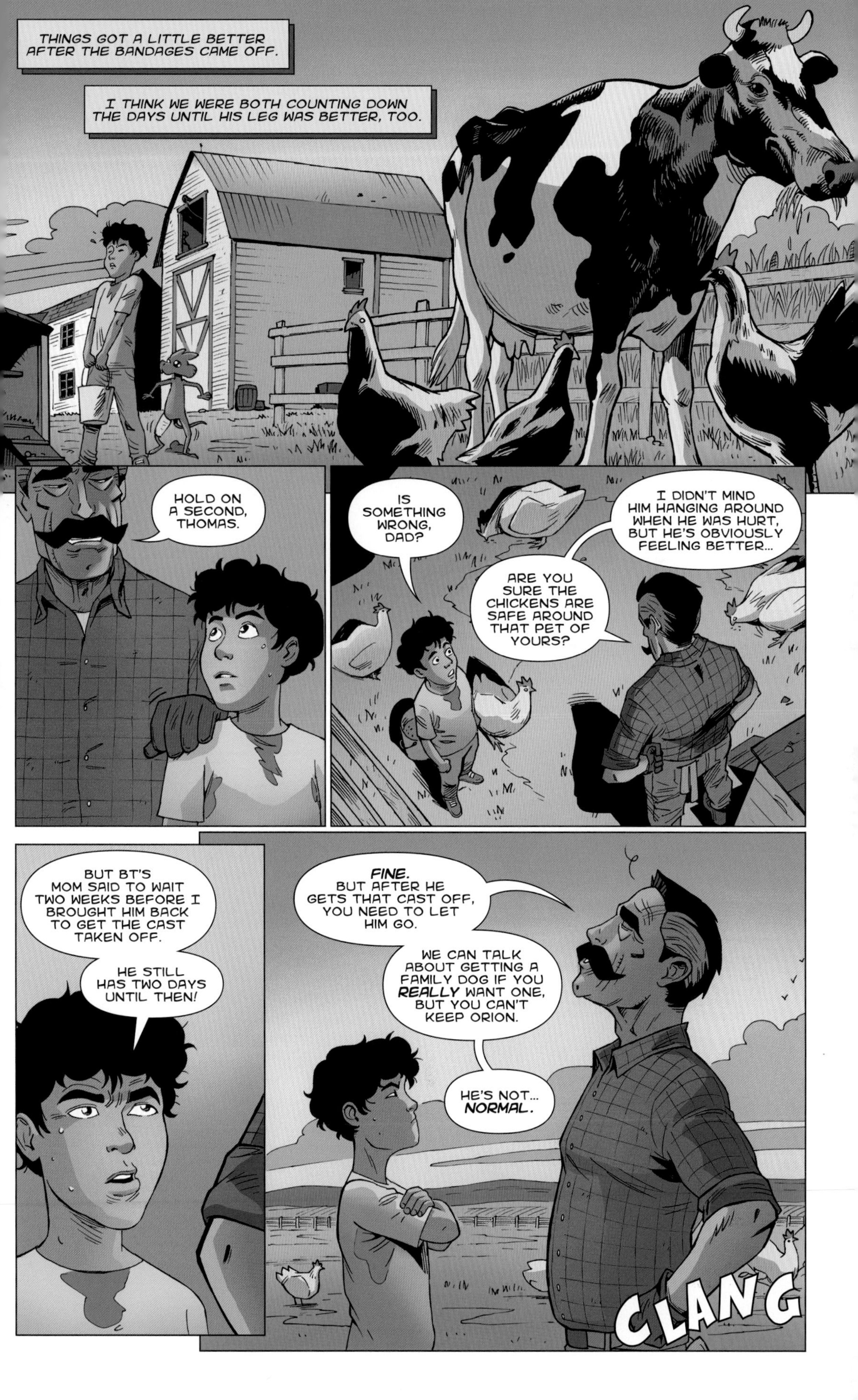
THINGS GOT A LITTLE BETTER AFTER THE BANDAGES CAME OFF.
I THINK WE WERE BOTH COUNTING DOWN THE DAYS UNTIL HIS LEG WAS BETTER, TOO.
HOLD ON A SECOND, THOMAS.
IS SOMETHING WRONG, DAD?
I DIDN'T MIND HIM HANGING AROUND WHEN HE WAS HURT, BUT HE'S OBVIOUSLY FEELING BETTER...
ARE YOU SURE THE CHICKENS ARE SAFE AROUND THAT PET OF YOURS?
BUT BT'S MOM SAID TO WAIT TWO WEEKS BEFORE I BROUGHT HIM BACK TO GET THE CAST TAKEN OFF.
HE STILL HAS TWO DAYS UNTIL THEN!
FINE. BUT AFTER HE GETS THAT CAST OFF, YOU NEED TO LET HIM GO.
WE CAN TALK ABOUT GETTING A FAMILY DOG IF YOU REALLY WANT ONE, BUT YOU CAN'T KEEP ORION.
HE'S NOT... NORMAL.
CLANG

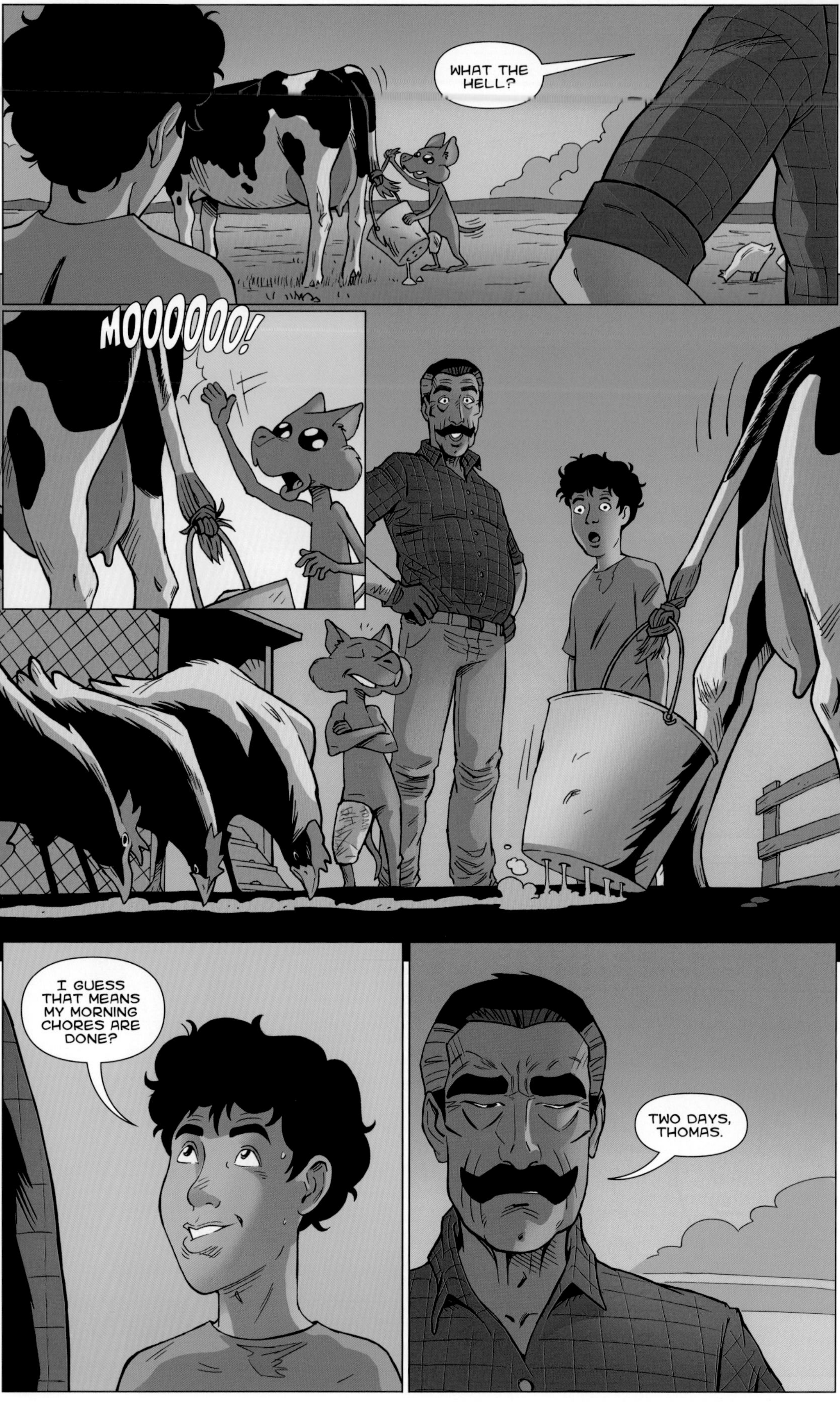
WHAT THE HELL?
MOOOOOO!
I GUESS THAT MEANS MY MORNING CHORES ARE DONE?
TWO DAYS, THOMAS.

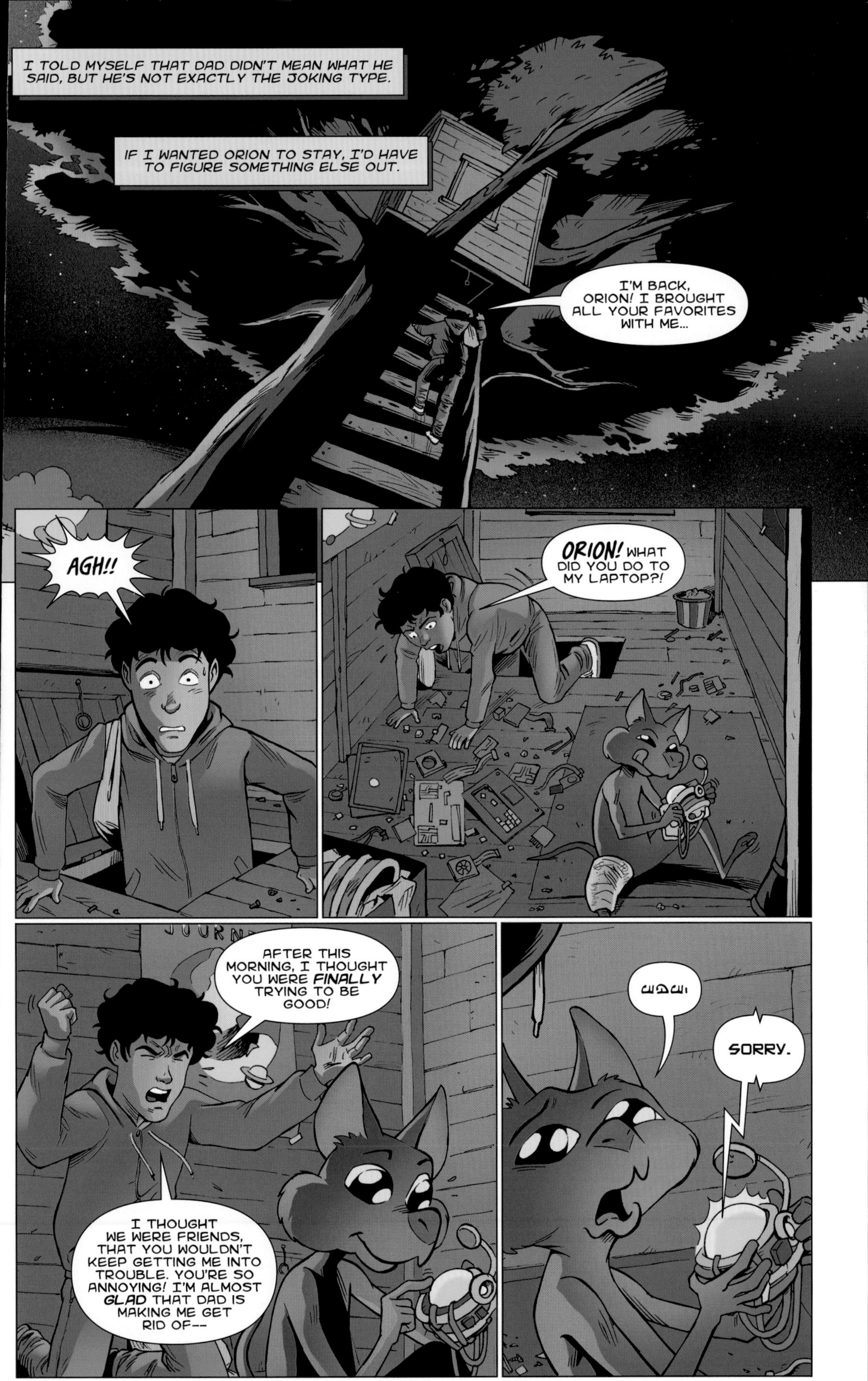
I TOLD MYSELF THAT DAD DIDN'T MEAN WHAT HE SAID, BUT HE'S NOT EXACTLY THE JOKING TYPE.
IF I WANTED ORION TO STAY, I'D HAVE TO FIGURE SOMETHING ELSE OUT.
I'M BACK, ORION! I BROUGHT ALL YOUR FAVORITES WITH ME...
AGH!!
ORION! WHAT DID YOU DO TO MY LAPTOP?!
AFTER THIS MORNING, I THOUGHT YOU WERE FINALLY TRYING TO BE GOOD!
I THOUGHT WE WERE FRIENDS, THAT YOU WOULDN'T KEEP GETTING ME INTO TROUBLE. YOU'RE SO ANNOYING! I'M ALMOST GLAD THAT DAD IS MAKING ME GET RID OF--
SORRY.

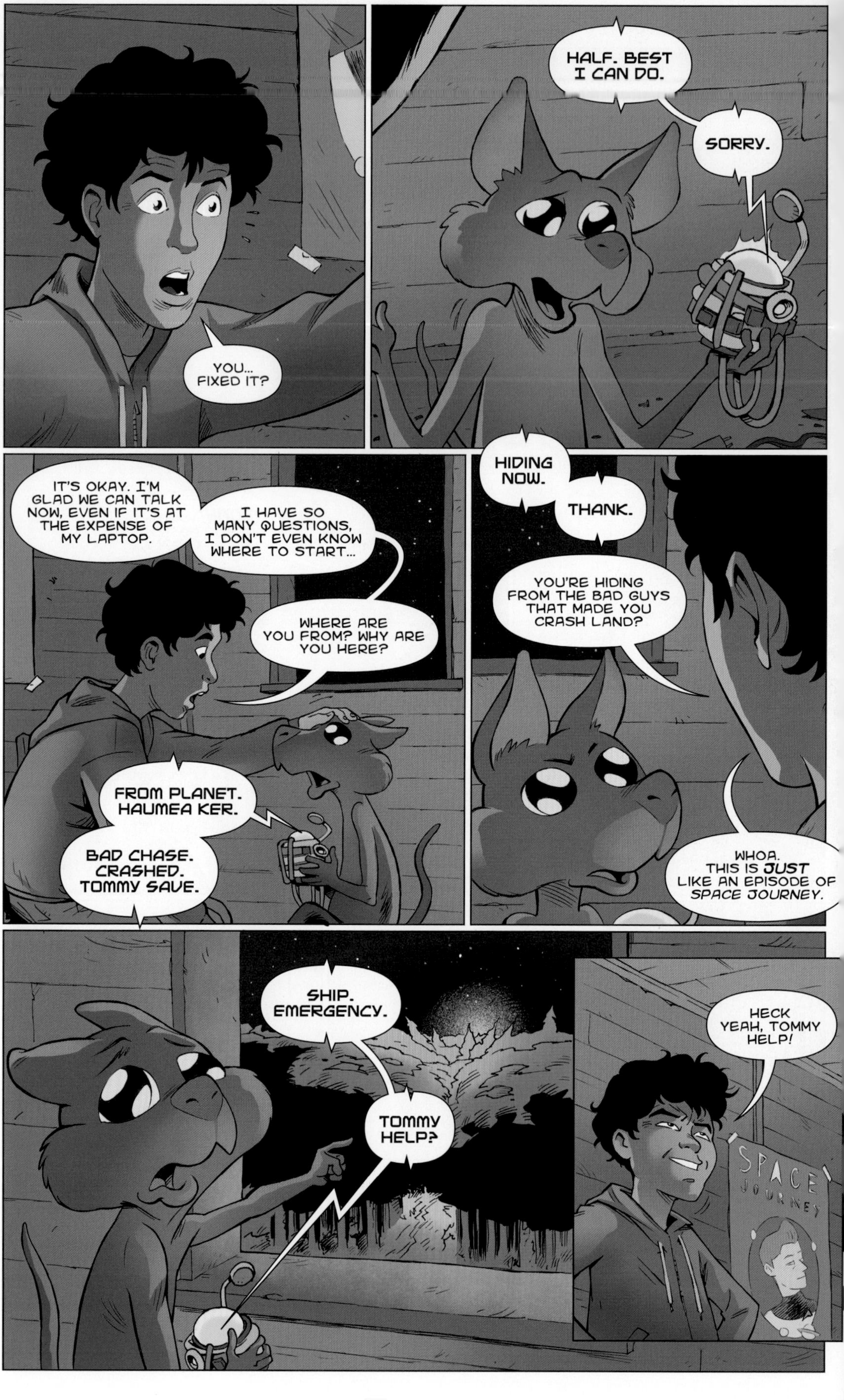
YOU... FIXED IT?
HALF. BEST I CAN DO.
SORRY.
IT'S OKAY. I'M GLAD WE CAN TALK NOW, EVEN IF IT'S AT THE EXPENSE OF MY LAPTOP.
I HAVE SO MANY QUESTIONS, I DON'T EVEN KNOW WHERE TO START...
WHERE ARE YOU FROM? WHY ARE YOU HERE?
FROM PLANET. HAUMEA KER.
BAD CHASE. CRASHED. TOMMY SAVE.
HIDING NOW.
THANK.
YOU'RE HIDING FROM THE BAD GUYS THAT MADE YOU CRASH LAND?
WHOA. THIS IS **JUST** LIKE AN EPISODE OF *SPACE JOURNEY*.
SHIP. EMERGENCY.
TOMMY HELP?
HECK YEAH, TOMMY HELP!
SPACE JOURNEY

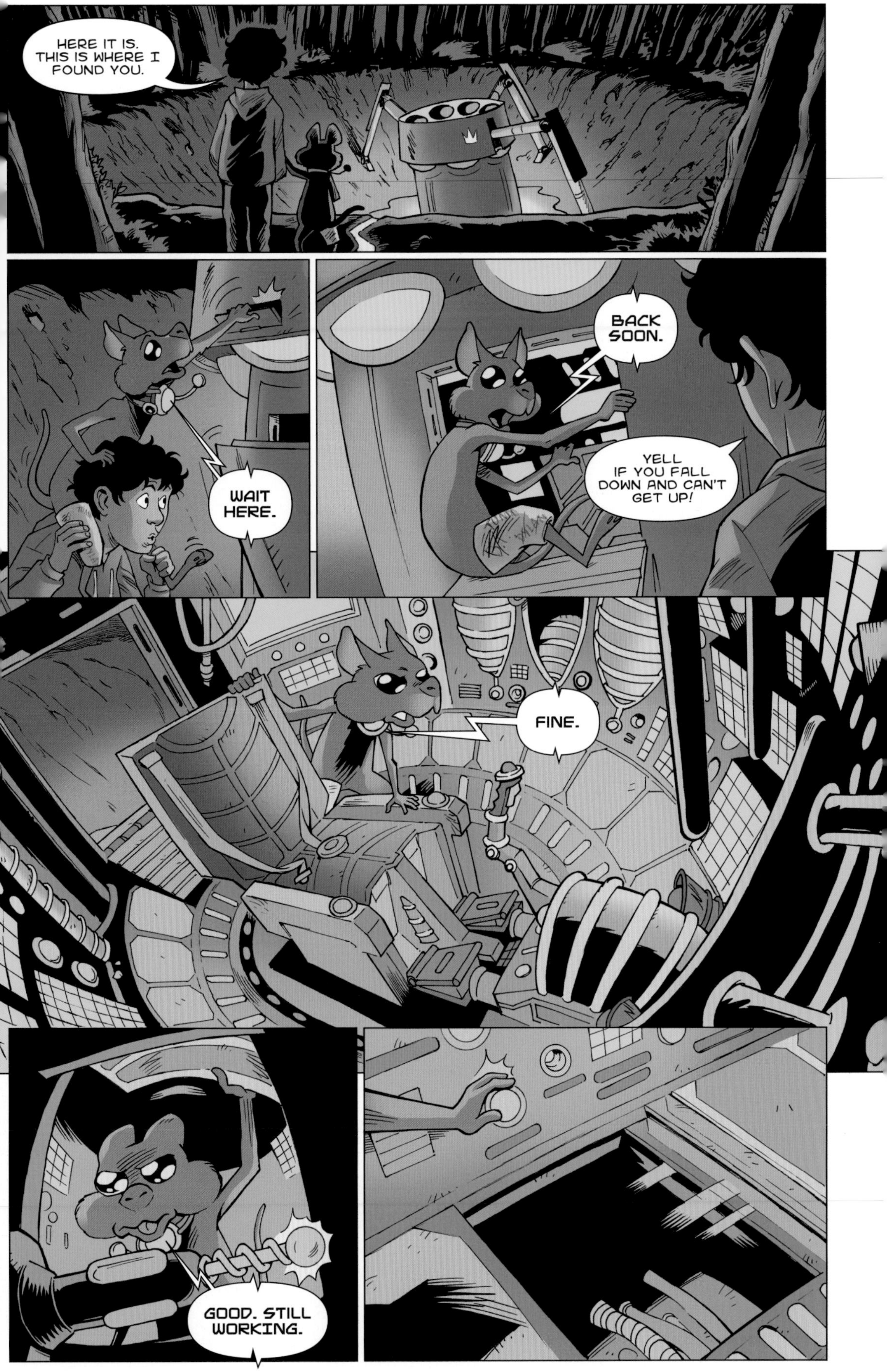
HERE IT IS. THIS IS WHERE I FOUND YOU.
WAIT HERE.
BACK SOON.
YELL IF YOU FALL DOWN AND CAN'T GET UP!
FINE.
GOOD. STILL WORKING.

NOT GOOD.
MAYBE WE SHOULD JUST COME BACK WHEN YOUR CAST IS GONE?
I BET EVEN BT WOULD OFFER TO HELP IF HE GOT TO SEE THE INSIDE OF A SPACESHIP!
THAT!
EXCREMENT!
"WHAT HAPPENED TO YOU LAST NIGHT?"

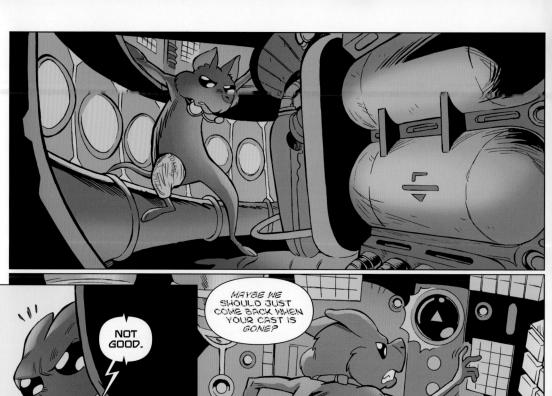

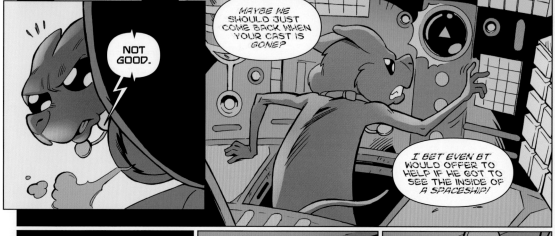

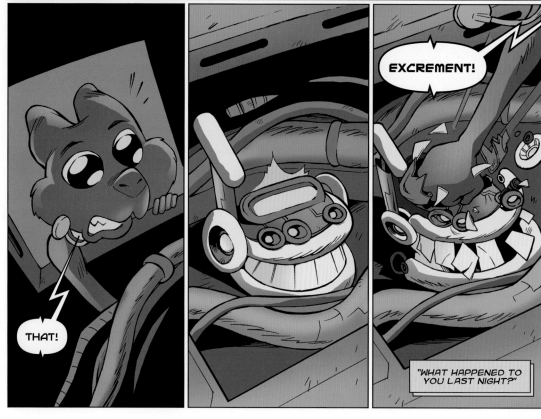

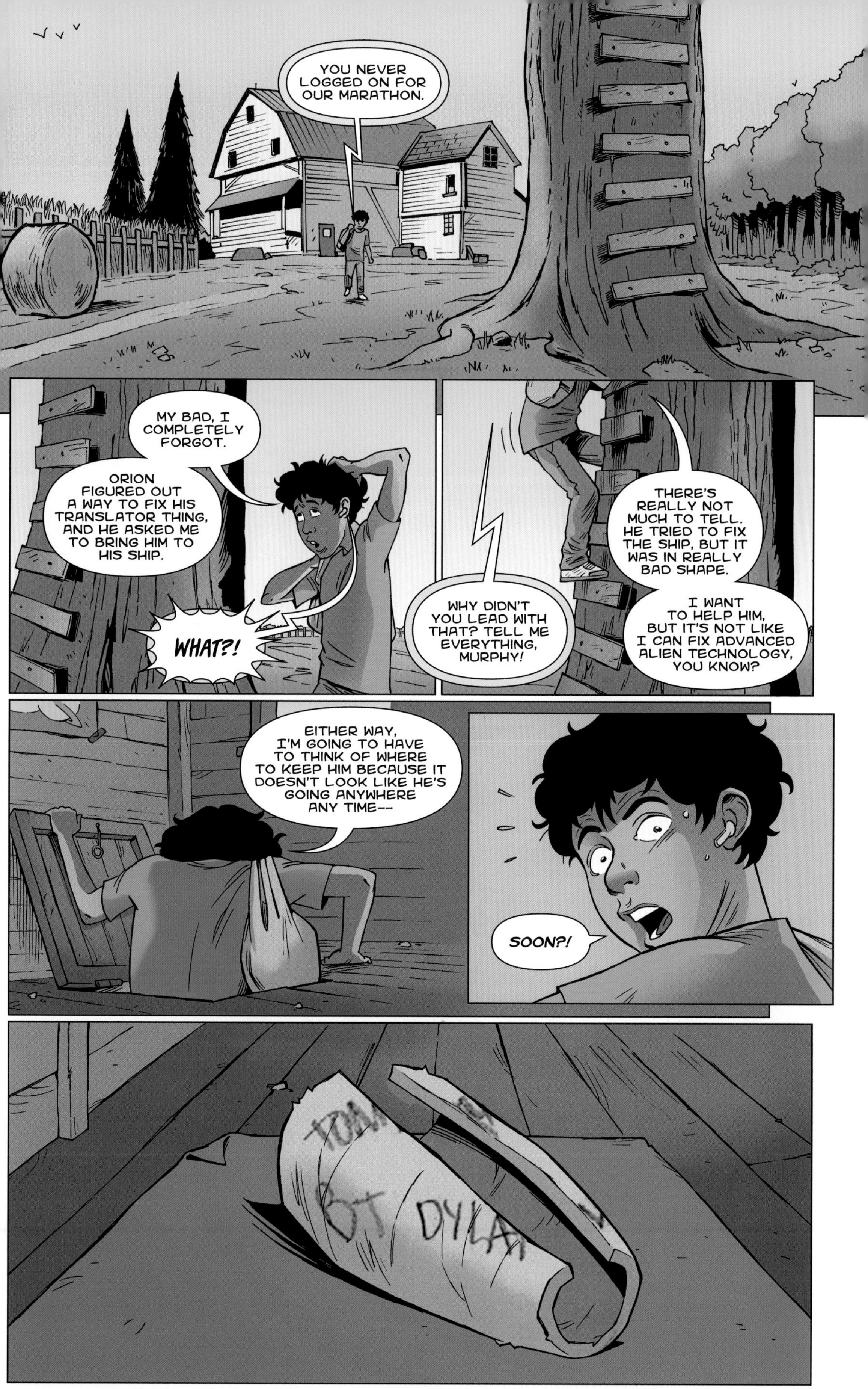

YOU NEVER LOGGED ON FOR OUR MARATHON.
MY BAD, I COMPLETELY FORGOT.
ORION FIGURED OUT A WAY TO FIX HIS TRANSLATOR THING, AND HE ASKED ME TO BRING HIM TO HIS SHIP.
WHAT?!
WHY DIDN'T YOU LEAD WITH THAT? TELL ME EVERYTHING, MURPHY!
THERE'S REALLY NOT MUCH TO TELL. HE TRIED TO FIX THE SHIP, BUT IT WAS IN REALLY BAD SHAPE.
I WANT TO HELP HIM, BUT IT'S NOT LIKE I CAN FIX ADVANCED ALIEN TECHNOLOGY, YOU KNOW?
EITHER WAY, I'M GOING TO HAVE TO THINK OF WHERE TO KEEP HIM BECAUSE IT DOESN'T LOOK LIKE HE'S GOING ANYWHERE ANY TIME--
SOON?!

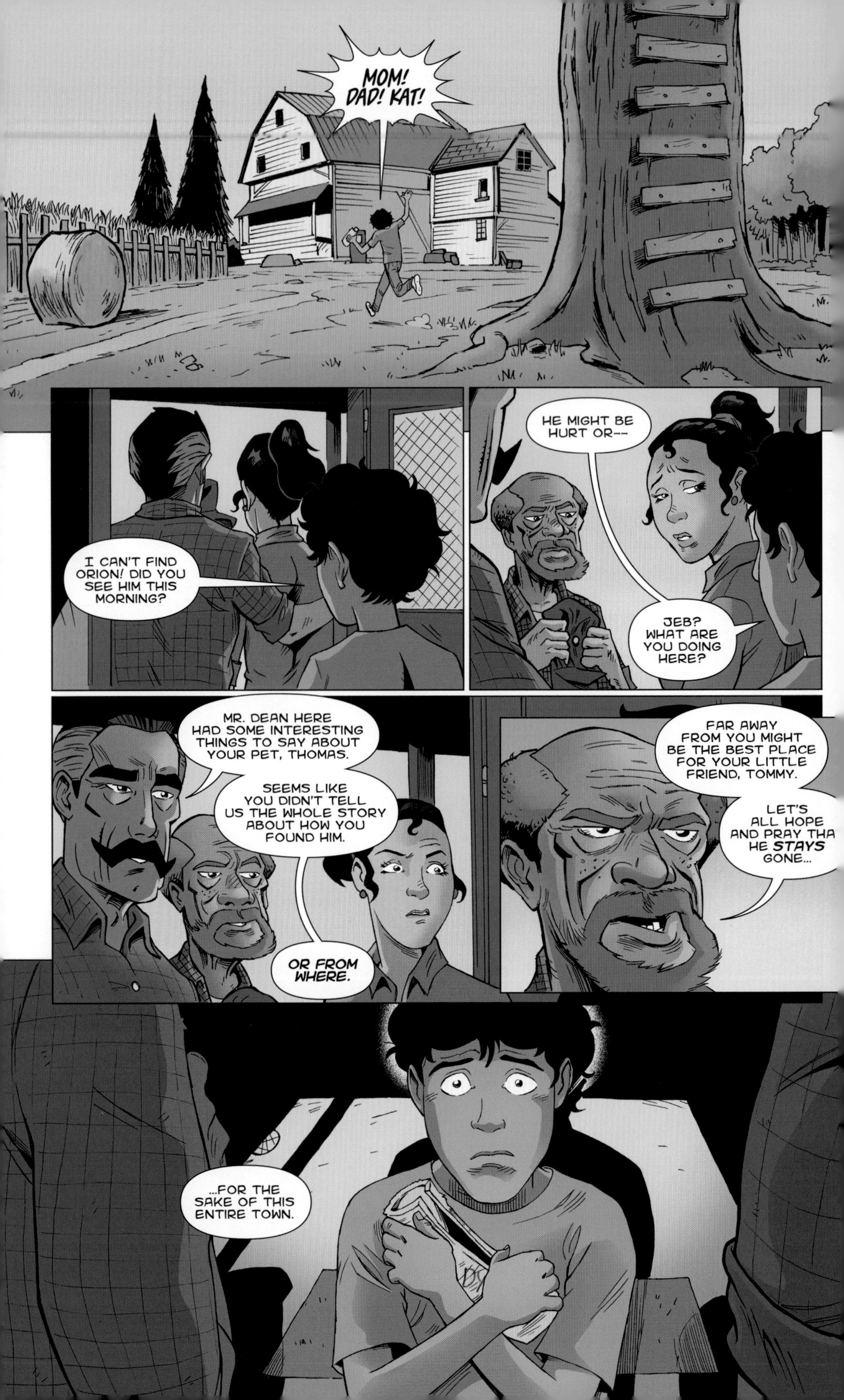
MOM! DAD! KAT!
I CAN'T FIND ORION! DID YOU SEE HIM THIS MORNING?
HE MIGHT BE HURT OR--
JEB? WHAT ARE YOU DOING HERE?
MR. DEAN HERE HAD SOME INTERESTING THINGS TO SAY ABOUT YOUR PET, THOMAS.
SEEMS LIKE YOU DIDN'T TELL US THE WHOLE STORY ABOUT HOW YOU FOUND HIM.
OR FROM WHERE.
FAR AWAY FROM YOU MIGHT BE THE BEST PLACE FOR YOUR LITTLE FRIEND, TOMMY.
LET'S ALL HOPE AND PRAY THA HE STAYS GONE...
...FOR THE SAKE OF THIS ENTIRE TOWN.

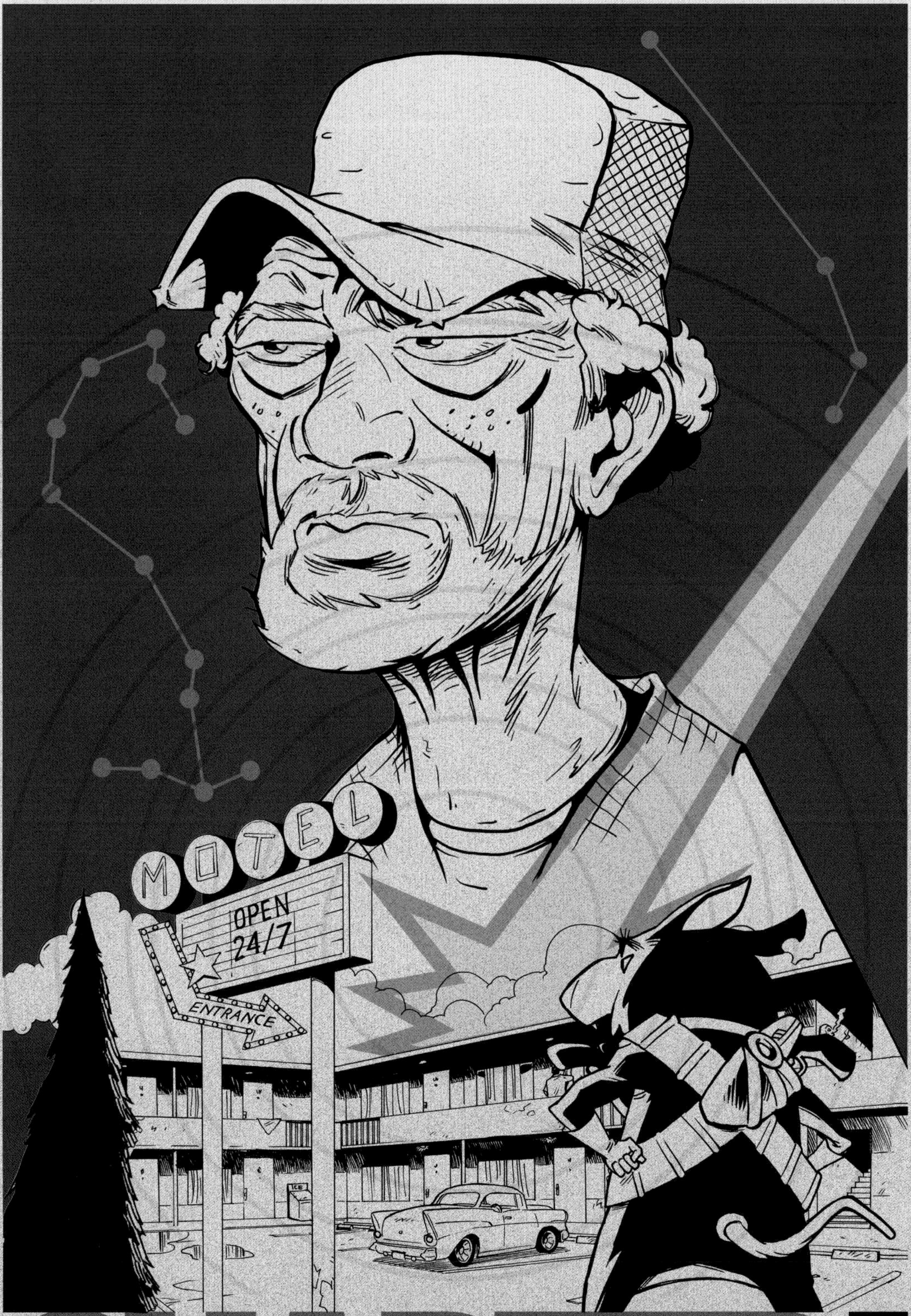
MOTEL
OPEN
24/7
ENTRANCE

CHAPTER THREE

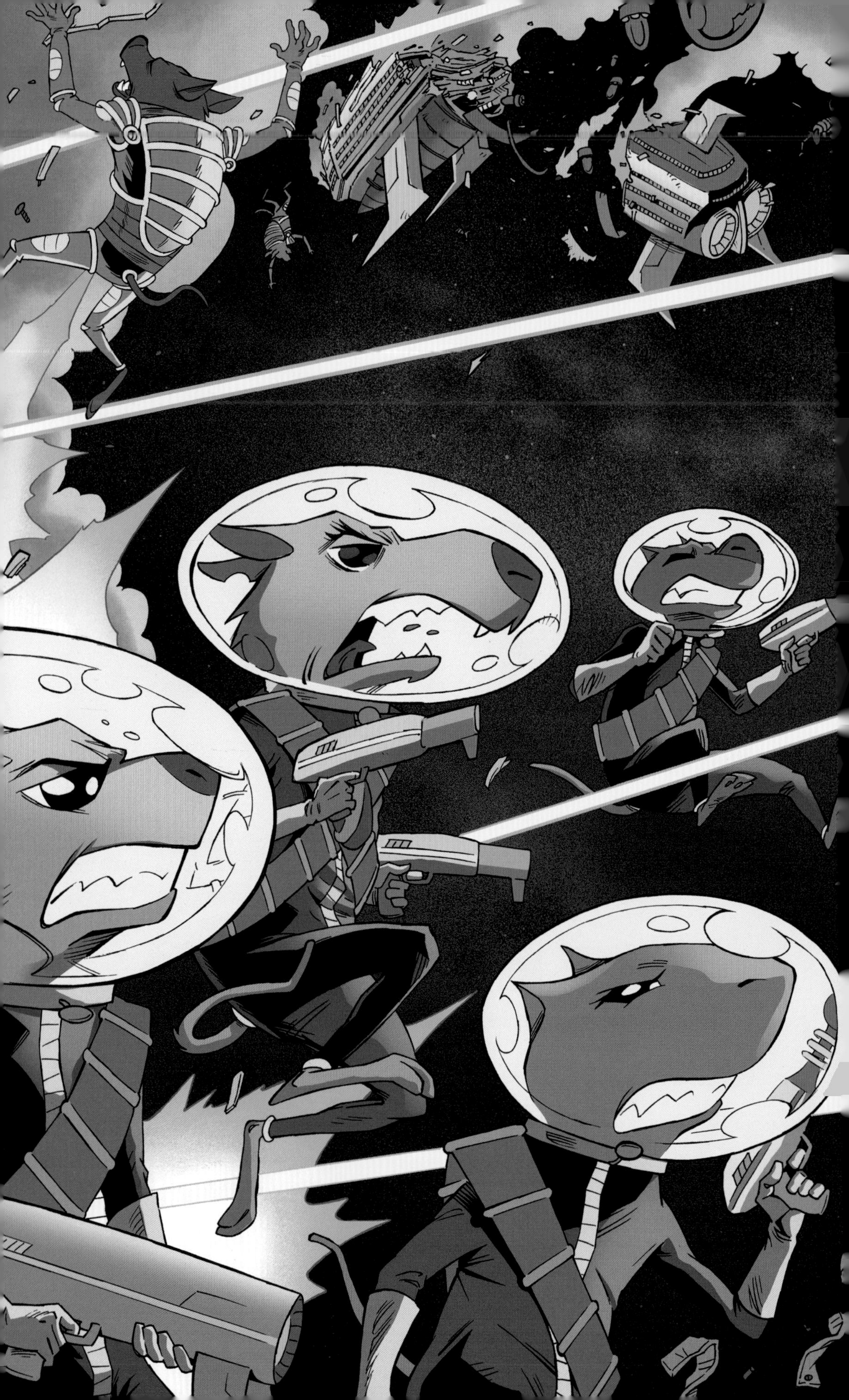

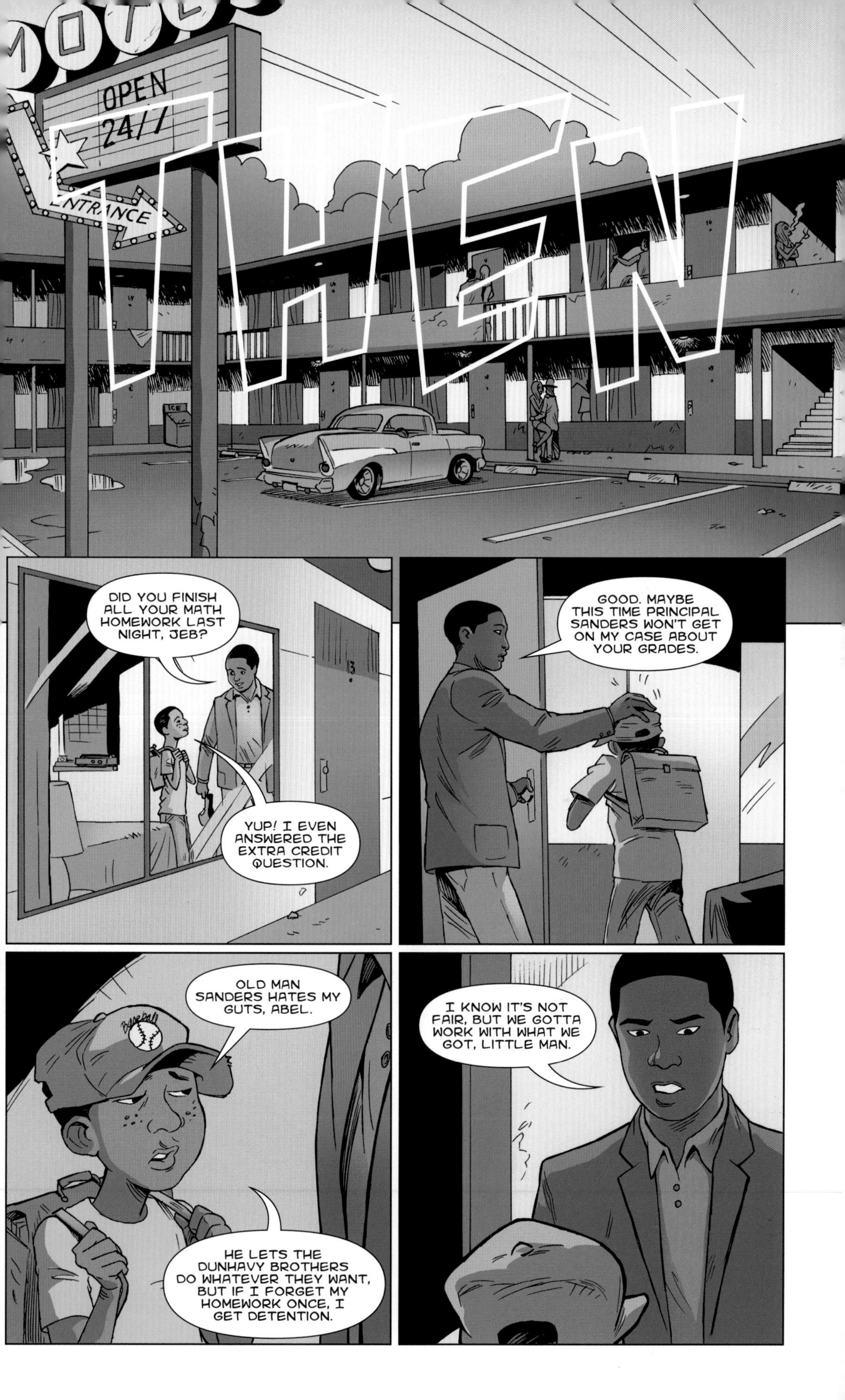
MOTEL
OPEN 24/7
ENTRANCE
THEN
ICE
DID YOU FINISH ALL YOUR MATH HOMEWORK LAST NIGHT, JEB?
YUP! I EVEN ANSWERED THE EXTRA CREDIT QUESTION.
13
GOOD. MAYBE THIS TIME PRINCIPAL SANDERS WON'T GET ON MY CASE ABOUT YOUR GRADES.
OLD MAN SANDERS HATES MY GUTS, ABEL.
HE LETS THE DUNHAVY BROTHERS DO WHATEVER THEY WANT, BUT IF I FORGET MY HOMEWORK ONCE, I GET DETENTION.
I KNOW IT'S NOT FAIR, BUT WE GOTTA WORK WITH WHAT WE GOT, LITTLE MAN.

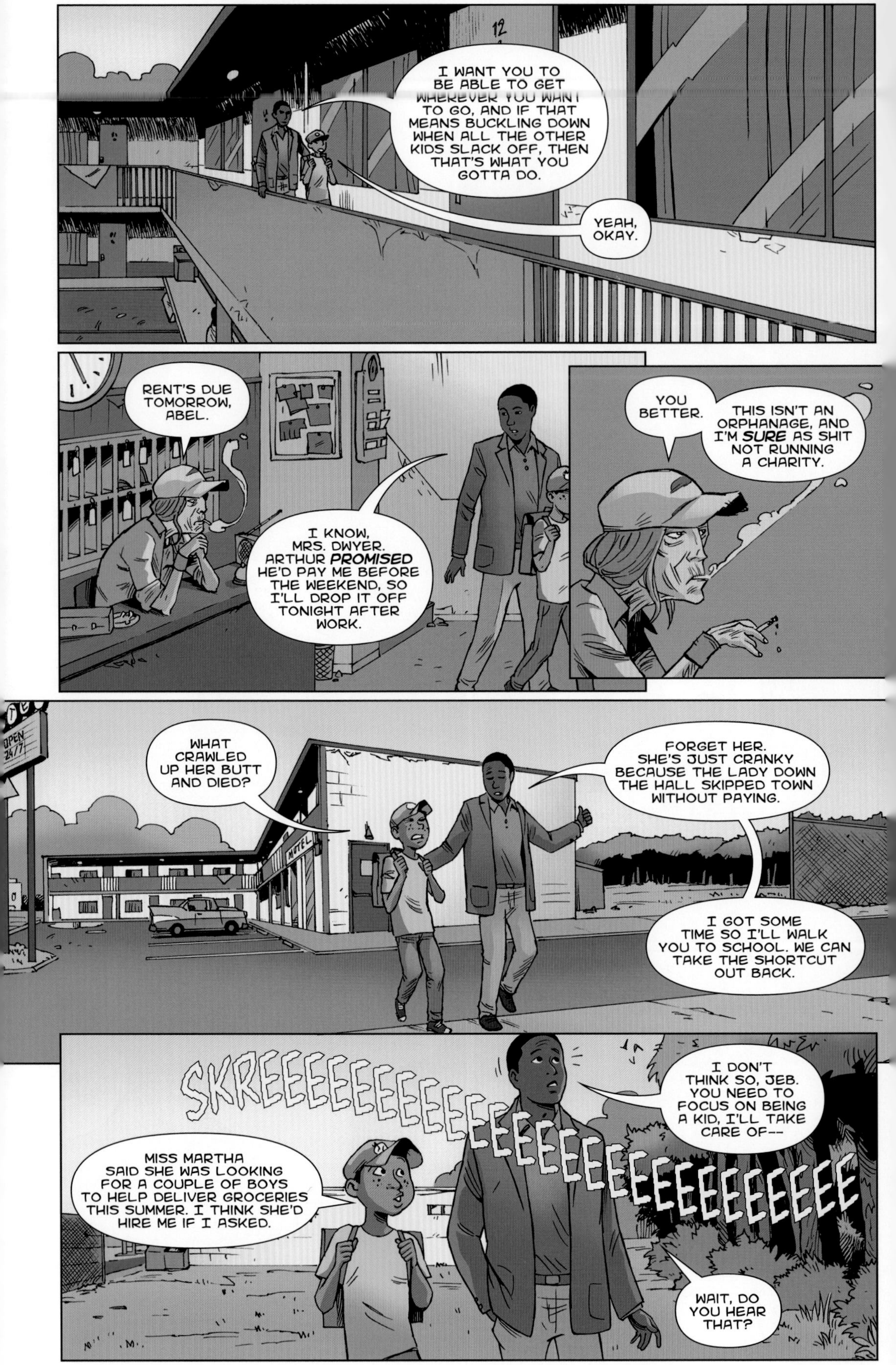
12
I WANT YOU TO BE ABLE TO GET WHEREVER YOU WANT TO GO, AND IF THAT MEANS BUCKLING DOWN WHEN ALL THE OTHER KIDS SLACK OFF, THEN THAT'S WHAT YOU GOTTA DO.
YEAH, OKAY.
RENT'S DUE TOMORROW, ABEL.
I KNOW, MRS. DWYER. ARTHUR **PROMISED** HE'D PAY ME BEFORE THE WEEKEND, SO I'LL DROP IT OFF TONIGHT AFTER WORK.
YOU BETTER.
THIS ISN'T AN ORPHANAGE, AND I'M ***SURE*** AS SHIT NOT RUNNING A CHARITY.
OPEN 24/7
MOTEL
WHAT CRAWLED UP HER BUTT AND DIED?
FORGET HER. SHE'S JUST CRANKY BECAUSE THE LADY DOWN THE HALL SKIPPED TOWN WITHOUT PAYING.
I GOT SOME TIME SO I'LL WALK YOU TO SCHOOL. WE CAN TAKE THE SHORTCUT OUT BACK.
MISS MARTHA SAID SHE WAS LOOKING FOR A COUPLE OF BOYS TO HELP DELIVER GROCERIES THIS SUMMER. I THINK SHE'D HIRE ME IF I ASKED.
I DON'T THINK SO, JEB. YOU NEED TO FOCUS ON BEING A KID, I'LL TAKE CARE OF--
SKREEEEEEEEEEEEEEEEEEEEEEEEEEEEEEEEEE
WAIT, DO YOU HEAR THAT?

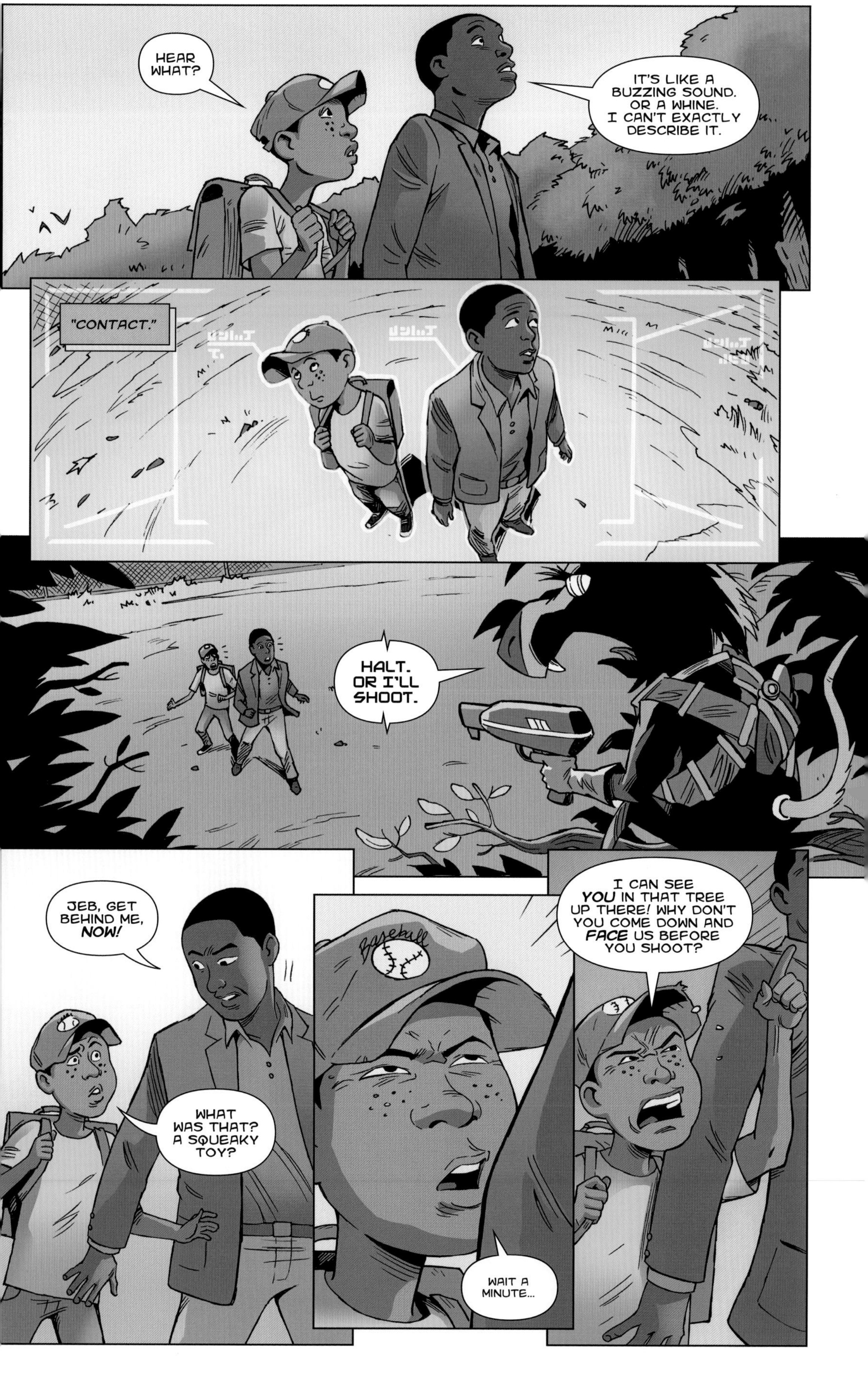
HEAR WHAT?
IT'S LIKE A BUZZING SOUND. OR A WHINE. I CAN'T EXACTLY DESCRIBE IT.
"CONTACT."
HALT. OR I'LL SHOOT.
JEB, GET BEHIND ME, NOW!
WHAT WAS THAT? A SQUEAKY TOY?
WAIT A MINUTE...
I CAN SEE YOU IN THAT TREE UP THERE! WHY DON'T YOU COME DOWN AND FACE US BEFORE YOU SHOOT?

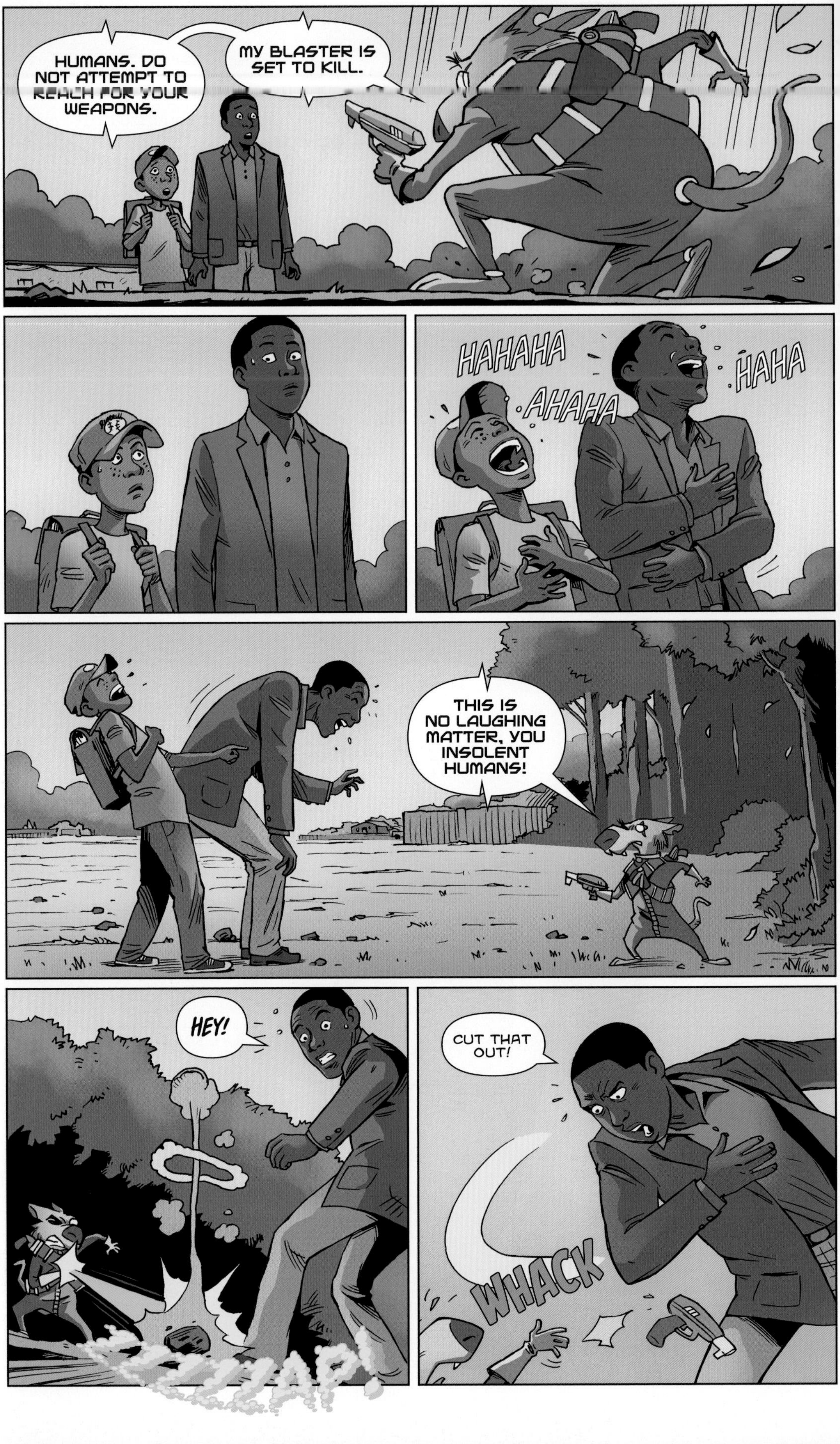

HUMANS. DO NOT ATTEMPT TO REACH FOR YOUR WEAPONS.
MY BLASTER IS SET TO KILL.
HAHAHA
AHAHA
HAHA
THIS IS NO LAUGHING MATTER, YOU INSOLENT HUMANS!
HEY!
ZZZAP!
CUT THAT OUT!
WHACK

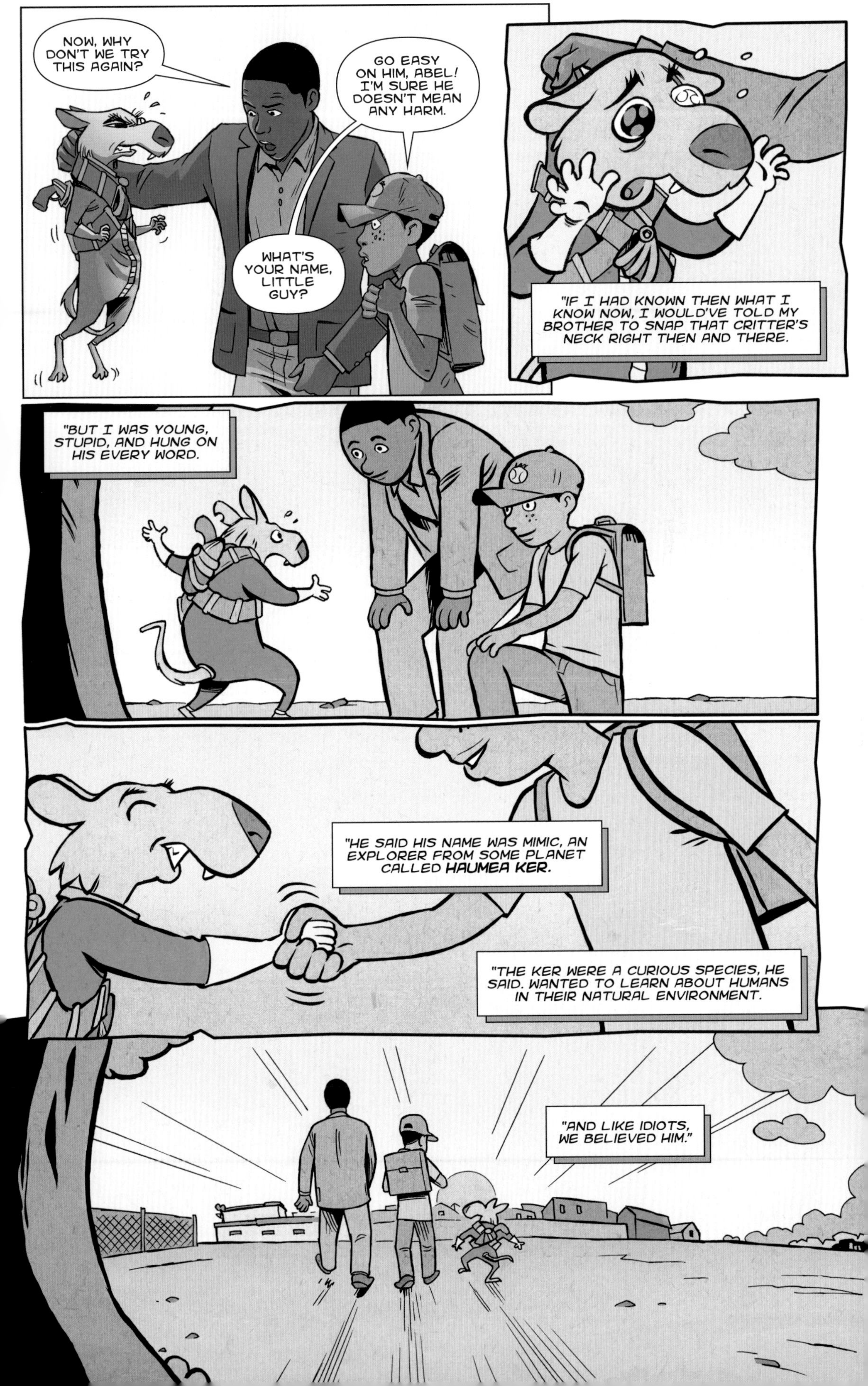
NOW, WHY DON'T WE TRY THIS AGAIN?
GO EASY ON HIM, ABEL! I'M SURE HE DOESN'T MEAN ANY HARM.
WHAT'S YOUR NAME, LITTLE GUY?
"IF I HAD KNOWN THEN WHAT I KNOW NOW, I WOULD'VE TOLD MY BROTHER TO SNAP THAT CRITTER'S NECK RIGHT THEN AND THERE.
"BUT I WAS YOUNG, STUPID, AND HUNG ON HIS EVERY WORD.
"HE SAID HIS NAME WAS MIMIC, AN EXPLORER FROM SOME PLANET CALLED **HAUMEA KER.**
"THE KER WERE A CURIOUS SPECIES, HE SAID. WANTED TO LEARN ABOUT HUMANS IN THEIR NATURAL ENVIRONMENT.
"AND LIKE IDIOTS, WE BELIEVED HIM."

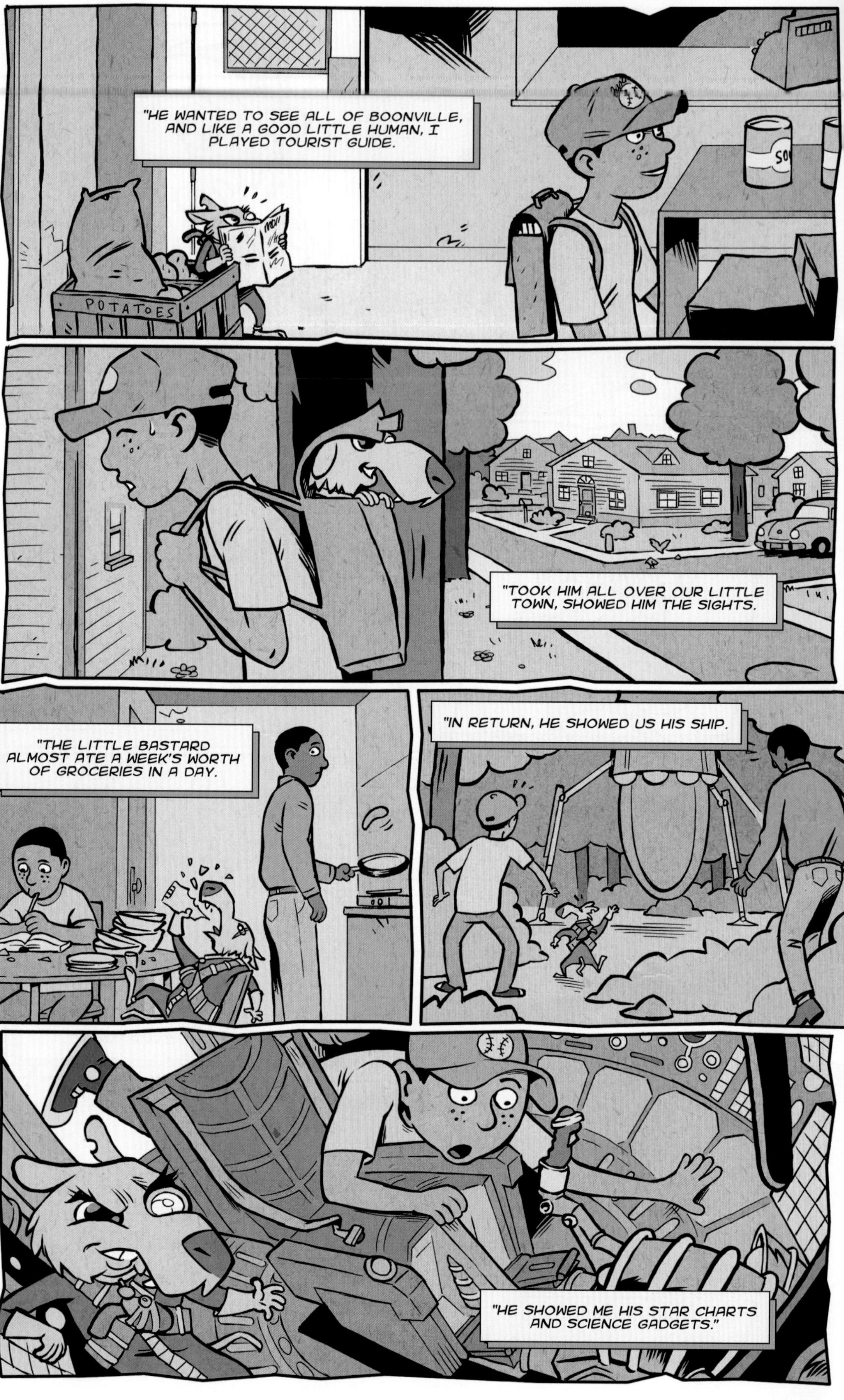
"HE WANTED TO SEE ALL OF BOONVILLE, AND LIKE A GOOD LITTLE HUMAN, I PLAYED TOURIST GUIDE.
POTATOES
"TOOK HIM ALL OVER OUR LITTLE TOWN, SHOWED HIM THE SIGHTS.
"THE LITTLE BASTARD ALMOST ATE A WEEK'S WORTH OF GROCERIES IN A DAY.
"IN RETURN, HE SHOWED US HIS SHIP.
"HE SHOWED ME HIS STAR CHARTS AND SCIENCE GADGETS."

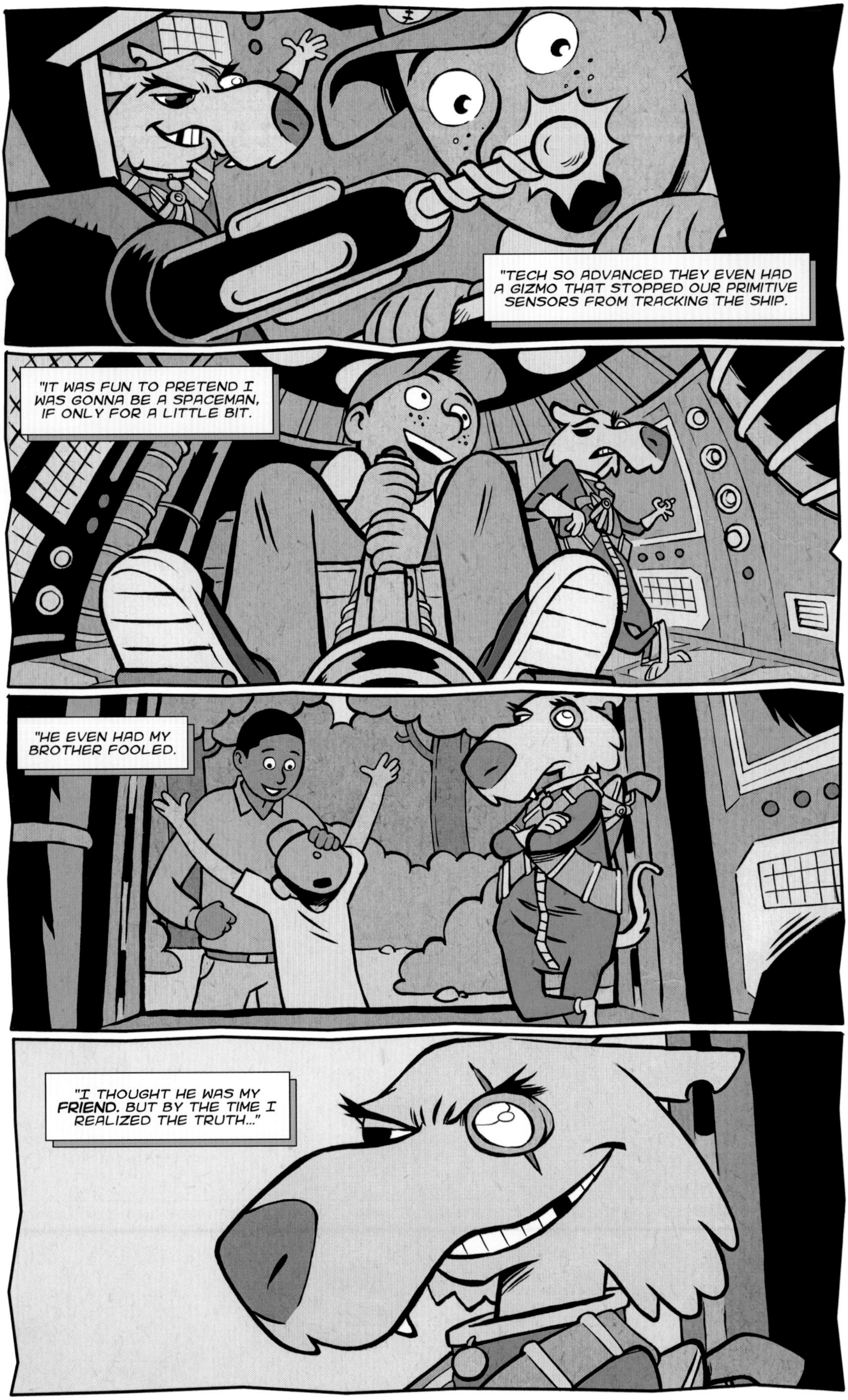
"TECH SO ADVANCED THEY EVEN HAD A GIZMO THAT STOPPED OUR PRIMITIVE SENSORS FROM TRACKING THE SHIP.
"IT WAS FUN TO PRETEND I WAS GONNA BE A SPACEMAN, IF ONLY FOR A LITTLE BIT.
"HE EVEN HAD MY BROTHER FOOLED.
"I THOUGHT HE WAS MY **FRIEND.** BUT BY THE TIME I REALIZED THE TRUTH..."

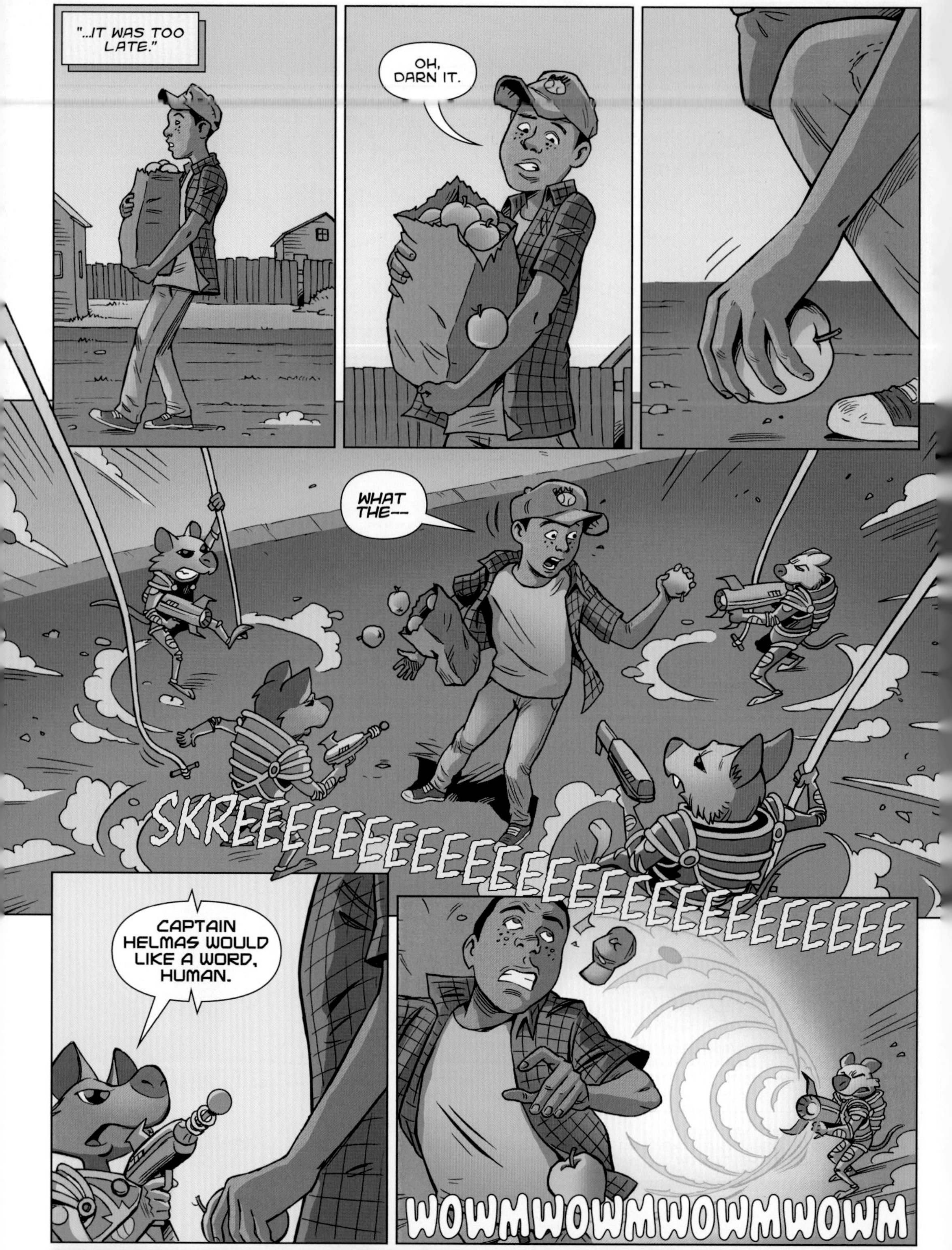
"...IT WAS TOO LATE."
OH, DARN IT.
WHAT THE--
SKREEEEEEEEEEEEEEEEEEEEEEEEEEEEE
CAPTAIN HELMAS WOULD LIKE A WORD, HUMAN.
WOWMWOWMWOWMWOWM

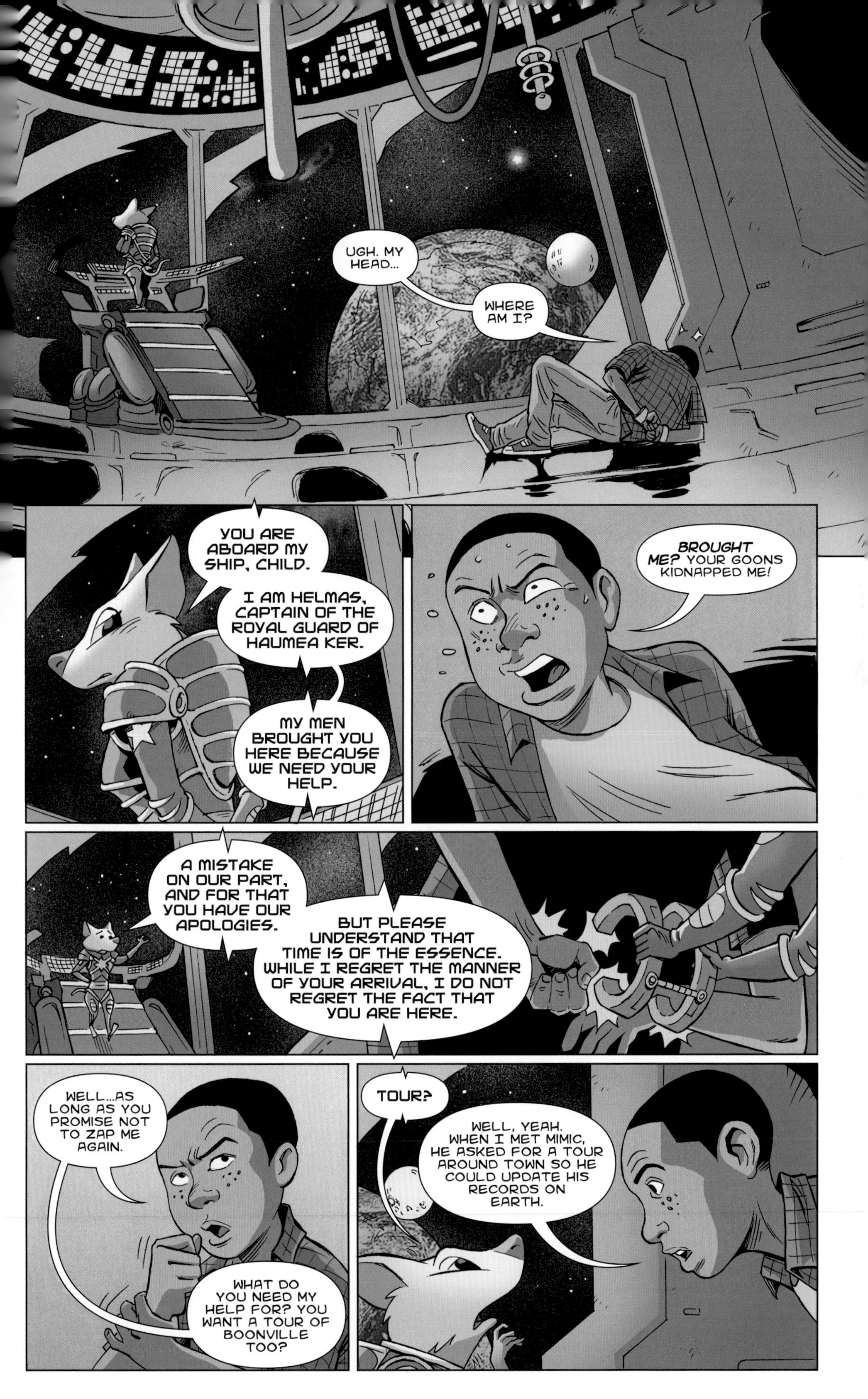
UGH. MY HEAD...
WHERE AM I?
YOU ARE ABOARD MY SHIP, CHILD.
I AM HELMAS, CAPTAIN OF THE ROYAL GUARD OF HAUMEA KER.
MY MEN BROUGHT YOU HERE BECAUSE WE NEED YOUR HELP.
BROUGHT ME? YOUR GOONS KIDNAPPED ME!
A MISTAKE ON OUR PART, AND FOR THAT YOU HAVE OUR APOLOGIES.
BUT PLEASE UNDERSTAND THAT TIME IS OF THE ESSENCE. WHILE I REGRET THE MANNER OF YOUR ARRIVAL, I DO NOT REGRET THE FACT THAT YOU ARE HERE.
WELL...AS LONG AS YOU PROMISE NOT TO ZAP ME AGAIN.
WHAT DO YOU NEED MY HELP FOR? YOU WANT A TOUR OF BOONVILLE TOO?
TOUR?
WELL, YEAH. WHEN I MET MIMIC, HE ASKED FOR A TOUR AROUND TOWN SO HE COULD UPDATE HIS RECORDS ON EARTH.

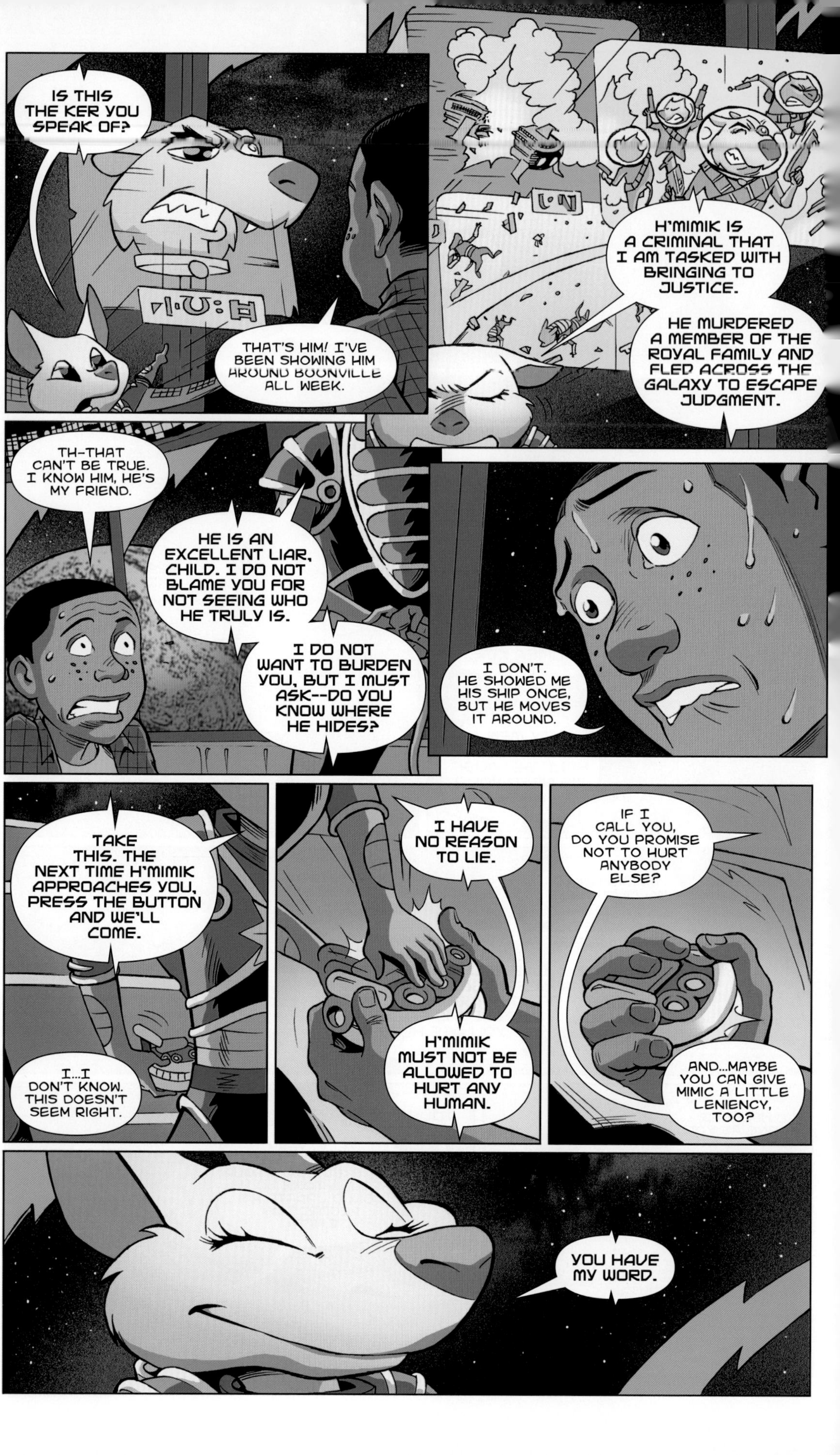
IS THIS THE KER YOU SPEAK OF?
THAT'S HIM! I'VE BEEN SHOWING HIM AROUND BOONVILLE ALL WEEK.
H'MIMIK IS A CRIMINAL THAT I AM TASKED WITH BRINGING TO JUSTICE.
HE MURDERED A MEMBER OF THE ROYAL FAMILY AND FLED ACROSS THE GALAXY TO ESCAPE JUDGMENT.
TH-THAT CAN'T BE TRUE. I KNOW HIM, HE'S MY FRIEND.
HE IS AN EXCELLENT LIAR, CHILD. I DO NOT BLAME YOU FOR NOT SEEING WHO HE TRULY IS.
I DO NOT WANT TO BURDEN YOU, BUT I MUST ASK--DO YOU KNOW WHERE HE HIDES?
I DON'T. HE SHOWED ME HIS SHIP ONCE, BUT HE MOVES IT AROUND.
TAKE THIS. THE NEXT TIME H'MIMIK APPROACHES YOU, PRESS THE BUTTON AND WE'LL COME.
I...I DON'T KNOW. THIS DOESN'T SEEM RIGHT.
I HAVE NO REASON TO LIE.
H'MIMIK MUST NOT BE ALLOWED TO HURT ANY HUMAN.
IF I CALL YOU, DO YOU PROMISE NOT TO HURT ANYBODY ELSE?
AND...MAYBE YOU CAN GIVE MIMIC A LITTLE LENIENCY, TOO?
YOU HAVE MY WORD.

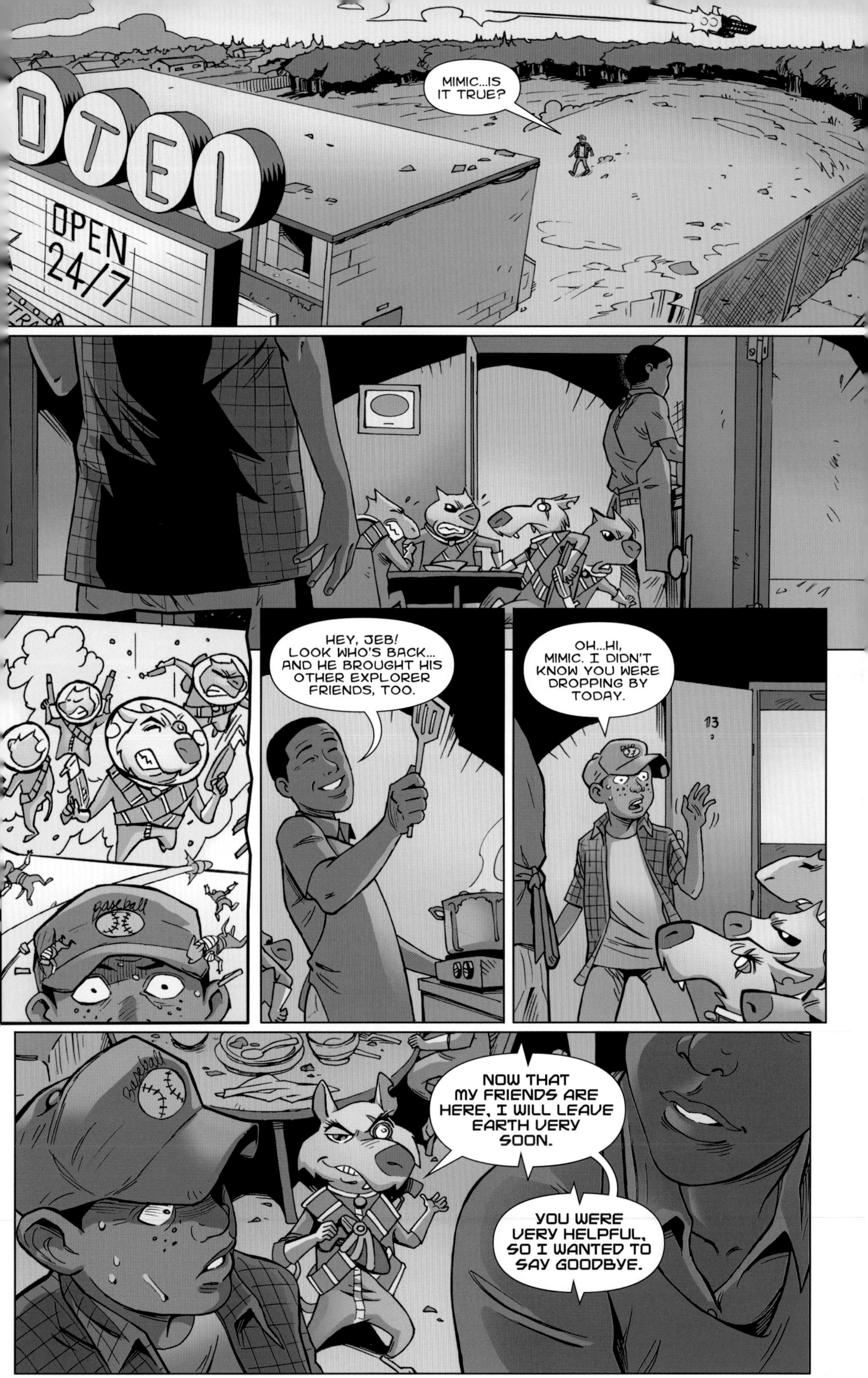

OTEL
OPEN 24/7
MIMIC...IS IT TRUE?
HEY, JEB! LOOK WHO'S BACK... AND HE BROUGHT HIS OTHER EXPLORER FRIENDS, TOO.
OH...HI, MIMIC. I DIDN'T KNOW YOU WERE DROPPING BY TODAY.
13
NOW THAT MY FRIENDS ARE HERE, I WILL LEAVE EARTH VERY SOON.
YOU WERE VERY HELPFUL, SO I WANTED TO SAY GOODBYE.

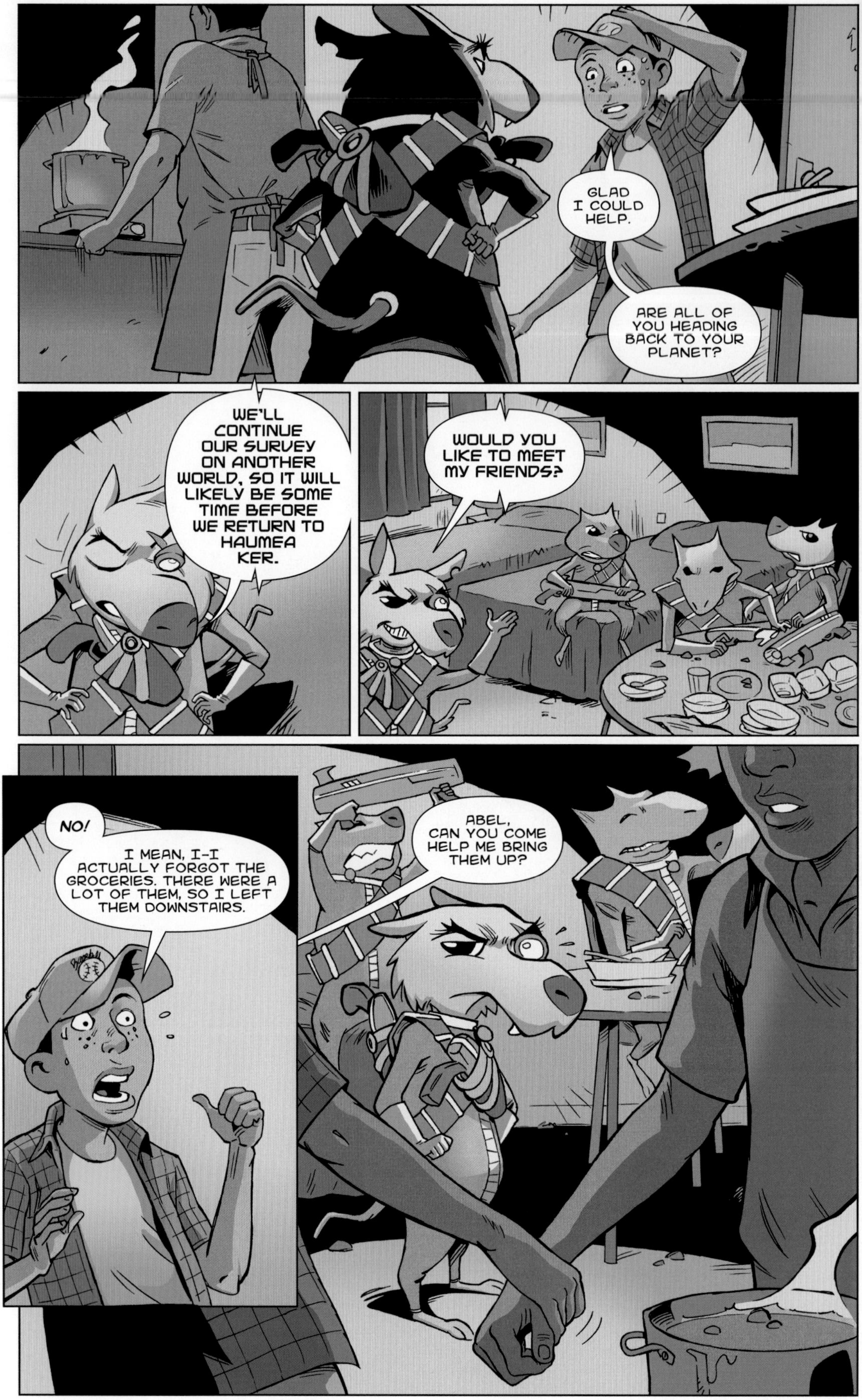
GLAD I COULD HELP.
ARE ALL OF YOU HEADING BACK TO YOUR PLANET?
WE'LL CONTINUE OUR SURVEY ON ANOTHER WORLD, SO IT WILL LIKELY BE SOME TIME BEFORE WE RETURN TO HAUMEA KER.
WOULD YOU LIKE TO MEET MY FRIENDS?
NO!
I MEAN, I-I ACTUALLY FORGOT THE GROCERIES. THERE WERE A LOT OF THEM, SO I LEFT THEM DOWNSTAIRS.
ABEL, CAN YOU COME HELP ME BRING THEM UP?

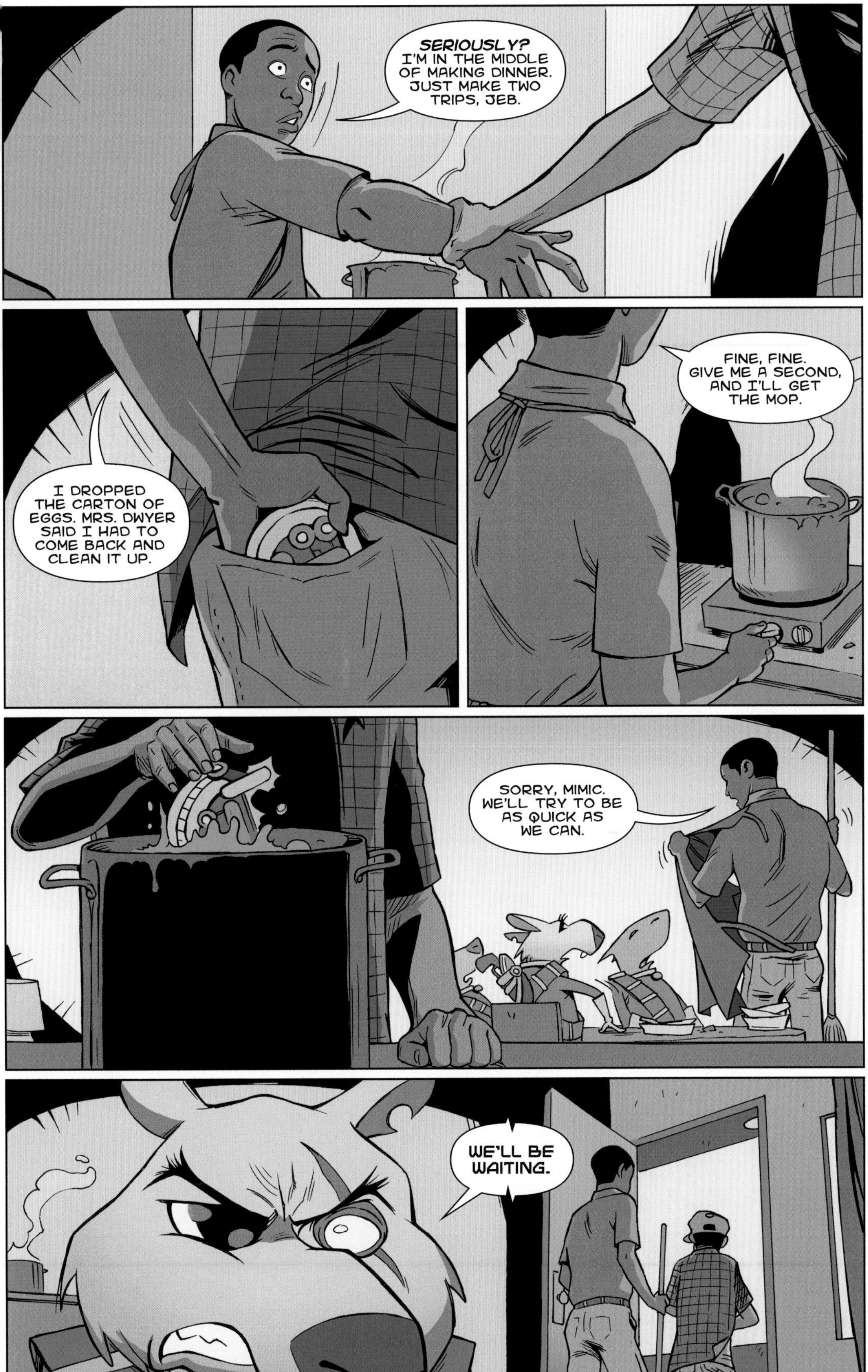
SERIOUSLY? I'M IN THE MIDDLE OF MAKING DINNER. JUST MAKE TWO TRIPS, JEB.
I DROPPED THE CARTON OF EGGS. MRS. DWYER SAID I HAD TO COME BACK AND CLEAN IT UP.
FINE, FINE. GIVE ME A SECOND, AND I'LL GET THE MOP.
SORRY, MIMIC. WE'LL TRY TO BE AS QUICK AS WE CAN.
WE'LL BE WAITING.

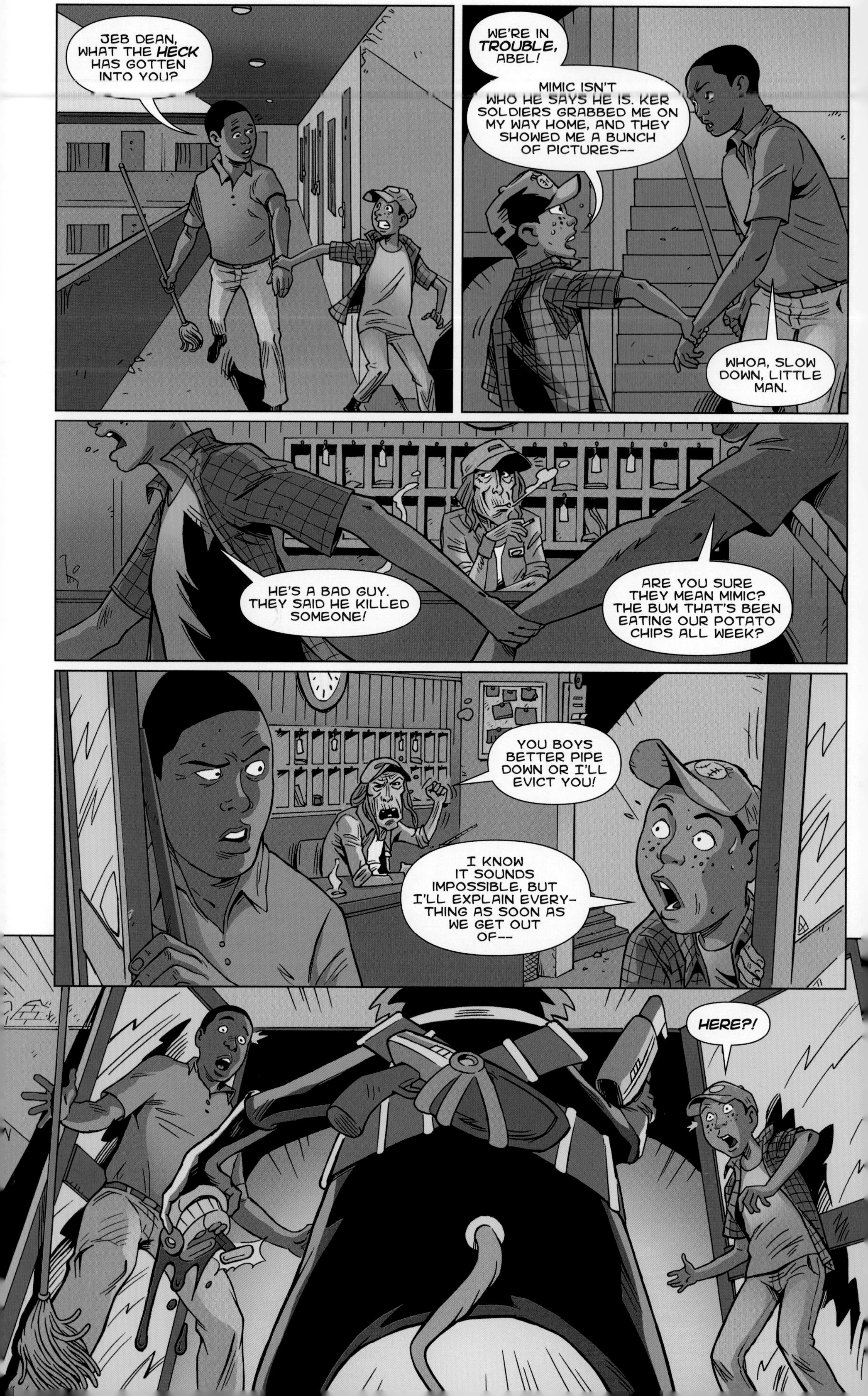
JEB DEAN, WHAT THE HECK HAS GOTTEN INTO YOU?
WE'RE IN TROUBLE, ABEL!
MIMIC ISN'T WHO HE SAYS HE IS. KER SOLDIERS GRABBED ME ON MY WAY HOME, AND THEY SHOWED ME A BUNCH OF PICTURES--
WHOA, SLOW DOWN, LITTLE MAN.
HE'S A BAD GUY. THEY SAID HE KILLED SOMEONE!
ARE YOU SURE THEY MEAN MIMIC? THE BUM THAT'S BEEN EATING OUR POTATO CHIPS ALL WEEK?
YOU BOYS BETTER PIPE DOWN OR I'LL EVICT YOU!
I KNOW IT SOUNDS IMPOSSIBLE, BUT I'LL EXPLAIN EVERY-THING AS SOON AS WE GET OUT OF--
HERE?!

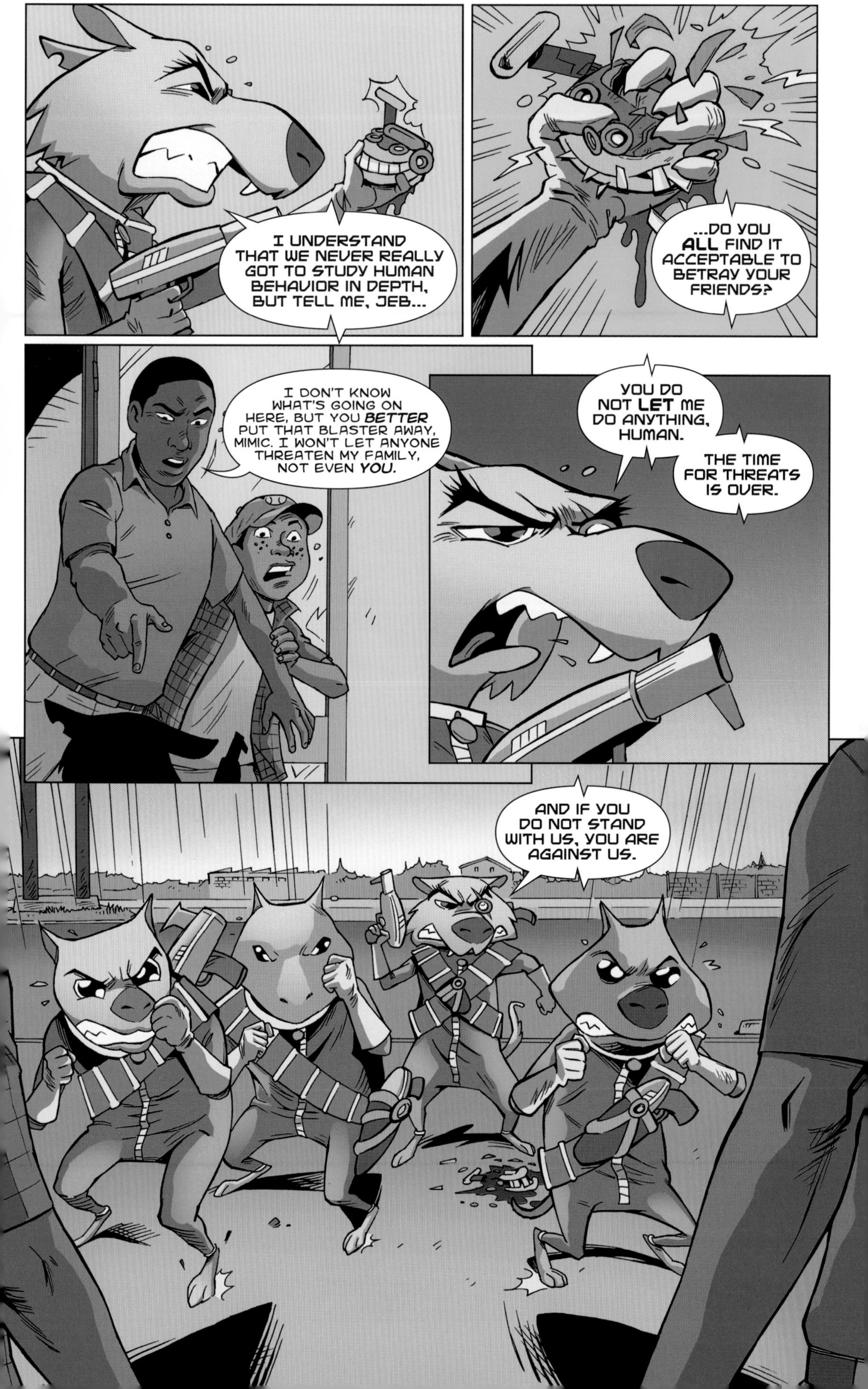
I UNDERSTAND THAT WE NEVER REALLY GOT TO STUDY HUMAN BEHAVIOR IN DEPTH, BUT TELL ME, JEB...
...DO YOU **ALL** FIND IT ACCEPTABLE TO BETRAY YOUR FRIENDS?
I DON'T KNOW WHAT'S GOING ON HERE, BUT YOU ***BETTER*** PUT THAT BLASTER AWAY, MIMIC. I WON'T LET ANYONE THREATEN MY FAMILY, NOT EVEN ***YOU.***
YOU DO NOT **LET** ME DO ANYTHING, HUMAN.
THE TIME FOR THREATS IS OVER.
AND IF YOU DO NOT STAND WITH US, YOU ARE AGAINST US.

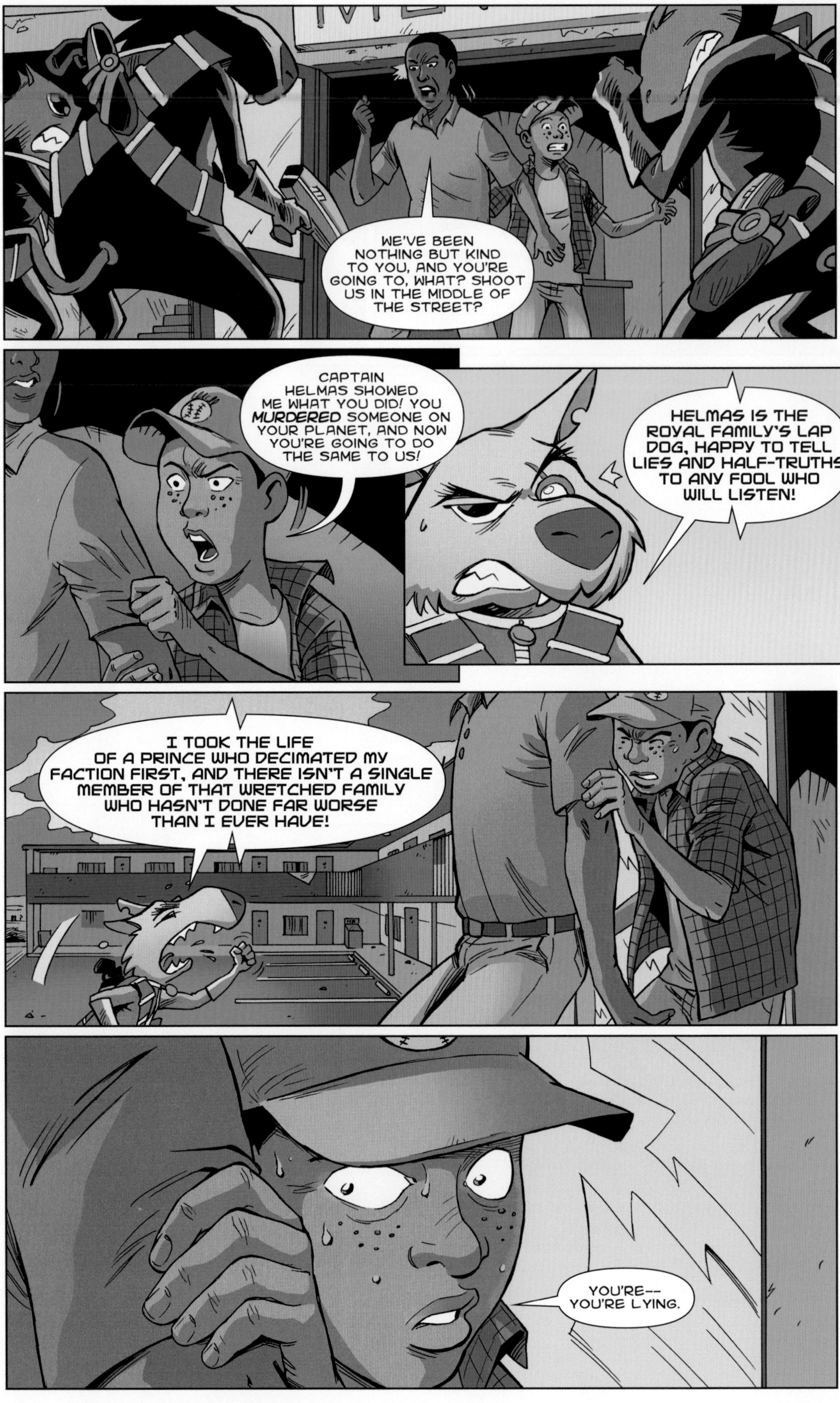
WE'VE BEEN NOTHING BUT KIND TO YOU, AND YOU'RE GOING TO, WHAT? SHOOT US IN THE MIDDLE OF THE STREET?
CAPTAIN HELMAS SHOWED ME WHAT YOU DID! YOU MURDERED SOMEONE ON YOUR PLANET, AND NOW YOU'RE GOING TO DO THE SAME TO US!
HELMAS IS THE ROYAL FAMILY'S LAP DOG, HAPPY TO TELL LIES AND HALF-TRUTHS TO ANY FOOL WHO WILL LISTEN!
I TOOK THE LIFE OF A PRINCE WHO DECIMATED MY FACTION FIRST, AND THERE ISN'T A SINGLE MEMBER OF THAT WRETCHED FAMILY WHO HASN'T DONE FAR WORSE THAN I EVER HAVE!
YOU'RE-- YOU'RE LYING.

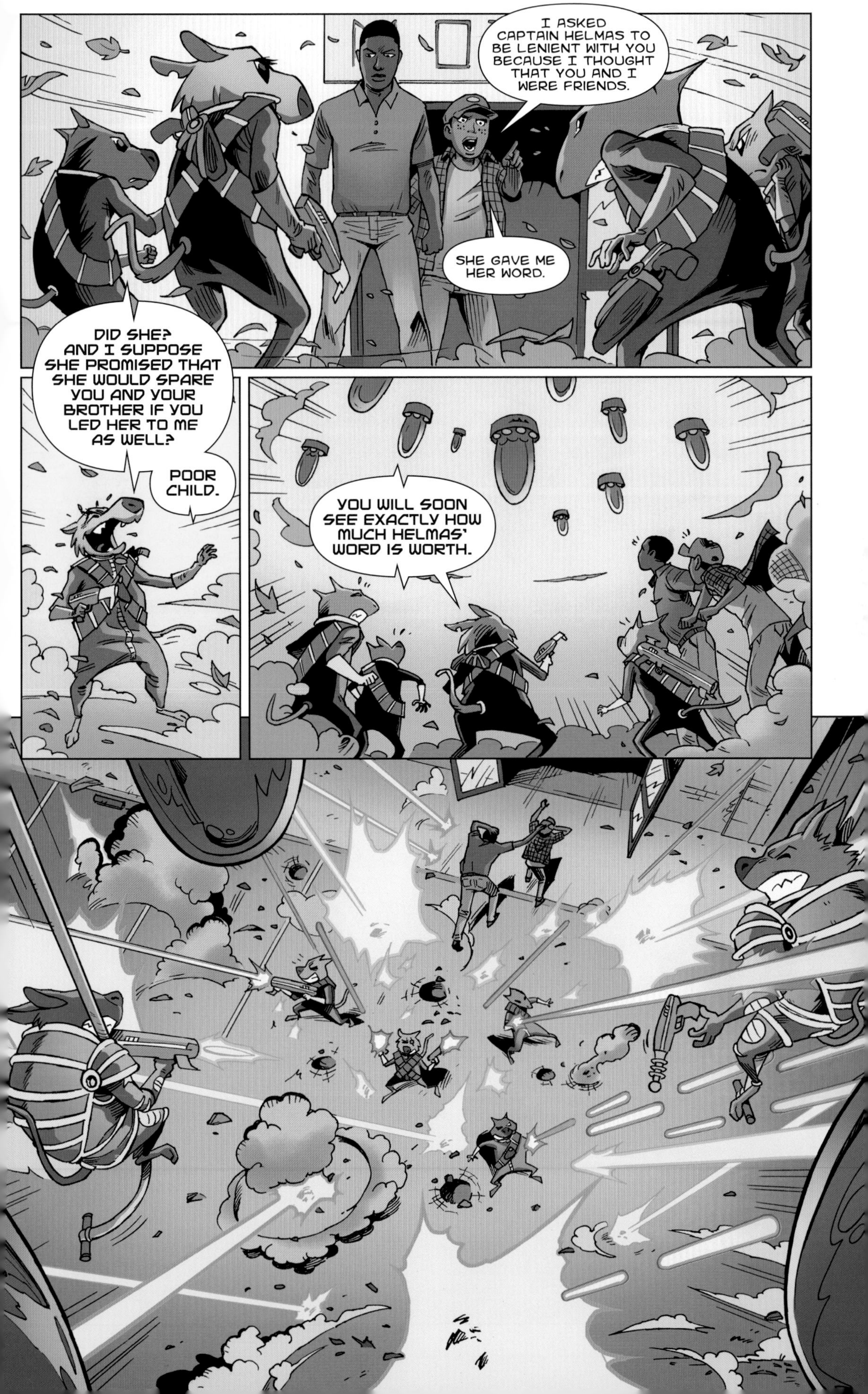
I ASKED CAPTAIN HELMAS TO BE LENIENT WITH YOU BECAUSE I THOUGHT THAT YOU AND I WERE FRIENDS.
SHE GAVE ME HER WORD.
DID SHE? AND I SUPPOSE SHE PROMISED THAT SHE WOULD SPARE YOU AND YOUR BROTHER IF YOU LED HER TO ME AS WELL?
POOR CHILD.
YOU WILL SOON SEE EXACTLY HOW MUCH HELMAS' WORD IS WORTH.

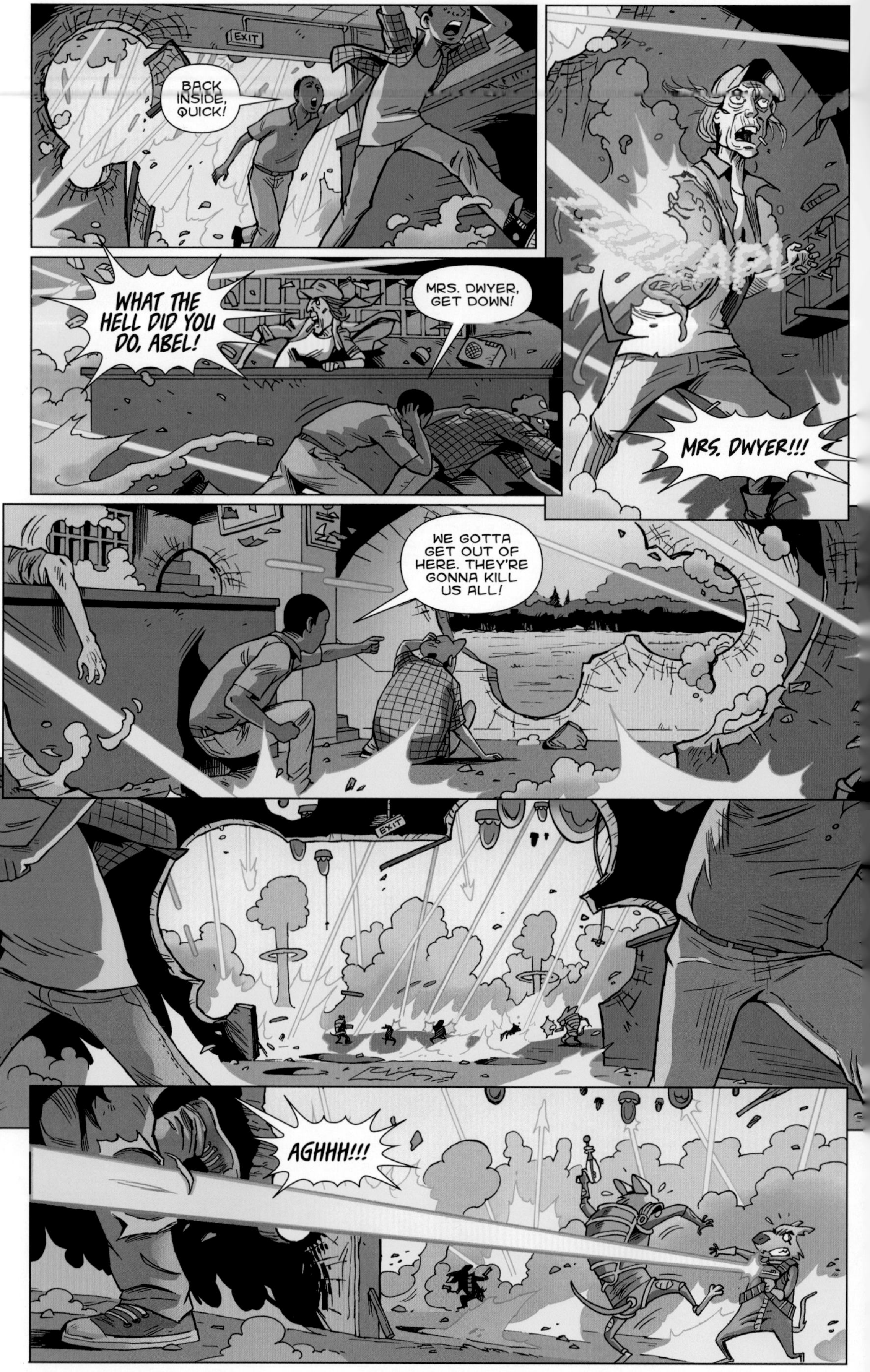
BACK INSIDE, QUICK!
WHAT THE HELL DID YOU DO, ABEL!
MRS. DWYER, GET DOWN!
MRS. DWYER!!!
WE GOTTA GET OUT OF HERE. THEY'RE GONNA KILL US ALL!
AGHHH!!!

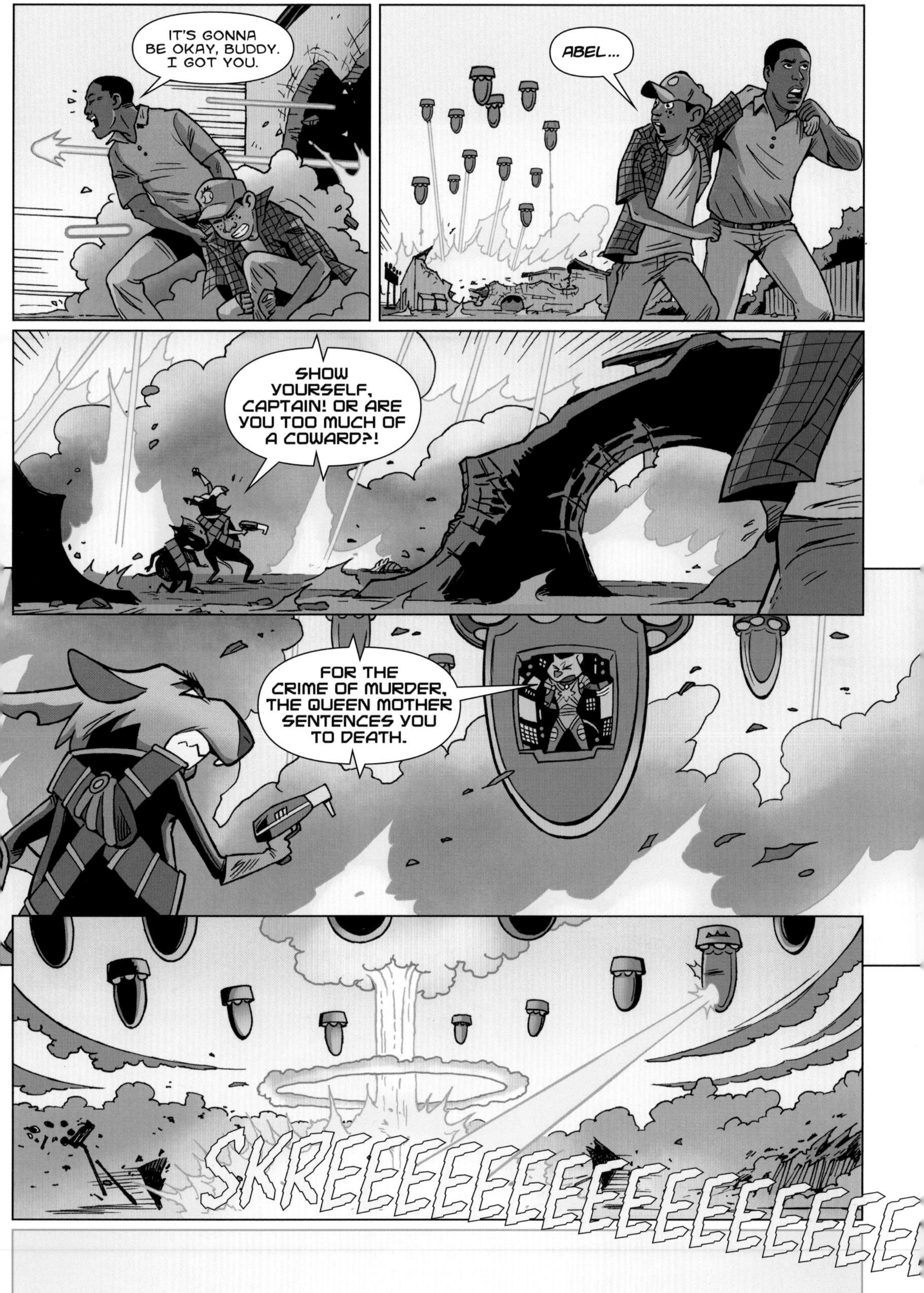
IT'S GONNA BE OKAY, BUDDY. I GOT YOU.
ABEL...
SHOW YOURSELF, CAPTAIN! OR ARE YOU TOO MUCH OF A COWARD?!
FOR THE CRIME OF MURDER, THE QUEEN MOTHER SENTENCES YOU TO DEATH.
SKREEEEEEEEEEEEEEEEEEEEEE

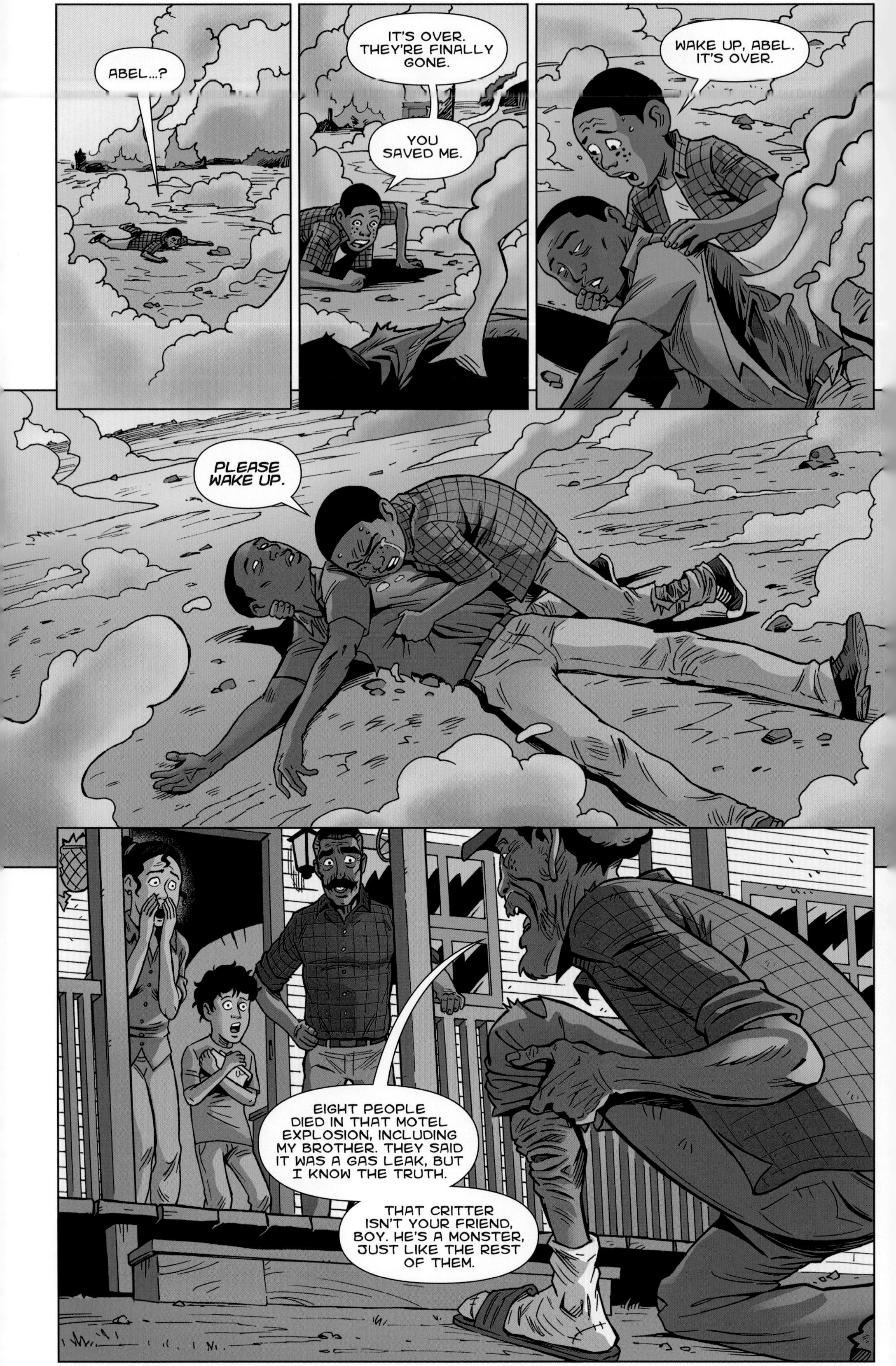
ABEL...?
IT'S OVER. THEY'RE FINALLY GONE.
YOU SAVED ME.
WAKE UP, ABEL. IT'S OVER.
PLEASE WAKE UP.
EIGHT PEOPLE DIED IN THAT MOTEL EXPLOSION, INCLUDING MY BROTHER. THEY SAID IT WAS A GAS LEAK, BUT I KNOW THE TRUTH.
THAT CRITTER ISN'T YOUR FRIEND, BOY. HE'S A MONSTER, JUST LIKE THE REST OF THEM.

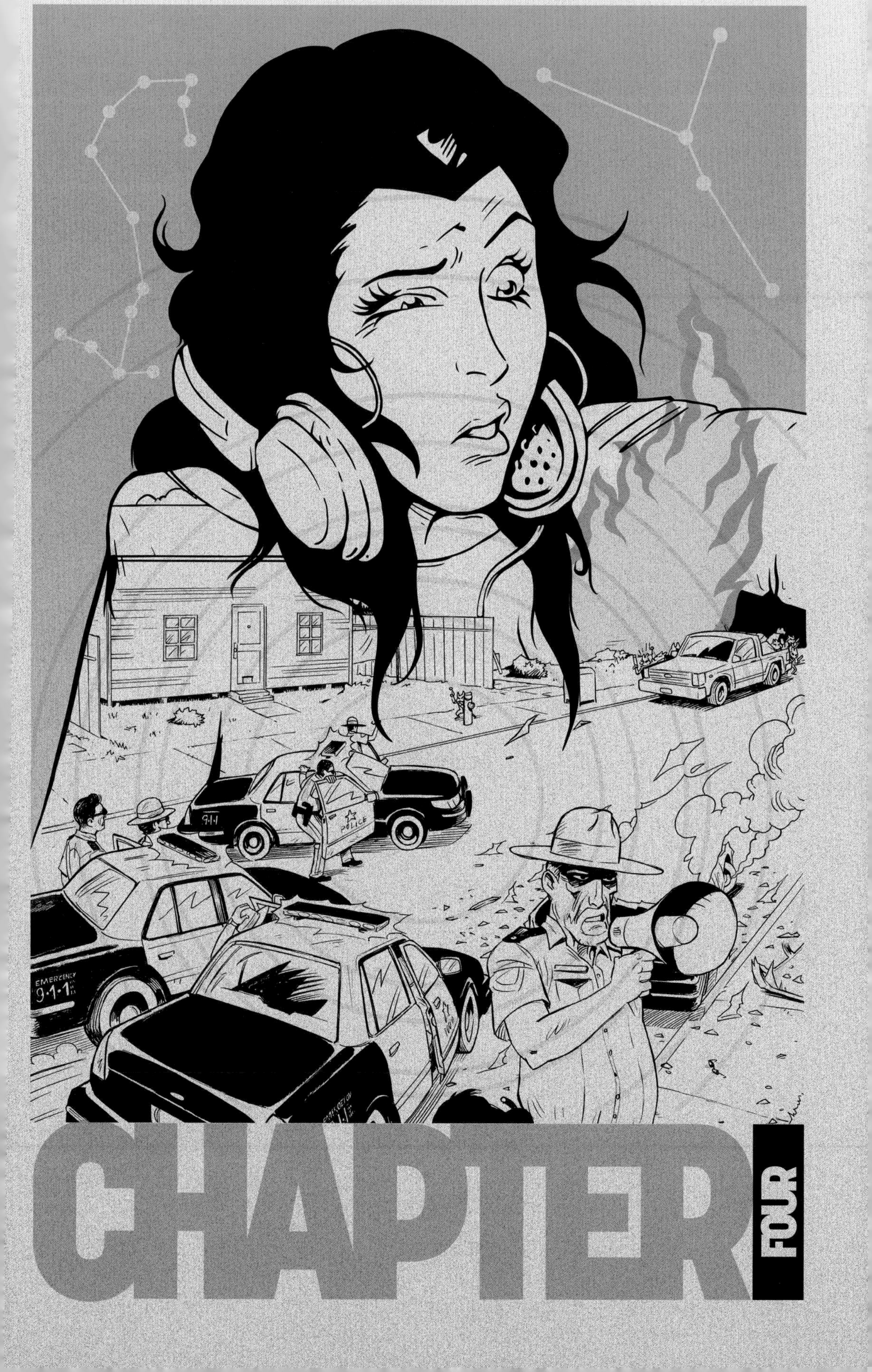
9·1·1
POLICE
EMERGENCY
9·1·1

CHAPTER FOUR

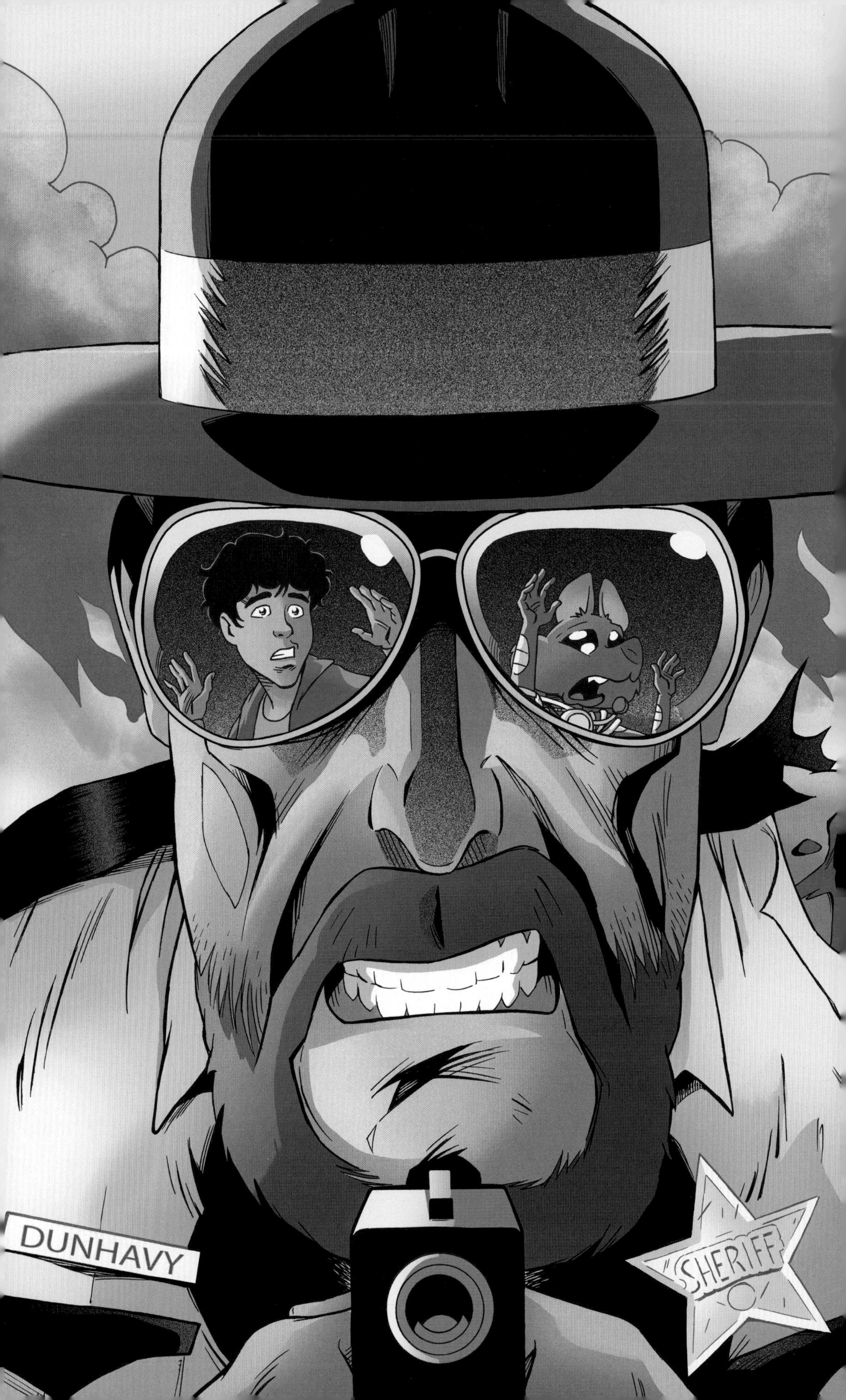
DUNHAVY
SHERIFF

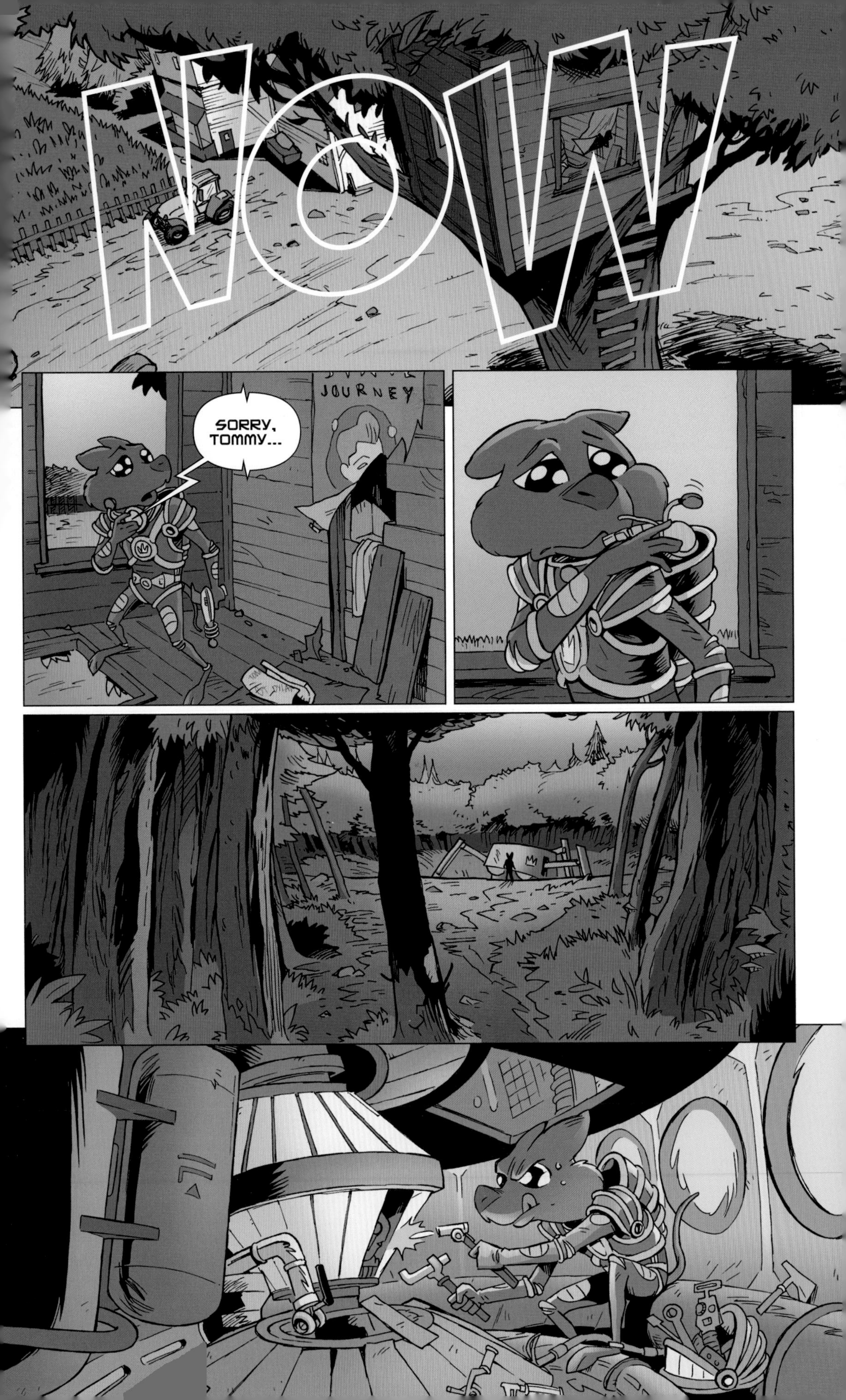
NOW
JOURNEY
SORRY, TOMMY...

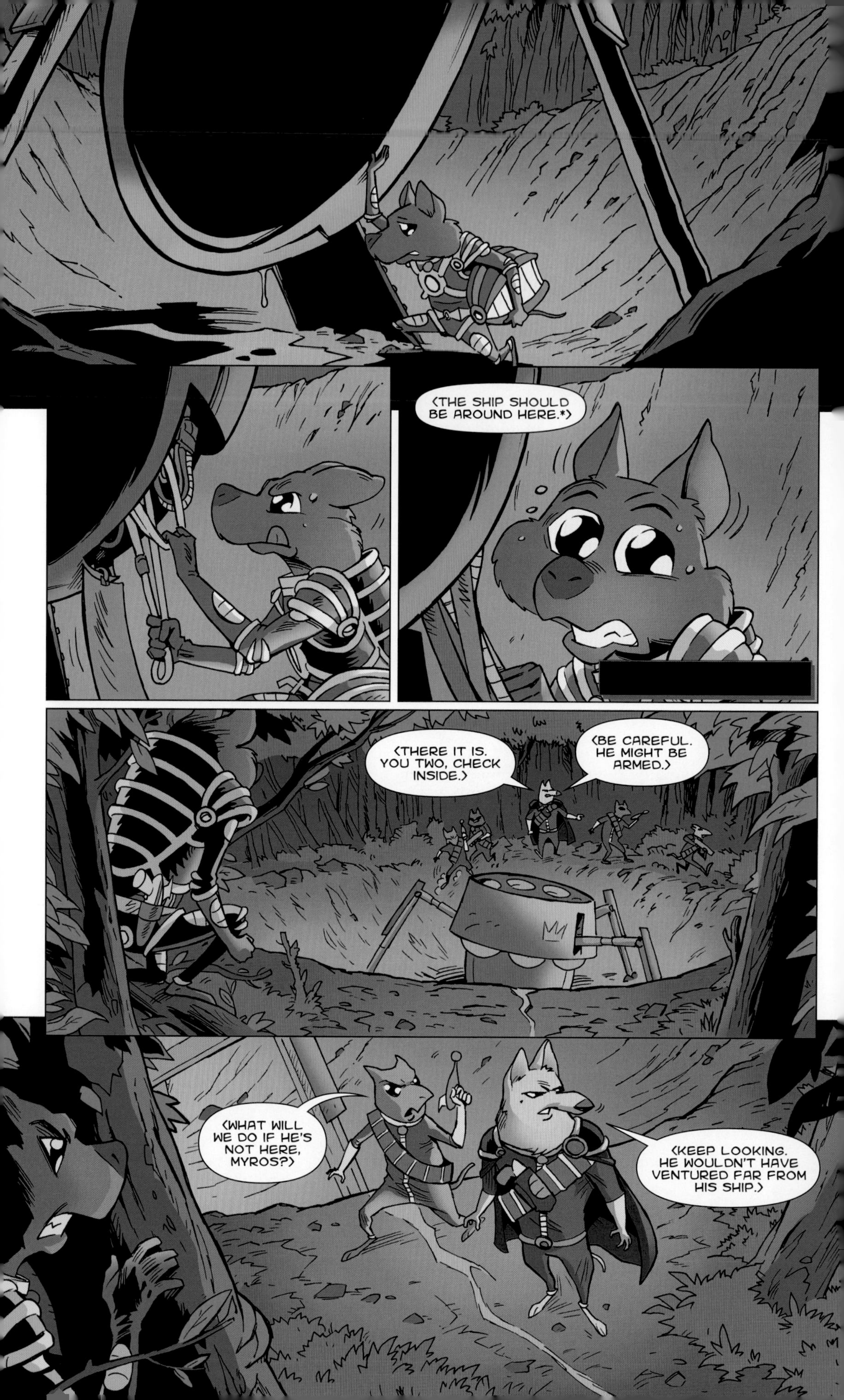
<THE SHIP SHOULD BE AROUND HERE.*>
[redacted]
<THERE IT IS. YOU TWO, CHECK INSIDE.>
<BE CAREFUL. HE MIGHT BE ARMED.>
<WHAT WILL WE DO IF HE'S NOT HERE, MYROS?>
<KEEP LOOKING. HE WOULDN'T HAVE VENTURED FAR FROM HIS SHIP.>

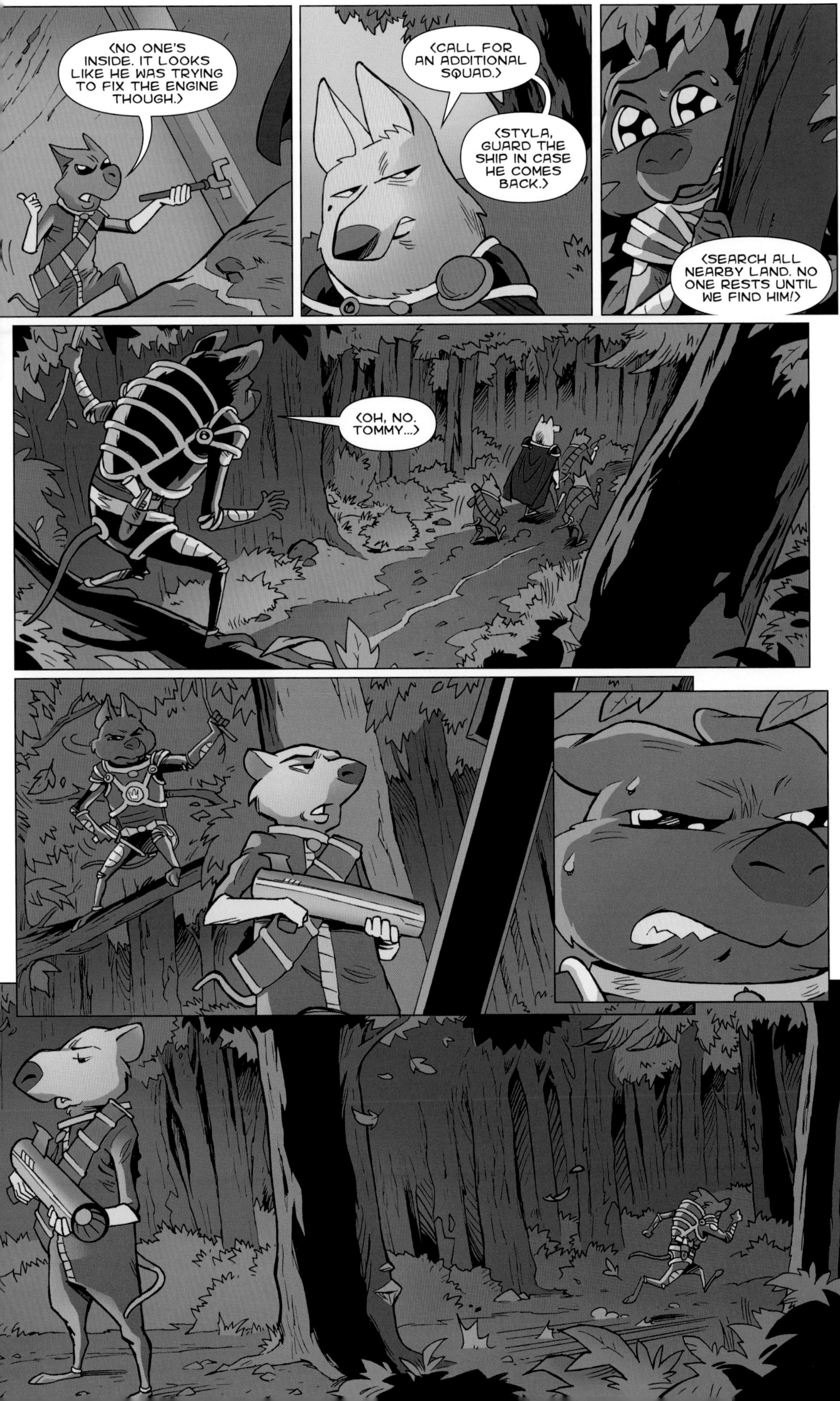

<NO ONE'S INSIDE. IT LOOKS LIKE HE WAS TRYING TO FIX THE ENGINE THOUGH.>
<CALL FOR AN ADDITIONAL SQUAD.>
<STYLA, GUARD THE SHIP IN CASE HE COMES BACK.>
<SEARCH ALL NEARBY LAND. NO ONE RESTS UNTIL WE FIND HIM!>
<OH, NO. TOMMY...>

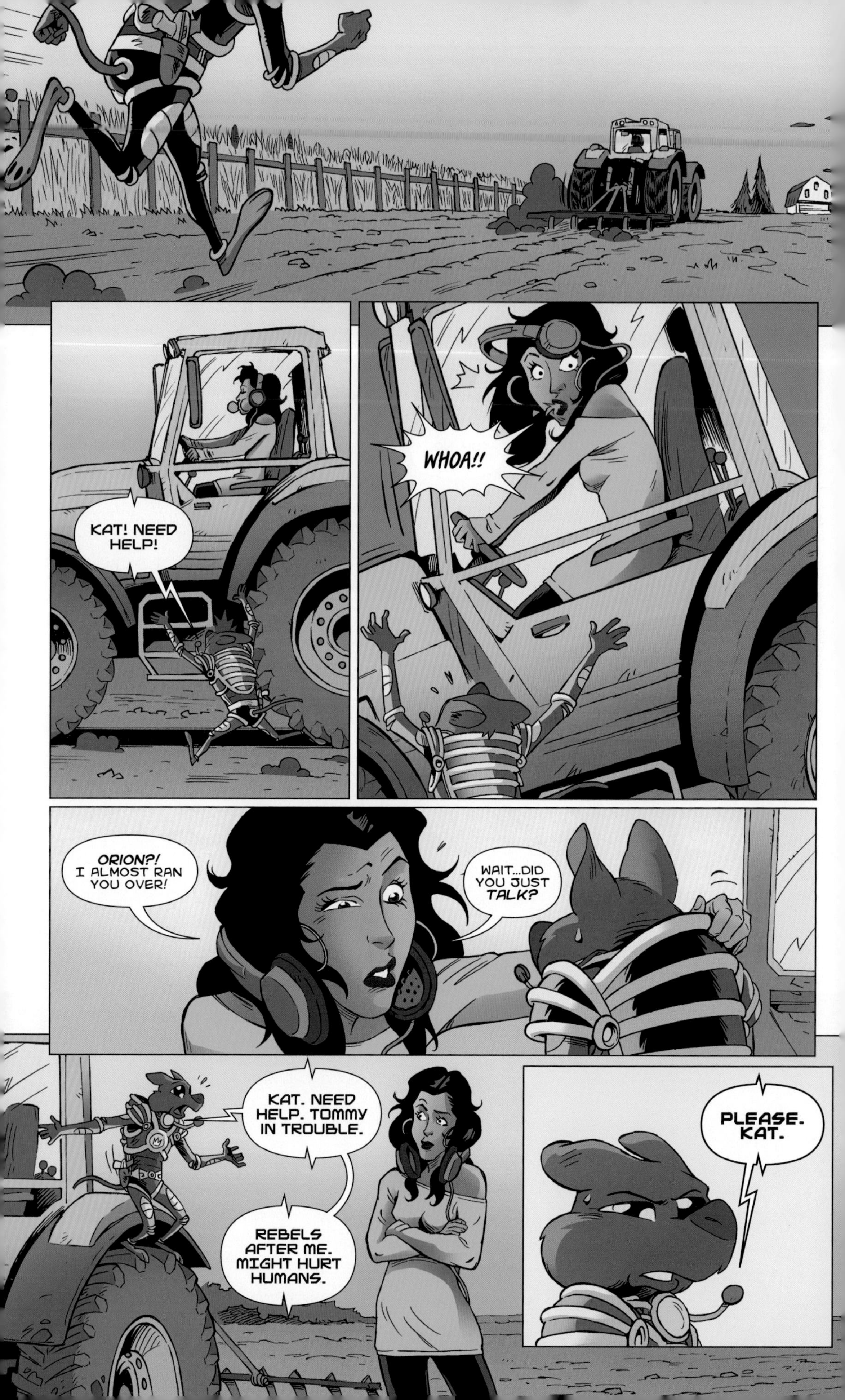
KAT! NEED HELP!
WHOA!!
ORION?! I ALMOST RAN YOU OVER!
WAIT...DID YOU JUST TALK?
KAT. NEED HELP. TOMMY IN TROUBLE.
REBELS AFTER ME. MIGHT HURT HUMANS.
PLEASE. KAT.

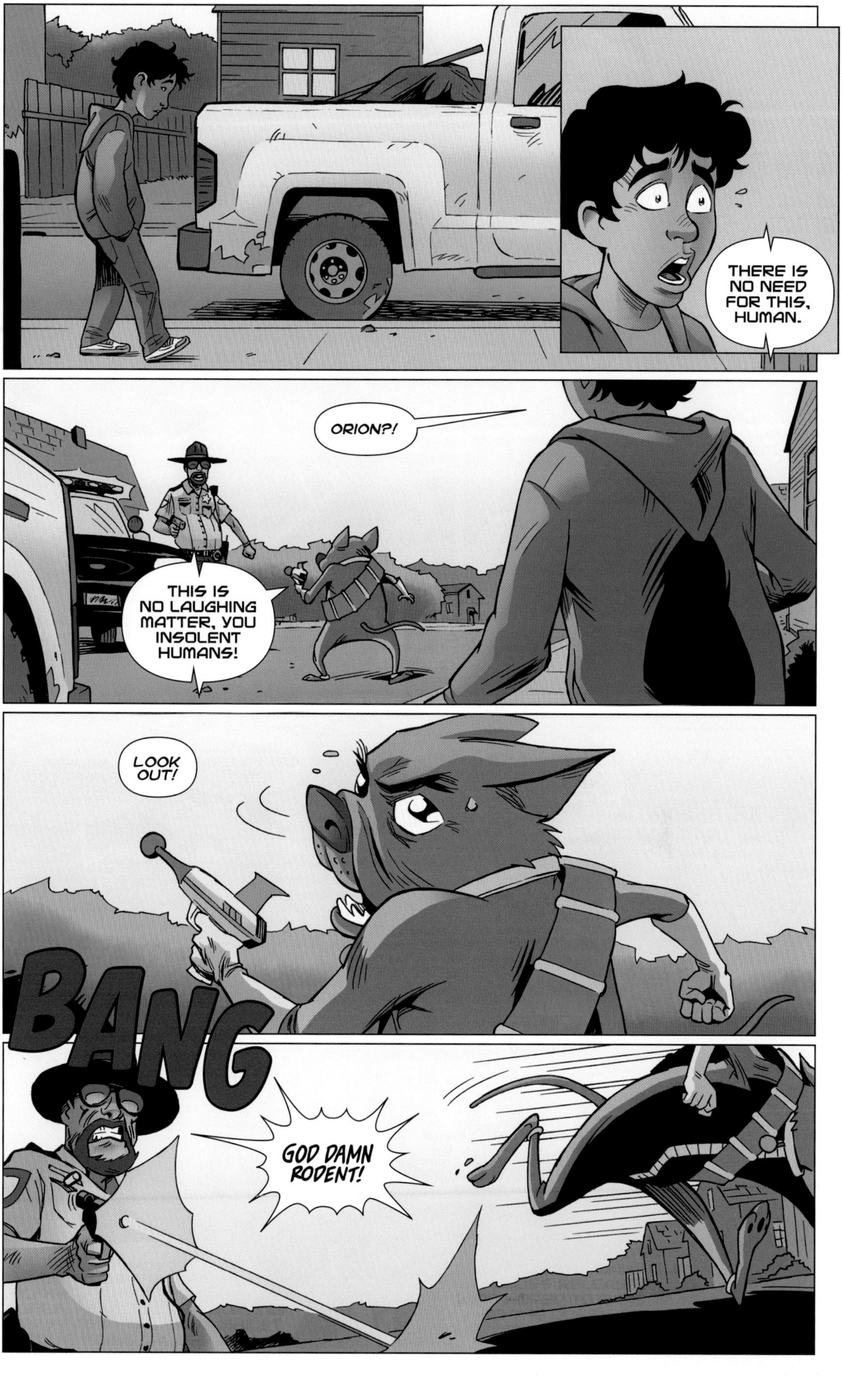
THERE IS NO NEED FOR THIS, HUMAN.
ORION?!
THIS IS NO LAUGHING MATTER, YOU INSOLENT HUMANS!
LOOK OUT!
BANG
GOD DAMN RODENT!

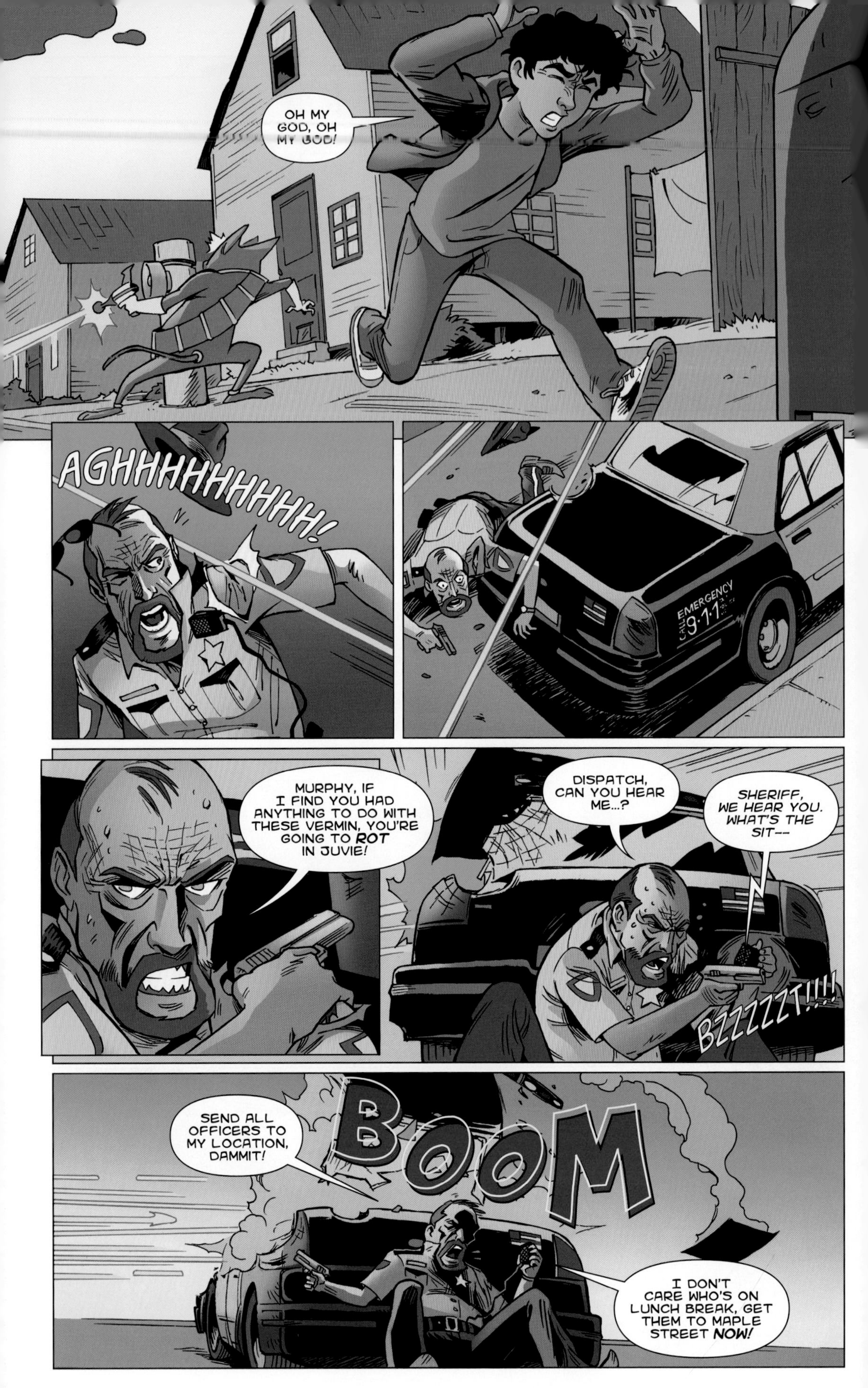
OH MY GOD, OH MY GOD!
AGHHHHHHHHHH!
EMERGENCY
CALL 9·1·1
MURPHY, IF I FIND YOU HAD ANYTHING TO DO WITH THESE VERMIN, YOU'RE GOING TO ROT IN JUVIE!
DISPATCH, CAN YOU HEAR ME...?
SHERIFF, WE HEAR YOU. WHAT'S THE SIT--
BZZZZZT!!!!
SEND ALL OFFICERS TO MY LOCATION, DAMMIT!
BOOM
I DON'T CARE WHO'S ON LUNCH BREAK, GET THEM TO MAPLE STREET NOW!

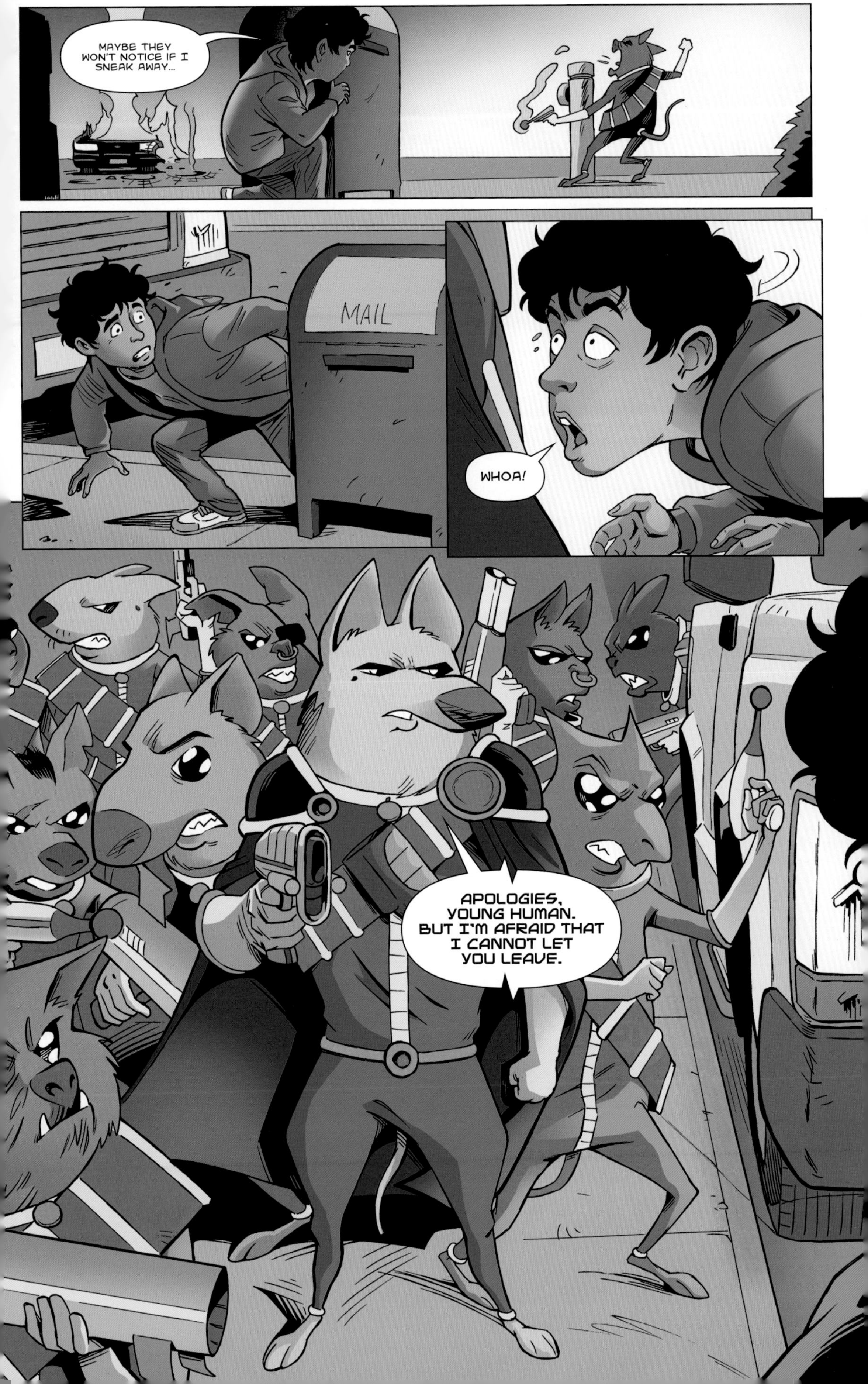
MAYBE THEY WON'T NOTICE IF I SNEAK AWAY...
MAIL
WHOA!
APOLOGIES, YOUNG HUMAN. BUT I'M AFRAID THAT I CANNOT LET YOU LEAVE.

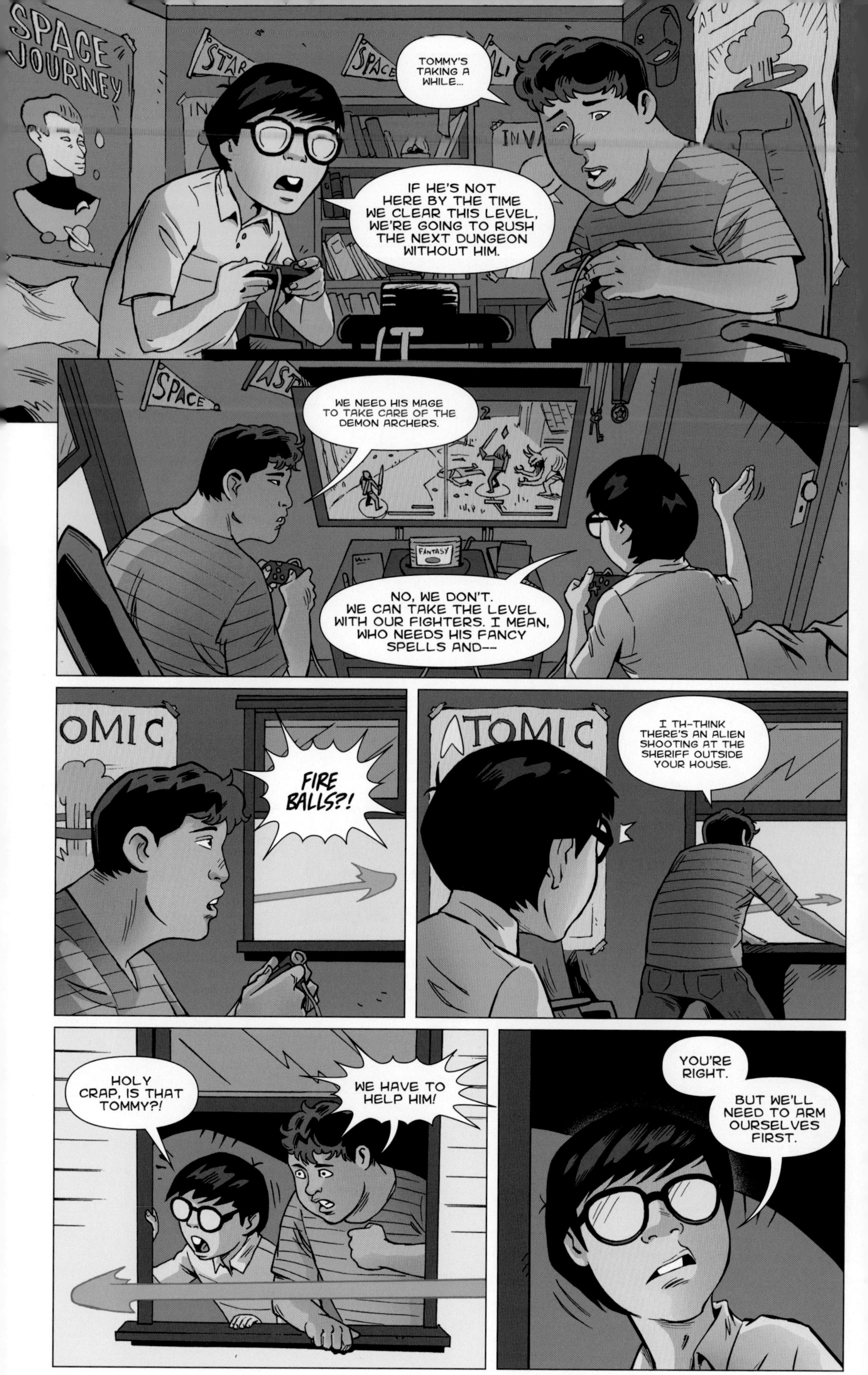
SPACE JOURNEY
TOMMY'S TAKING A WHILE...
IF HE'S NOT HERE BY THE TIME WE CLEAR THIS LEVEL, WE'RE GOING TO RUSH THE NEXT DUNGEON WITHOUT HIM.
WE NEED HIS MAGE TO TAKE CARE OF THE DEMON ARCHERS.
FANTASY
NO, WE DON'T. WE CAN TAKE THE LEVEL WITH OUR FIGHTERS. I MEAN, WHO NEEDS HIS FANCY SPELLS AND--
FIRE BALLS?!
I TH-THINK THERE'S AN ALIEN SHOOTING AT THE SHERIFF OUTSIDE YOUR HOUSE.
HOLY CRAP, IS THAT TOMMY?!
WE HAVE TO HELP HIM!
YOU'RE RIGHT.
BUT WE'LL NEED TO ARM OURSELVES FIRST.

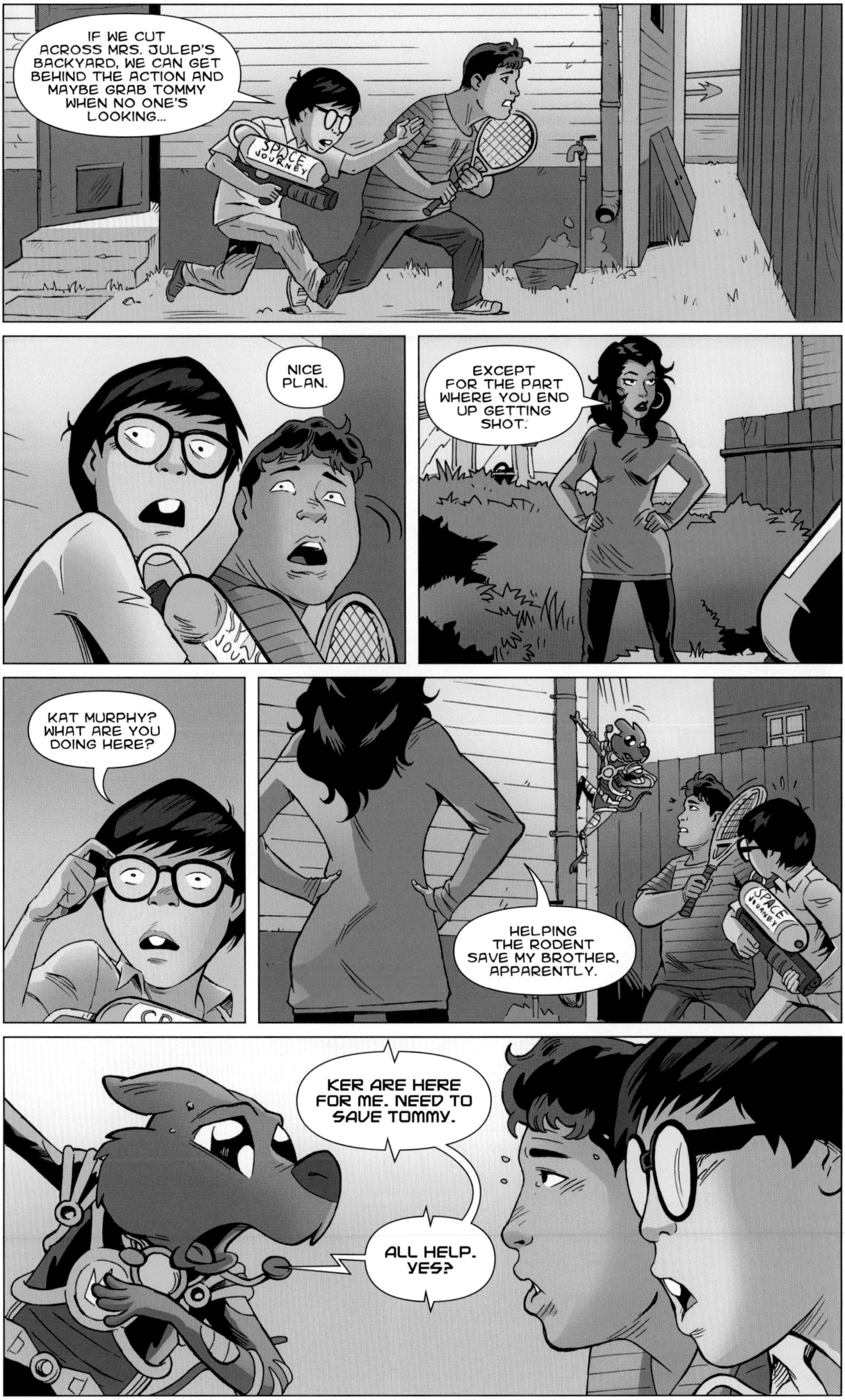
IF WE CUT ACROSS MRS. JULEP'S BACKYARD, WE CAN GET BEHIND THE ACTION AND MAYBE GRAB TOMMY WHEN NO ONE'S LOOKING...
SPACE JOURNEY
NICE PLAN.
EXCEPT FOR THE PART WHERE YOU END UP GETTING SHOT.
KAT MURPHY? WHAT ARE YOU DOING HERE?
HELPING THE RODENT SAVE MY BROTHER, APPARENTLY.
SPACE JOURNEY
KER ARE HERE FOR ME. NEED TO SAVE TOMMY.
ALL HELP. YES?

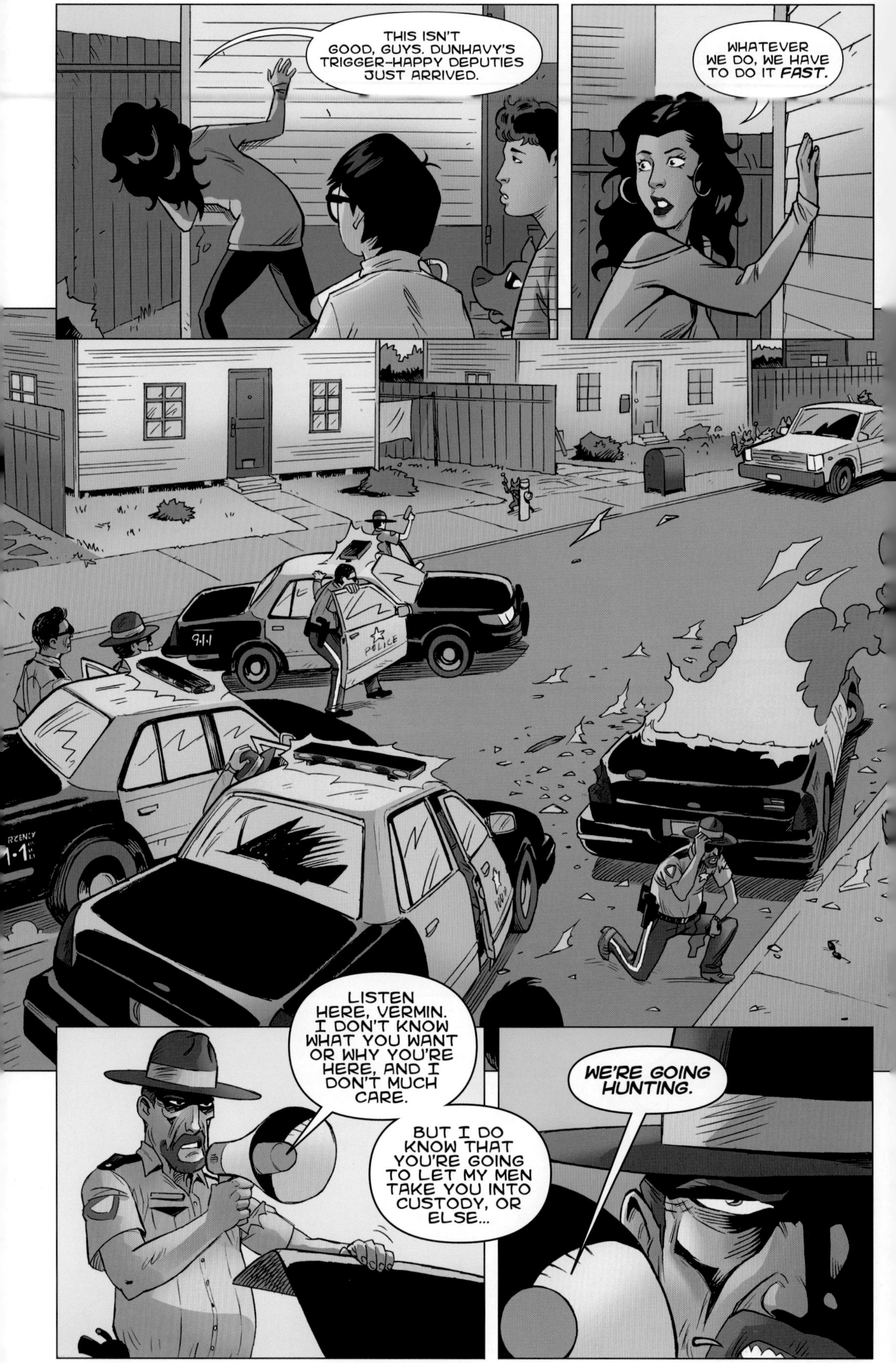
THIS ISN'T GOOD, GUYS. DUNHAVY'S TRIGGER-HAPPY DEPUTIES JUST ARRIVED.
WHATEVER WE DO, WE HAVE TO DO IT FAST.
POLICE
9-1-1
LISTEN HERE, VERMIN. I DON'T KNOW WHAT YOU WANT OR WHY YOU'RE HERE, AND I DON'T MUCH CARE.
BUT I DO KNOW THAT YOU'RE GOING TO LET MY MEN TAKE YOU INTO CUSTODY, OR ELSE...
WE'RE GOING HUNTING.

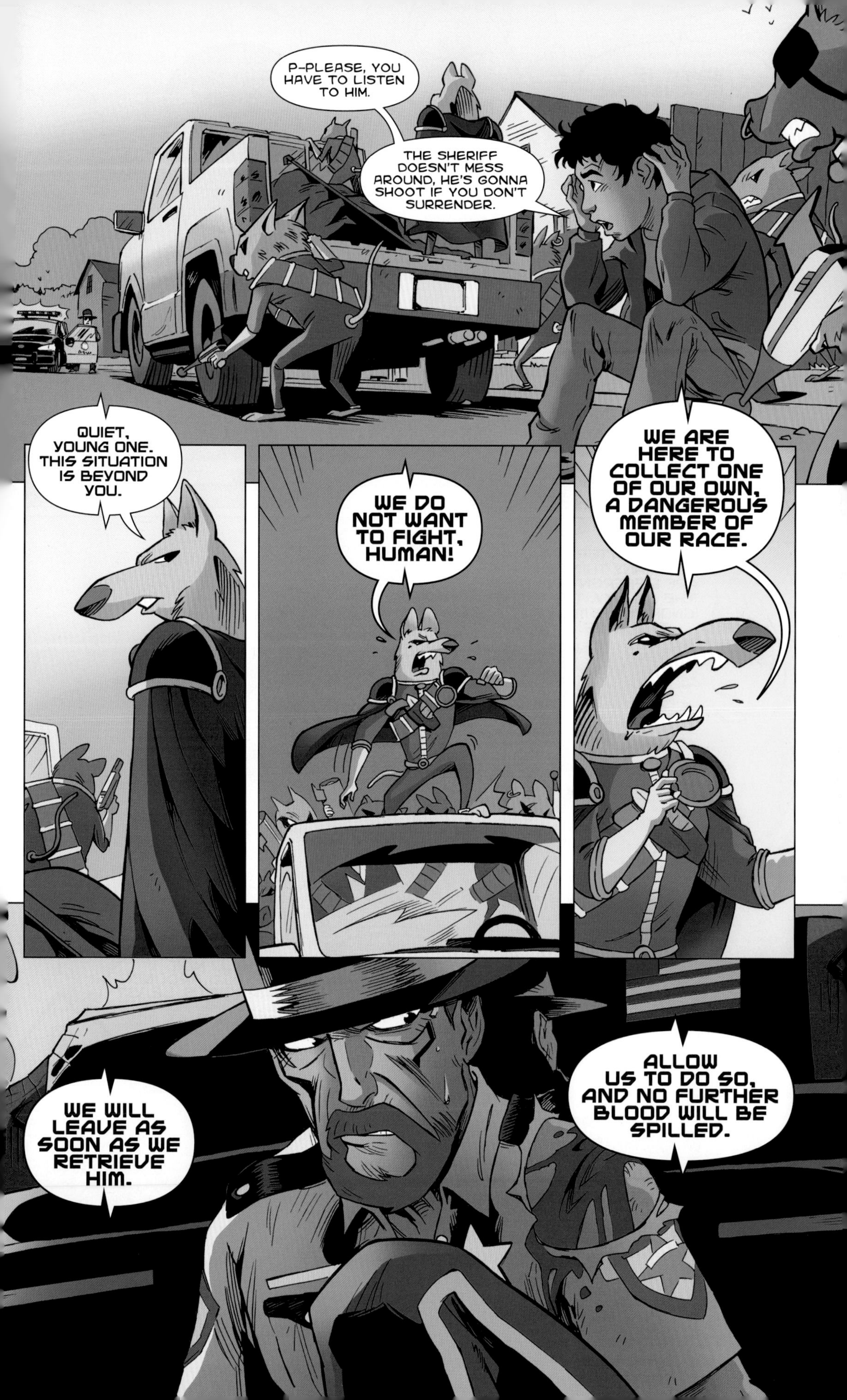
P-PLEASE, YOU HAVE TO LISTEN TO HIM.
THE SHERIFF DOESN'T MESS AROUND, HE'S GONNA SHOOT IF YOU DON'T SURRENDER.
QUIET, YOUNG ONE. THIS SITUATION IS BEYOND YOU.
WE DO NOT WANT TO FIGHT, HUMAN!
WE ARE HERE TO COLLECT ONE OF OUR OWN, A DANGEROUS MEMBER OF OUR RACE.
WE WILL LEAVE AS SOON AS WE RETRIEVE HIM.
ALLOW US TO DO SO, AND NO FURTHER BLOOD WILL BE SPILLED.

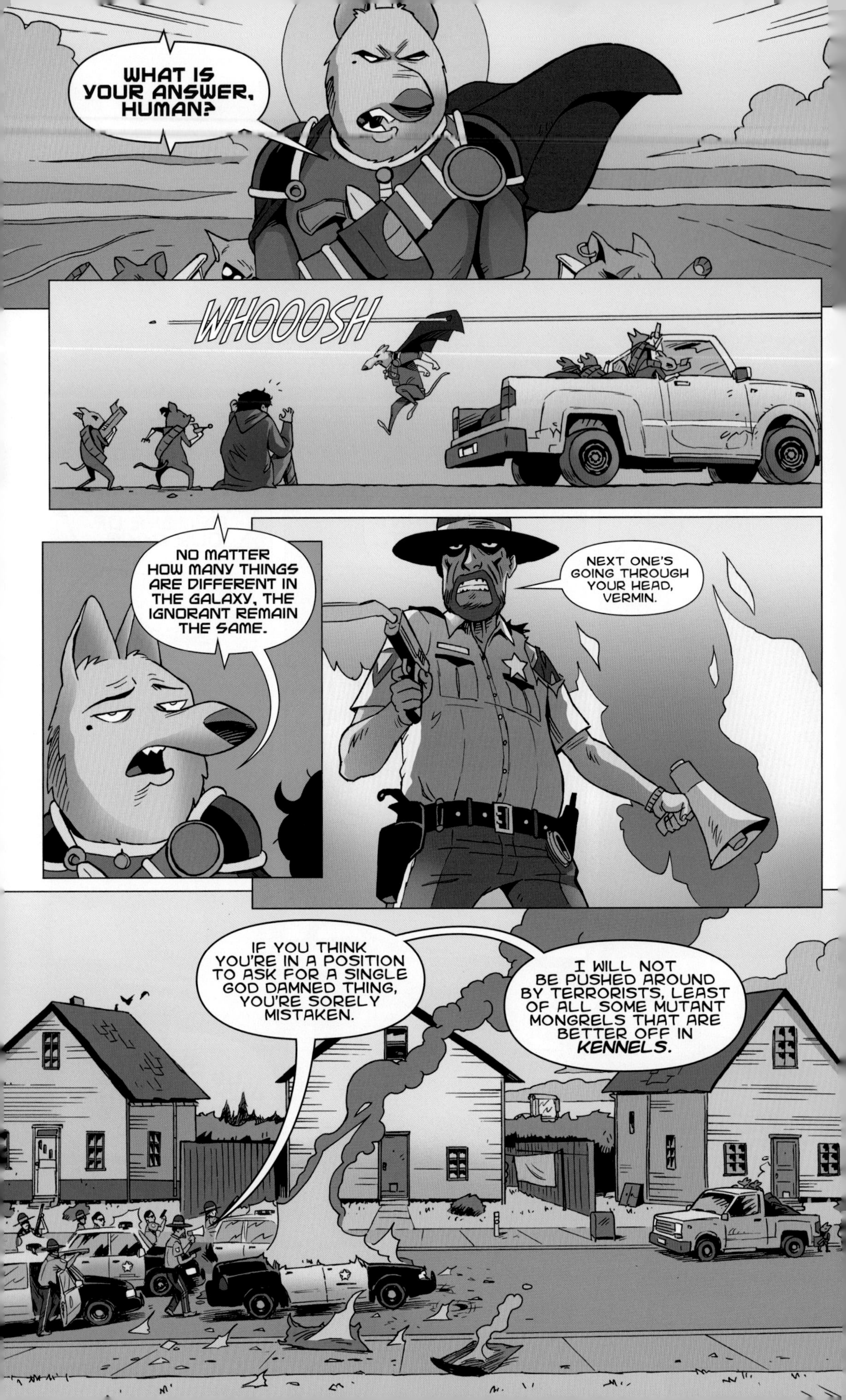
WHAT IS YOUR ANSWER, HUMAN?
WHOOOSH
NO MATTER HOW MANY THINGS ARE DIFFERENT IN THE GALAXY, THE IGNORANT REMAIN THE SAME.
NEXT ONE'S GOING THROUGH YOUR HEAD, VERMIN.
IF YOU THINK YOU'RE IN A POSITION TO ASK FOR A SINGLE GOD DAMNED THING, YOU'RE SORELY MISTAKEN.
I WILL NOT BE PUSHED AROUND BY TERRORISTS, LEAST OF ALL SOME MUTANT MONGRELS THAT ARE BETTER OFF IN *KENNELS.*

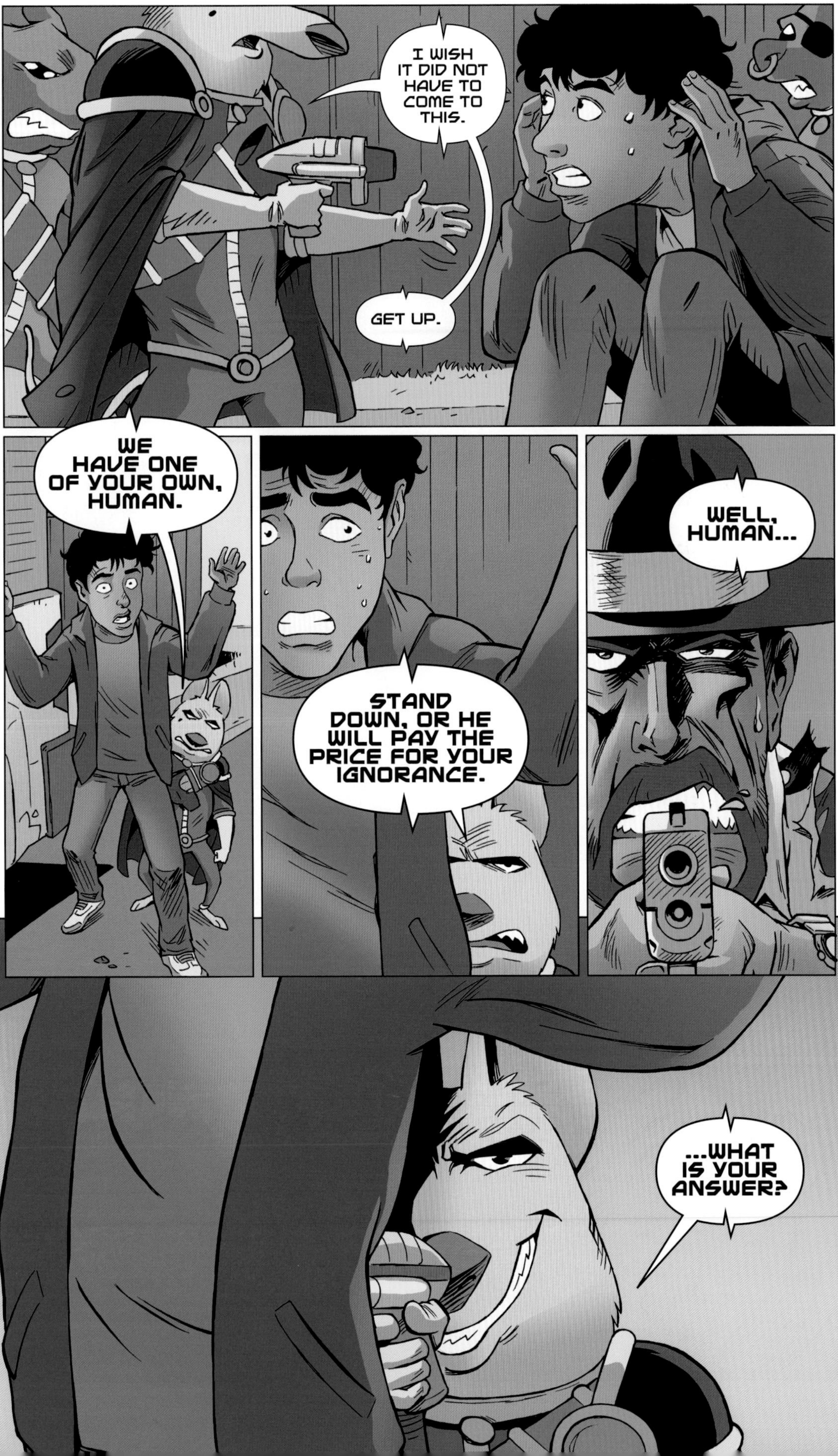
I WISH IT DID NOT HAVE TO COME TO THIS.
GET UP.
WE HAVE ONE OF YOUR OWN, HUMAN.
STAND DOWN, OR HE WILL PAY THE PRICE FOR YOUR IGNORANCE.
WELL, HUMAN...
...WHAT IS YOUR ANSWER?

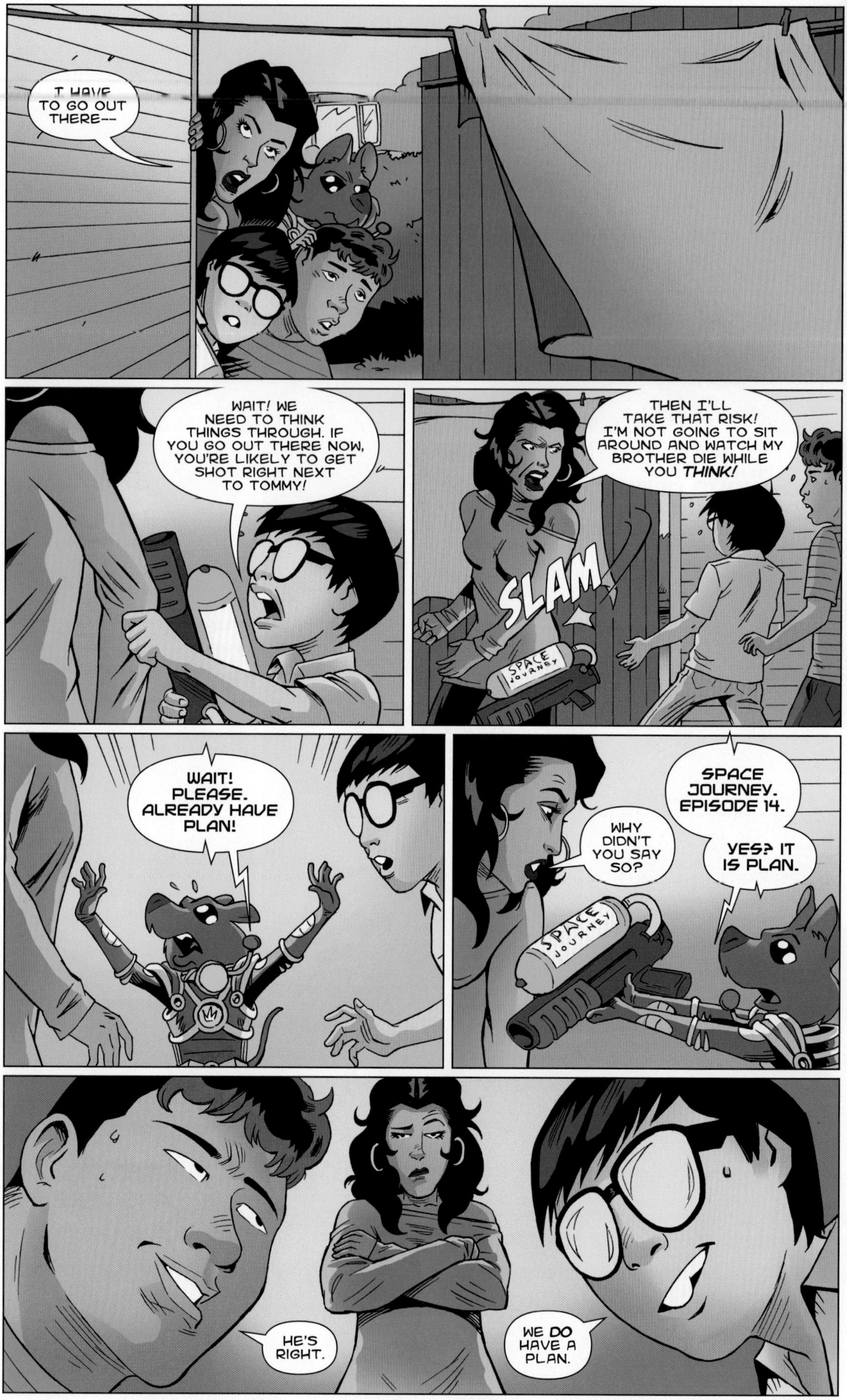
I HAVE TO GO OUT THERE--
WAIT! WE NEED TO THINK THINGS THROUGH. IF YOU GO OUT THERE NOW, YOU'RE LIKELY TO GET SHOT RIGHT NEXT TO TOMMY!
THEN I'LL TAKE THAT RISK! I'M NOT GOING TO SIT AROUND AND WATCH MY BROTHER DIE WHILE YOU THINK!
SLAM
SPACE JOURNEY
WAIT! PLEASE. ALREADY HAVE PLAN!
SPACE JOURNEY. EPISODE 14.
WHY DIDN'T YOU SAY SO?
YES? IT IS PLAN.
SPACE JOURNEY
HE'S RIGHT.
WE DO HAVE A PLAN.

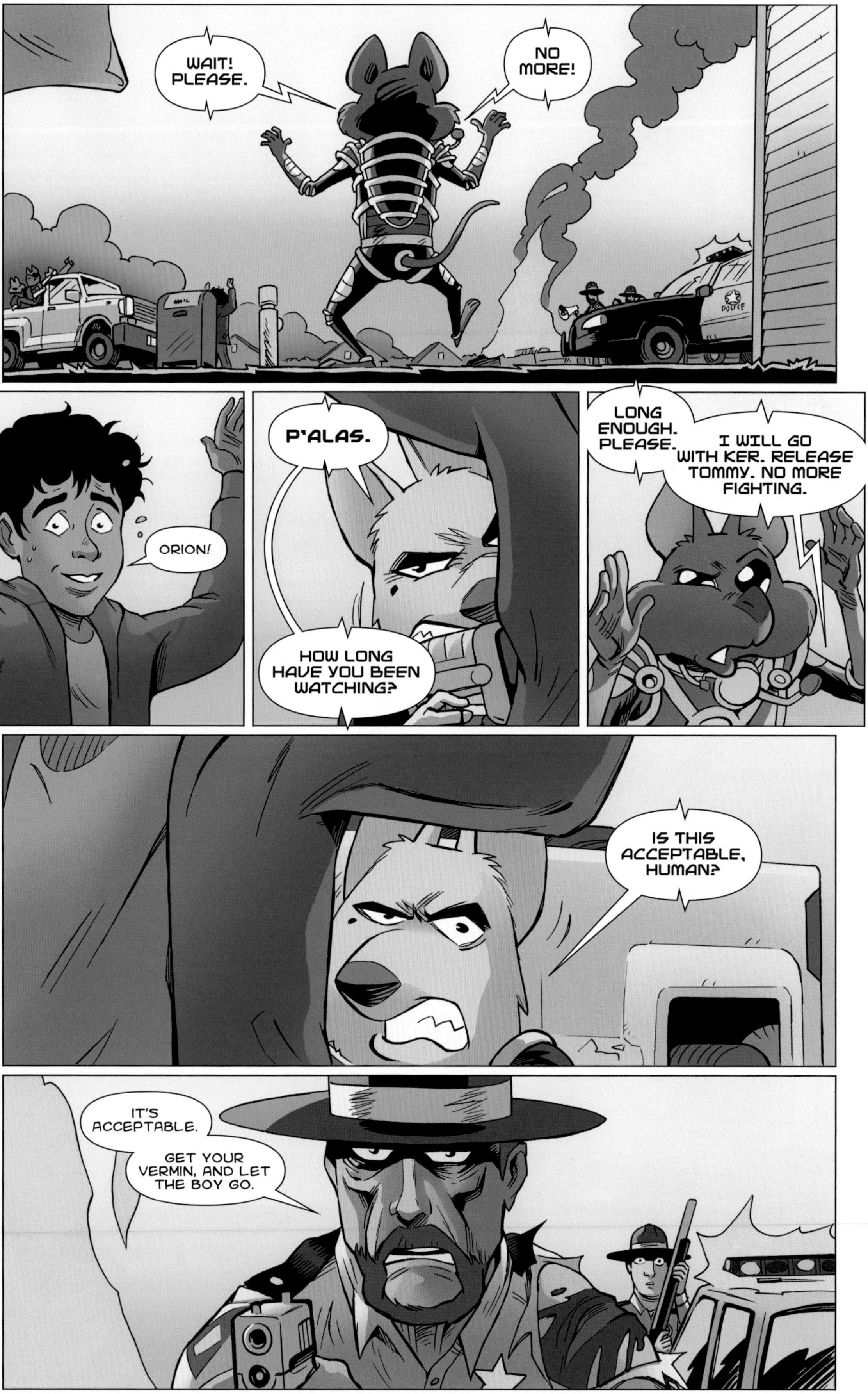
WAIT! PLEASE.
NO MORE!
MAIL
POLICE
ORION!
P'ALAS.
HOW LONG HAVE YOU BEEN WATCHING?
LONG ENOUGH. PLEASE.
I WILL GO WITH KER. RELEASE TOMMY. NO MORE FIGHTING.
IS THIS ACCEPTABLE, HUMAN?
IT'S ACCEPTABLE.
GET YOUR VERMIN, AND LET THE BOY GO.

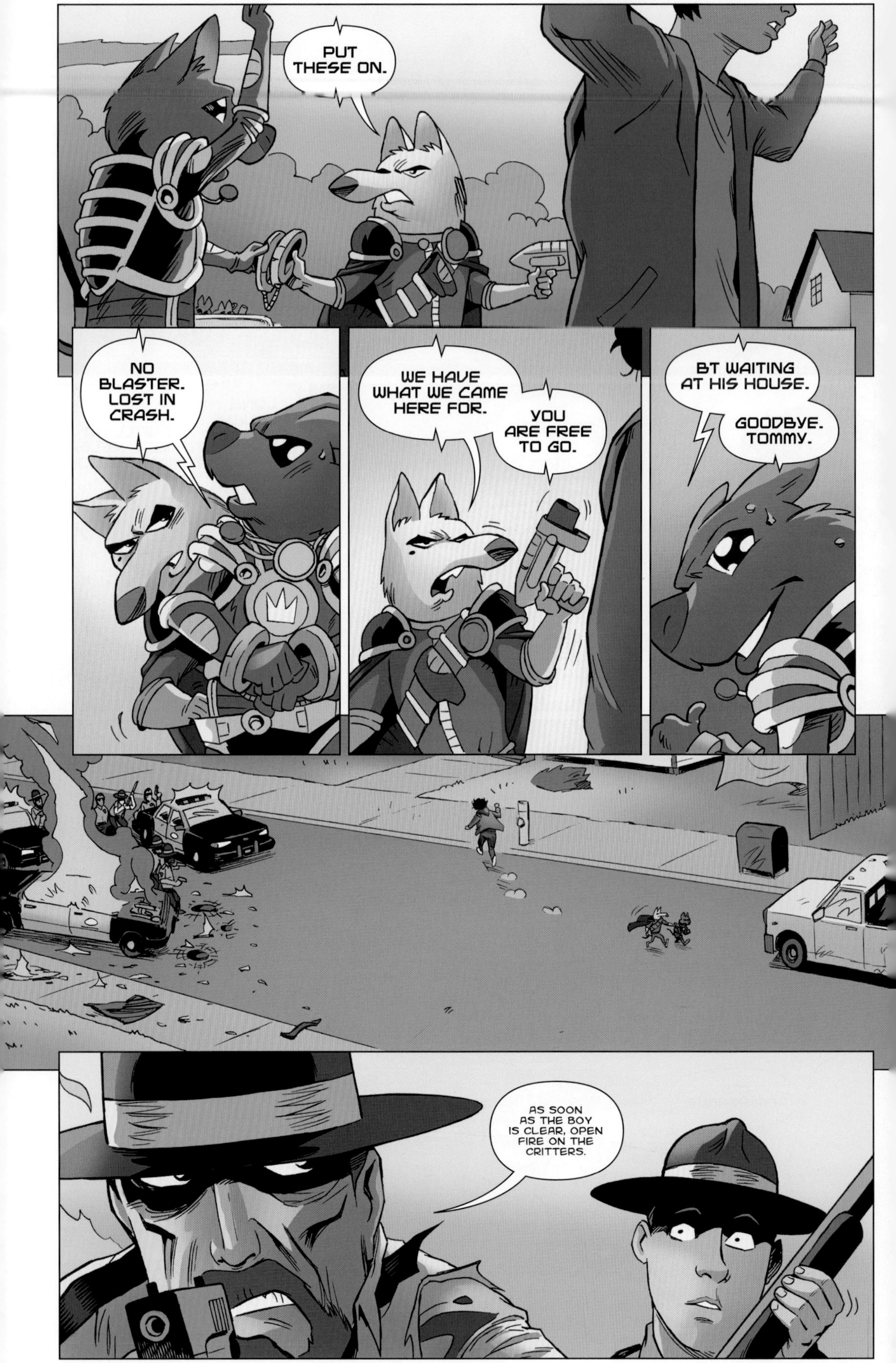
PUT THESE ON.
NO BLASTER. LOST IN CRASH.
WE HAVE WHAT WE CAME HERE FOR.
YOU ARE FREE TO GO.
BT WAITING AT HIS HOUSE.
GOODBYE. TOMMY.
AS SOON AS THE BOY IS CLEAR, OPEN FIRE ON THE CRITTERS.

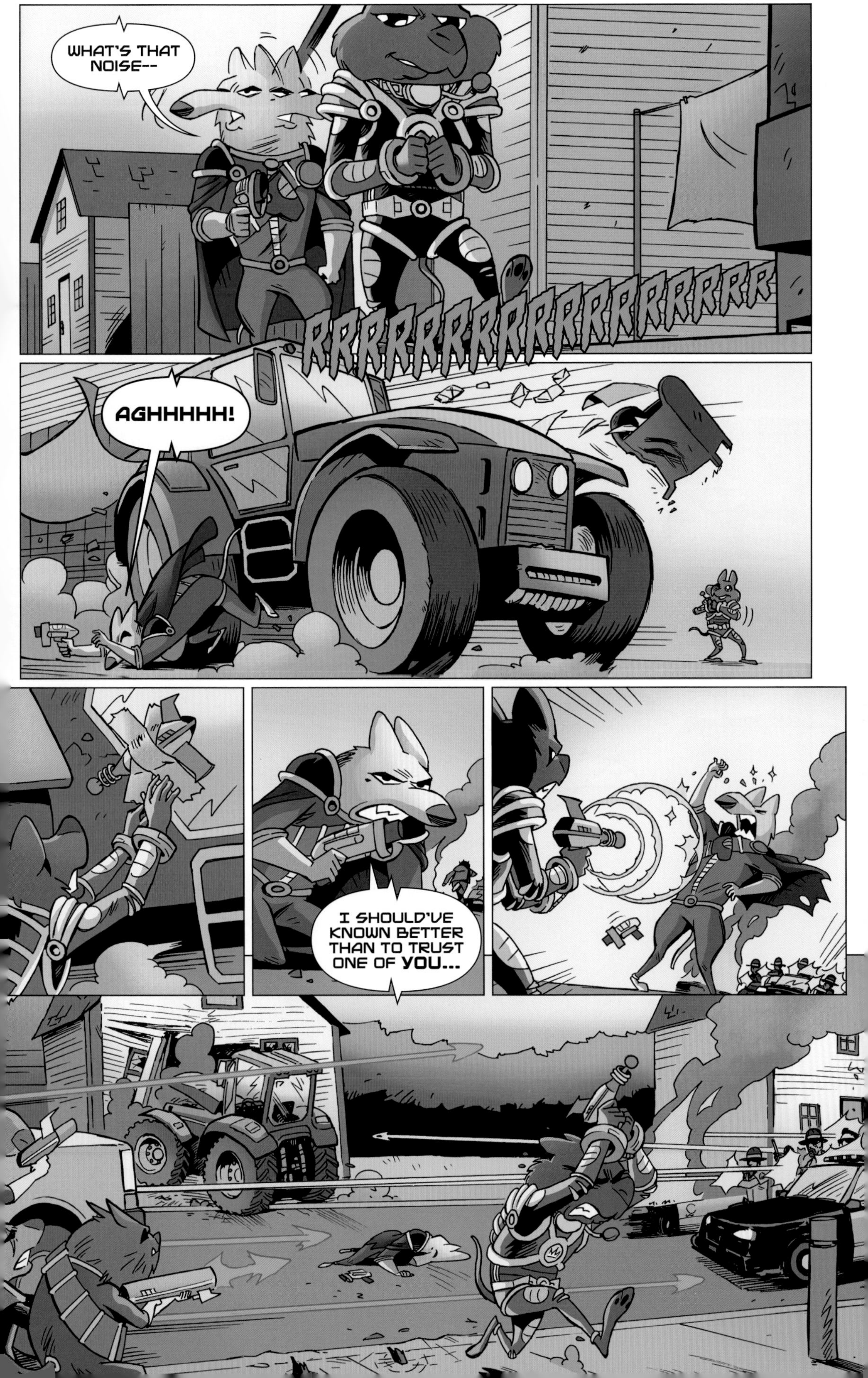
WHAT'S THAT NOISE--
RRRRRRRRRRRRRRRRRRRRRRR
AGHHHHH!
I SHOULD'VE KNOWN BETTER THAN TO TRUST ONE OF YOU...

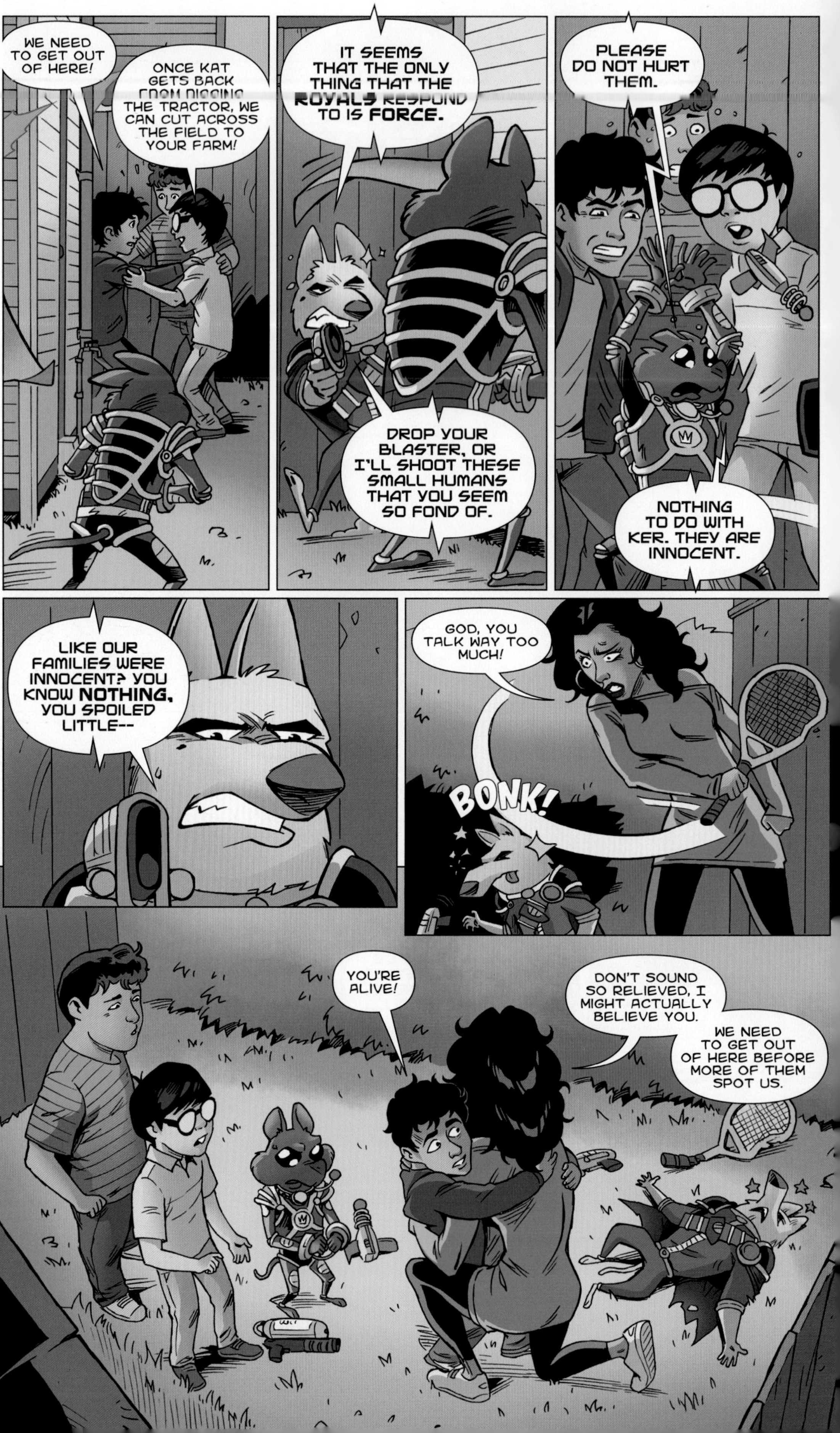
WE NEED TO GET OUT OF HERE!
ONCE KAT GETS BACK FROM DIGGING THE TRACTOR, WE CAN CUT ACROSS THE FIELD TO YOUR FARM!
IT SEEMS THAT THE ONLY THING THAT THE ROYALS RESPOND TO IS FORCE.
DROP YOUR BLASTER, OR I'LL SHOOT THESE SMALL HUMANS THAT YOU SEEM SO FOND OF.
PLEASE DO NOT HURT THEM.
NOTHING TO DO WITH KER. THEY ARE INNOCENT.
LIKE OUR FAMILIES WERE INNOCENT? YOU KNOW NOTHING, YOU SPOILED LITTLE--
GOD, YOU TALK WAY TOO MUCH!
BONK!
YOU'RE ALIVE!
DON'T SOUND SO RELIEVED, I MIGHT ACTUALLY BELIEVE YOU.
WE NEED TO GET OUT OF HERE BEFORE MORE OF THEM SPOT US.

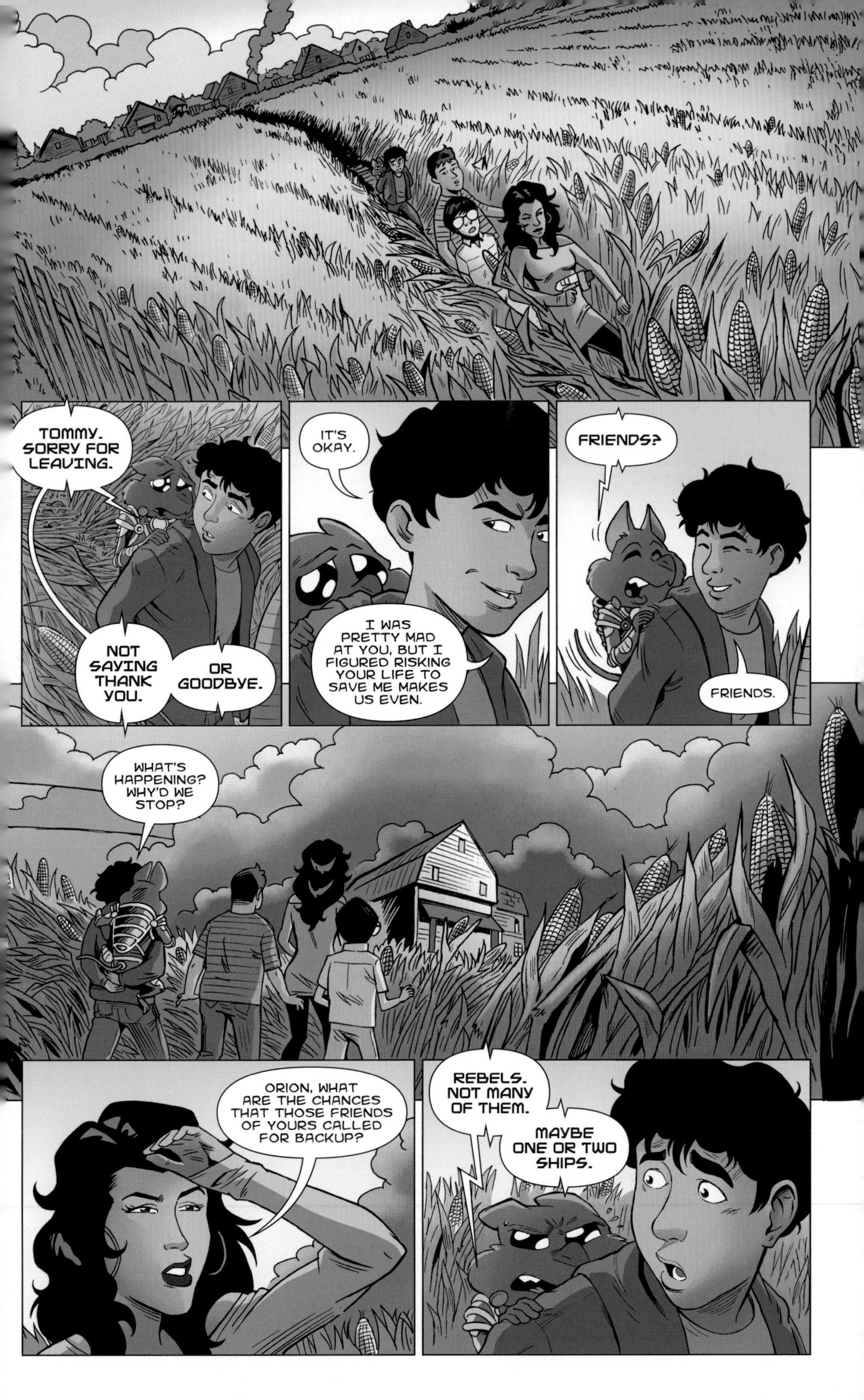
TOMMY. SORRY FOR LEAVING.
NOT SAYING THANK YOU.
OR GOODBYE.
IT'S OKAY.
I WAS PRETTY MAD AT YOU, BUT I FIGURED RISKING YOUR LIFE TO SAVE ME MAKES US EVEN.
FRIENDS?
FRIENDS.
WHAT'S HAPPENING? WHY'D WE STOP?
ORION, WHAT ARE THE CHANCES THAT THOSE FRIENDS OF YOURS CALLED FOR BACKUP?
REBELS. NOT MANY OF THEM.
MAYBE ONE OR TWO SHIPS.

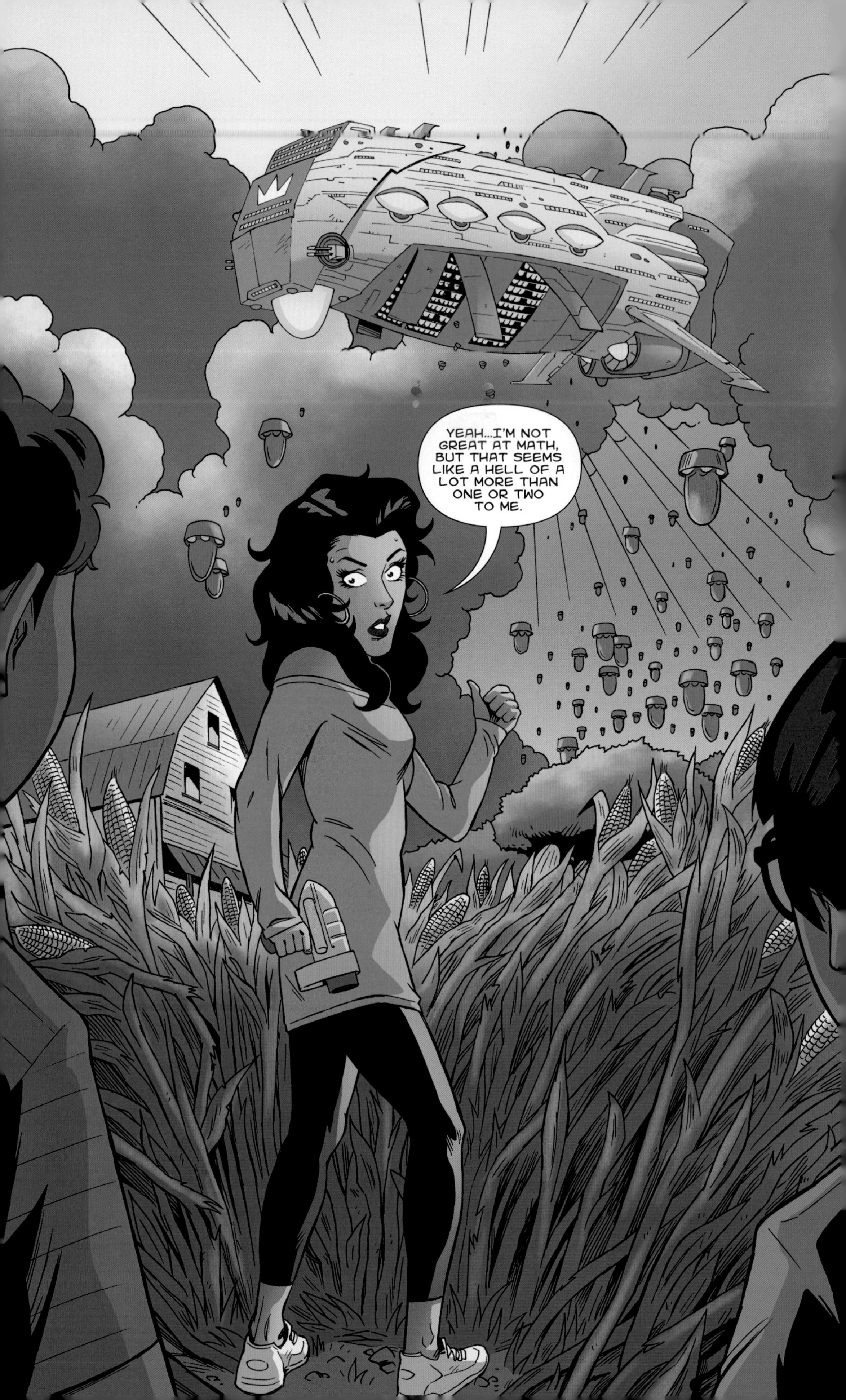
YEAH...I'M NOT GREAT AT MATH, BUT THAT SEEMS LIKE A HELL OF A LOT MORE THAN ONE OR TWO TO ME.

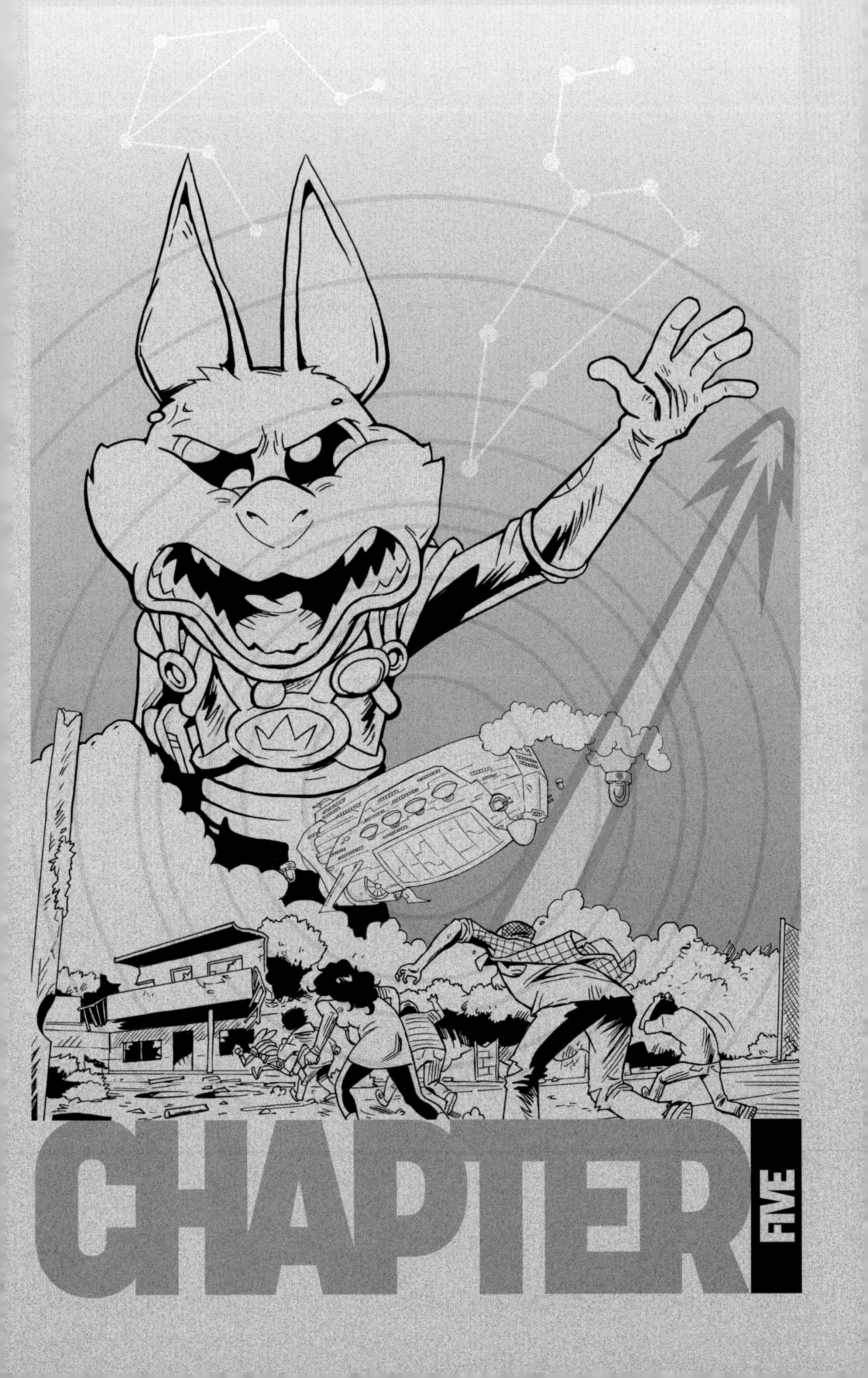

CHAPTER FIVE

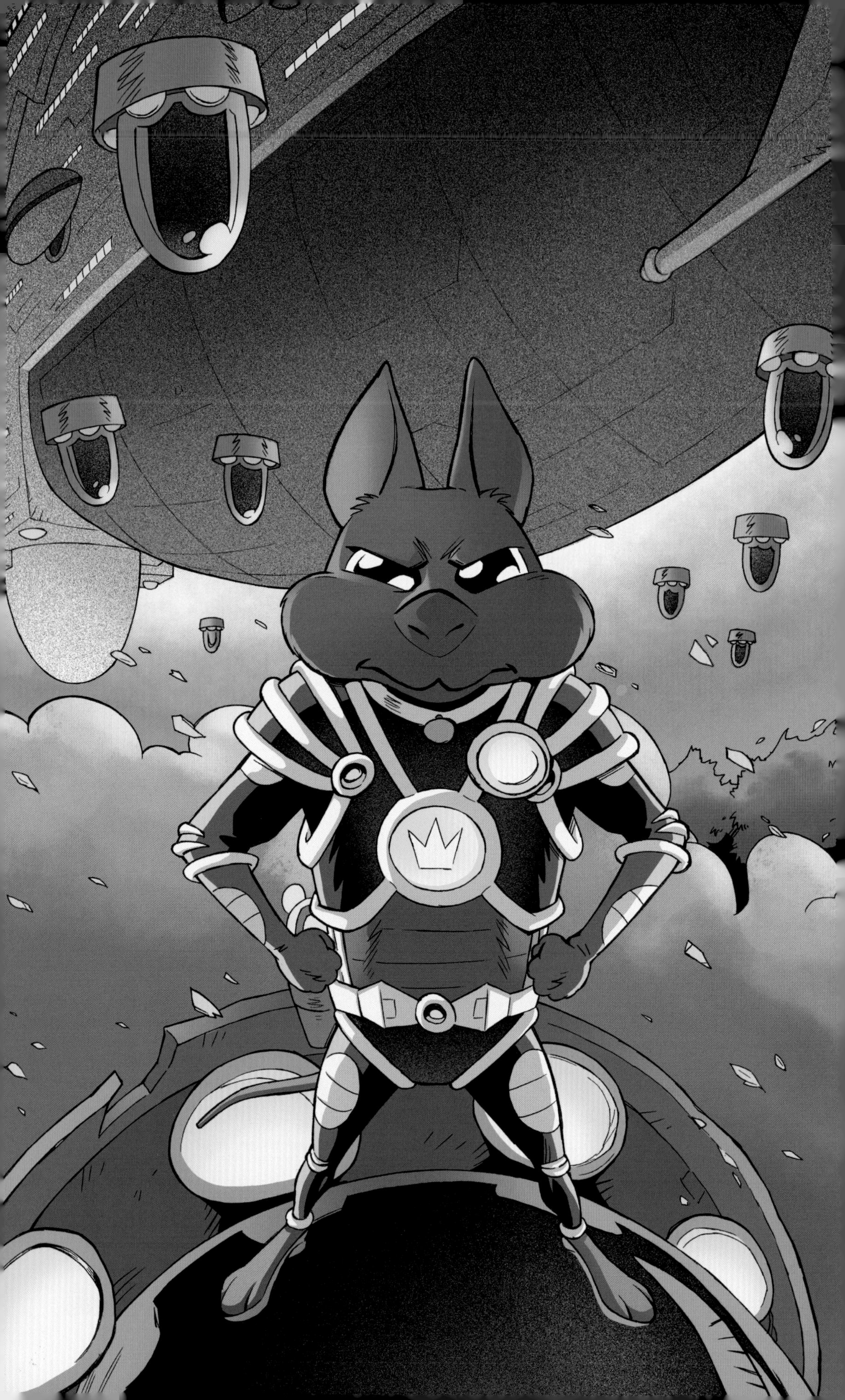

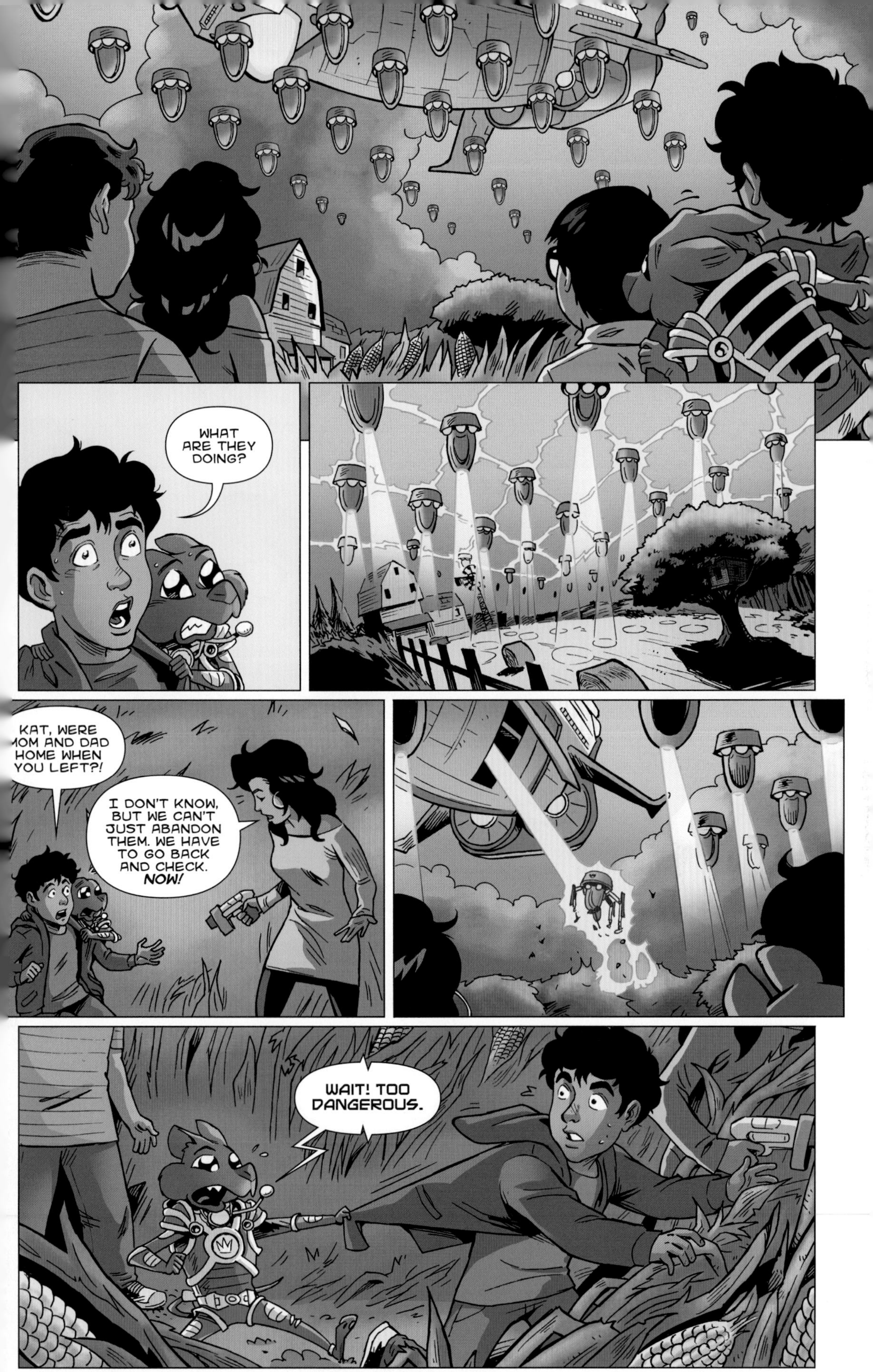
WHAT ARE THEY DOING?
KAT, WERE MOM AND DAD HOME WHEN YOU LEFT?!
I DON'T KNOW, BUT WE CAN'T JUST ABANDON THEM. WE HAVE TO GO BACK AND CHECK. NOW!
WAIT! TOO DANGEROUS.

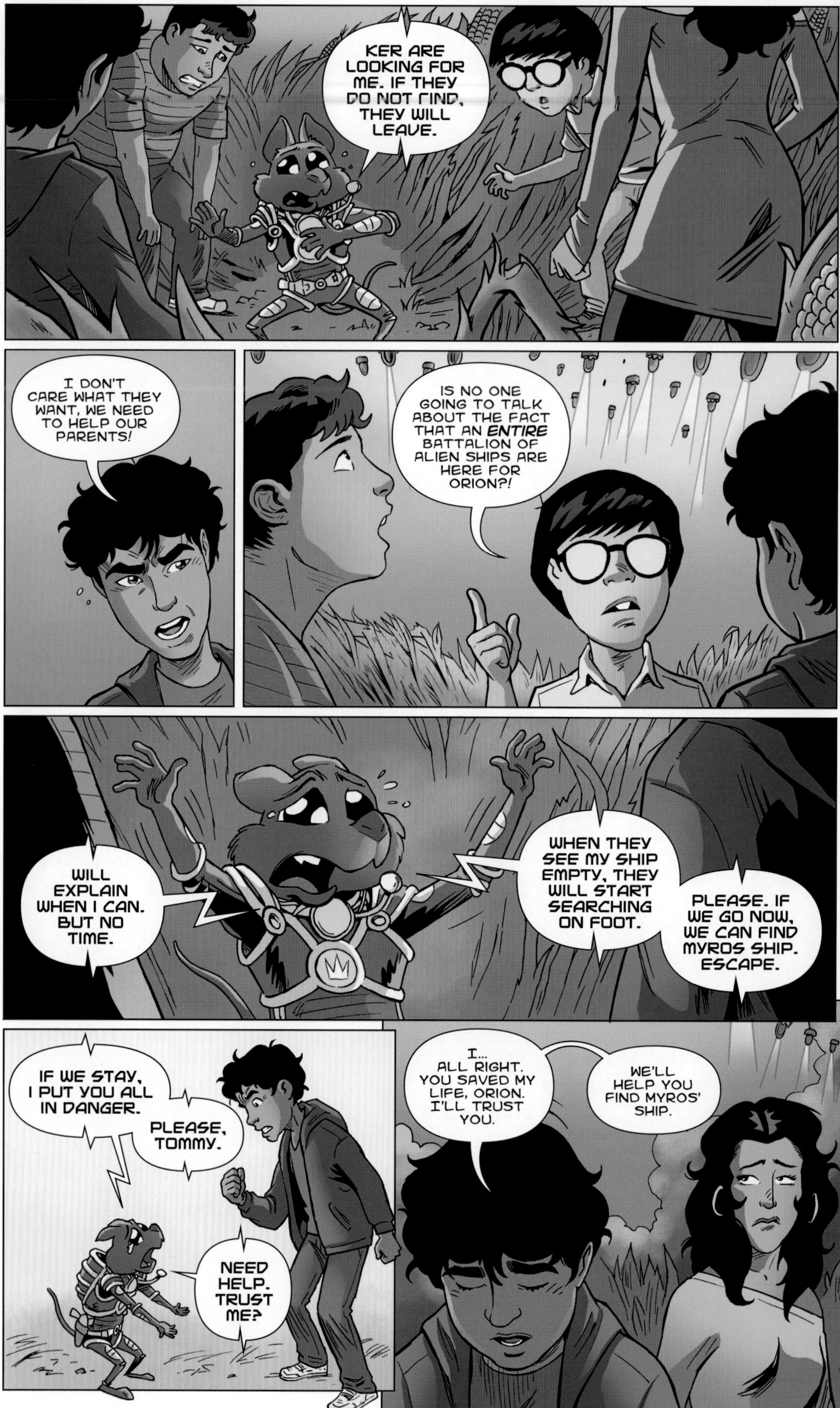
KER ARE LOOKING FOR ME. IF THEY DO NOT FIND, THEY WILL LEAVE.
I DON'T CARE WHAT THEY WANT, WE NEED TO HELP OUR PARENTS!
IS NO ONE GOING TO TALK ABOUT THE FACT THAT AN *ENTIRE* BATTALION OF ALIEN SHIPS ARE HERE FOR ORION?!
WILL EXPLAIN WHEN I CAN. BUT NO TIME.
WHEN THEY SEE MY SHIP EMPTY, THEY WILL START SEARCHING ON FOOT.
PLEASE. IF WE GO NOW, WE CAN FIND MYROS SHIP. ESCAPE.
IF WE STAY, I PUT YOU ALL IN DANGER.
PLEASE, TOMMY.
NEED HELP. TRUST ME?
I... ALL RIGHT. YOU SAVED MY LIFE, ORION. I'LL TRUST YOU.
WE'LL HELP YOU FIND MYROS' SHIP.

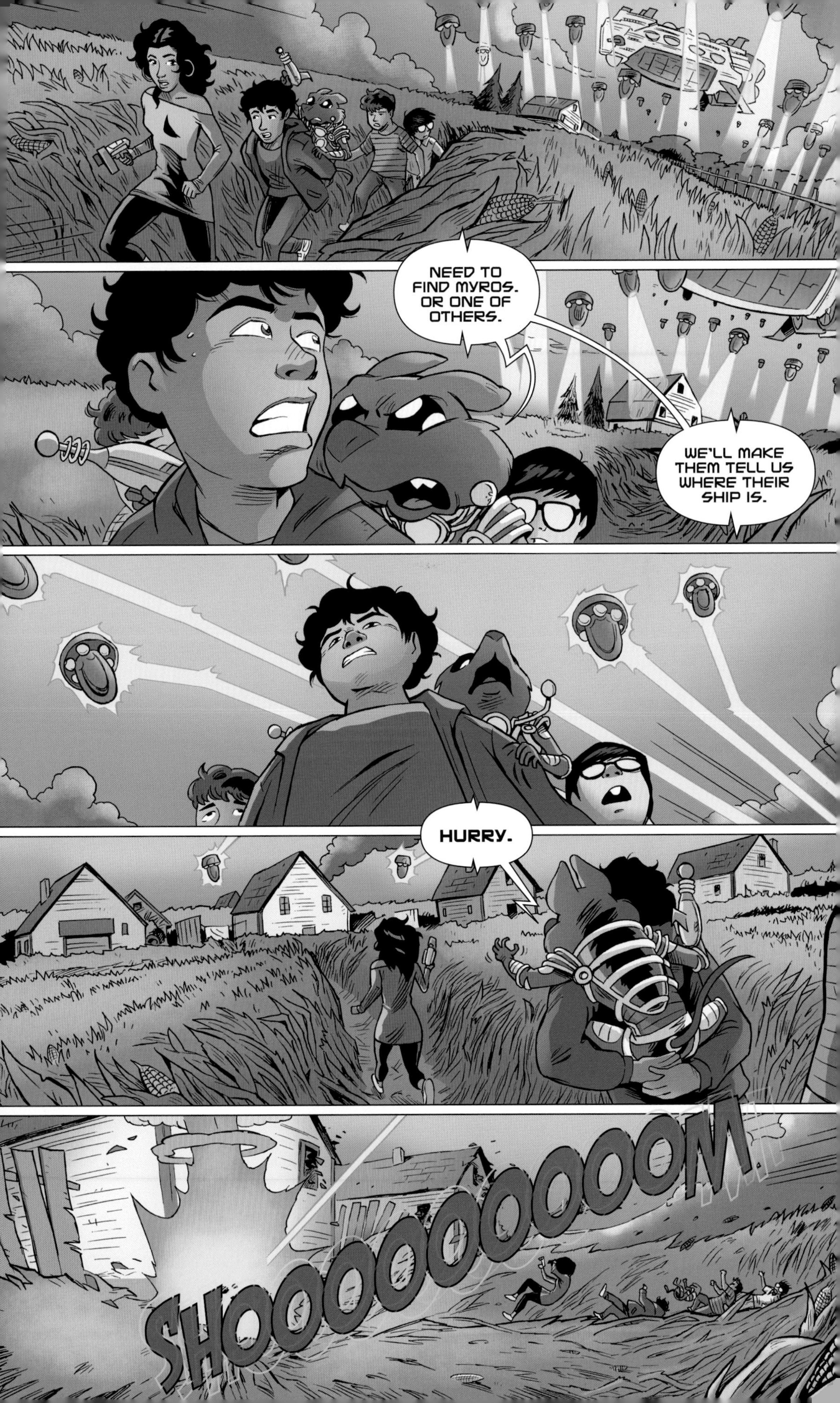
NEED TO FIND MYROS. OR ONE OF OTHERS.
WE'LL MAKE THEM TELL US WHERE THEIR SHIP IS.
HURRY.
SHOOOOOOOOOOOM

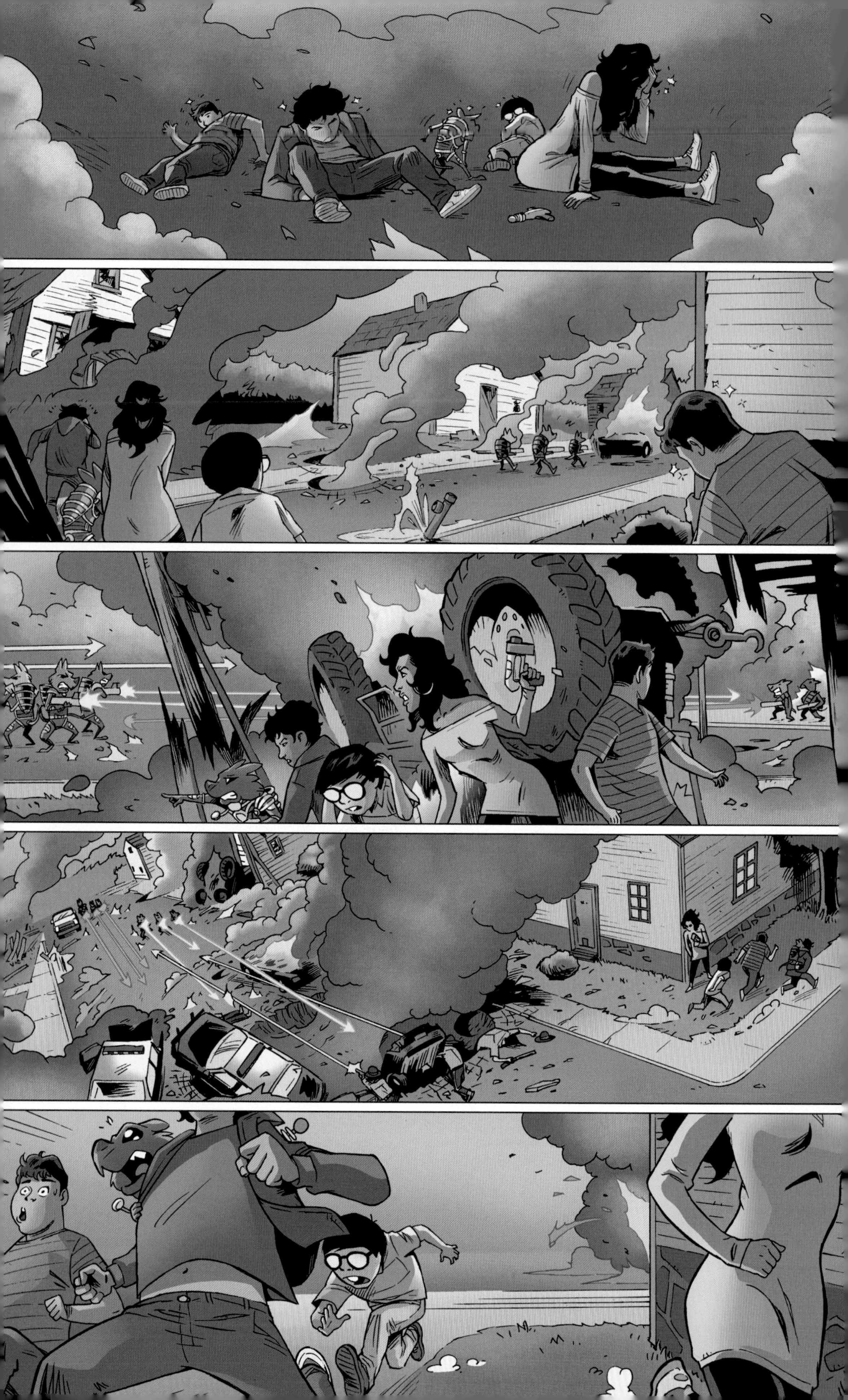

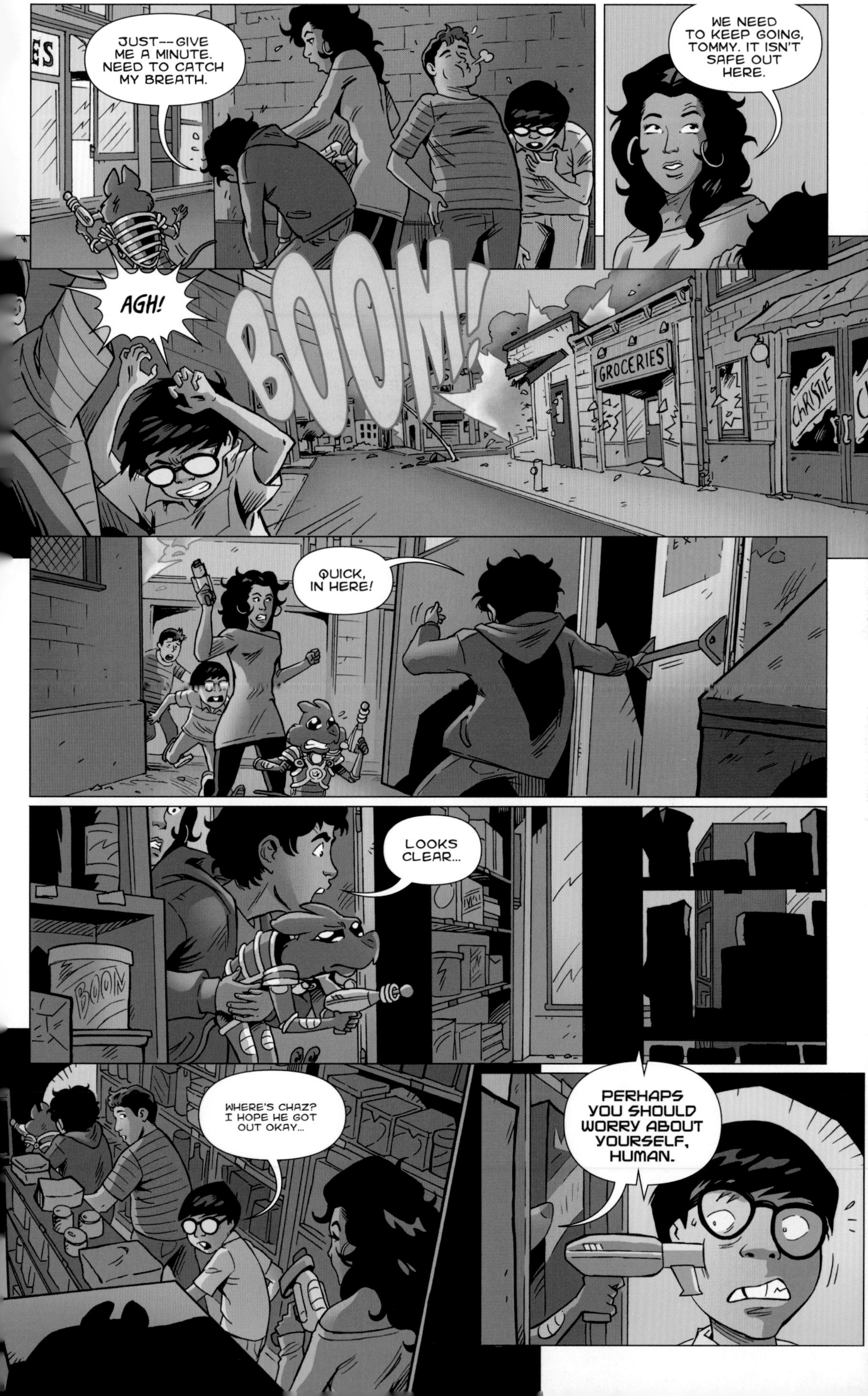
JUST--GIVE ME A MINUTE. NEED TO CATCH MY BREATH.
WE NEED TO KEEP GOING, TOMMY. IT ISN'T SAFE OUT HERE.
AGH!
BOOM!
GROCERIES
CHRISTIE
QUICK, IN HERE!
LOOKS CLEAR...
WHERE'S CHAZ? I HOPE HE GOT OUT OKAY...
PERHAPS YOU SHOULD WORRY ABOUT YOURSELF, HUMAN.

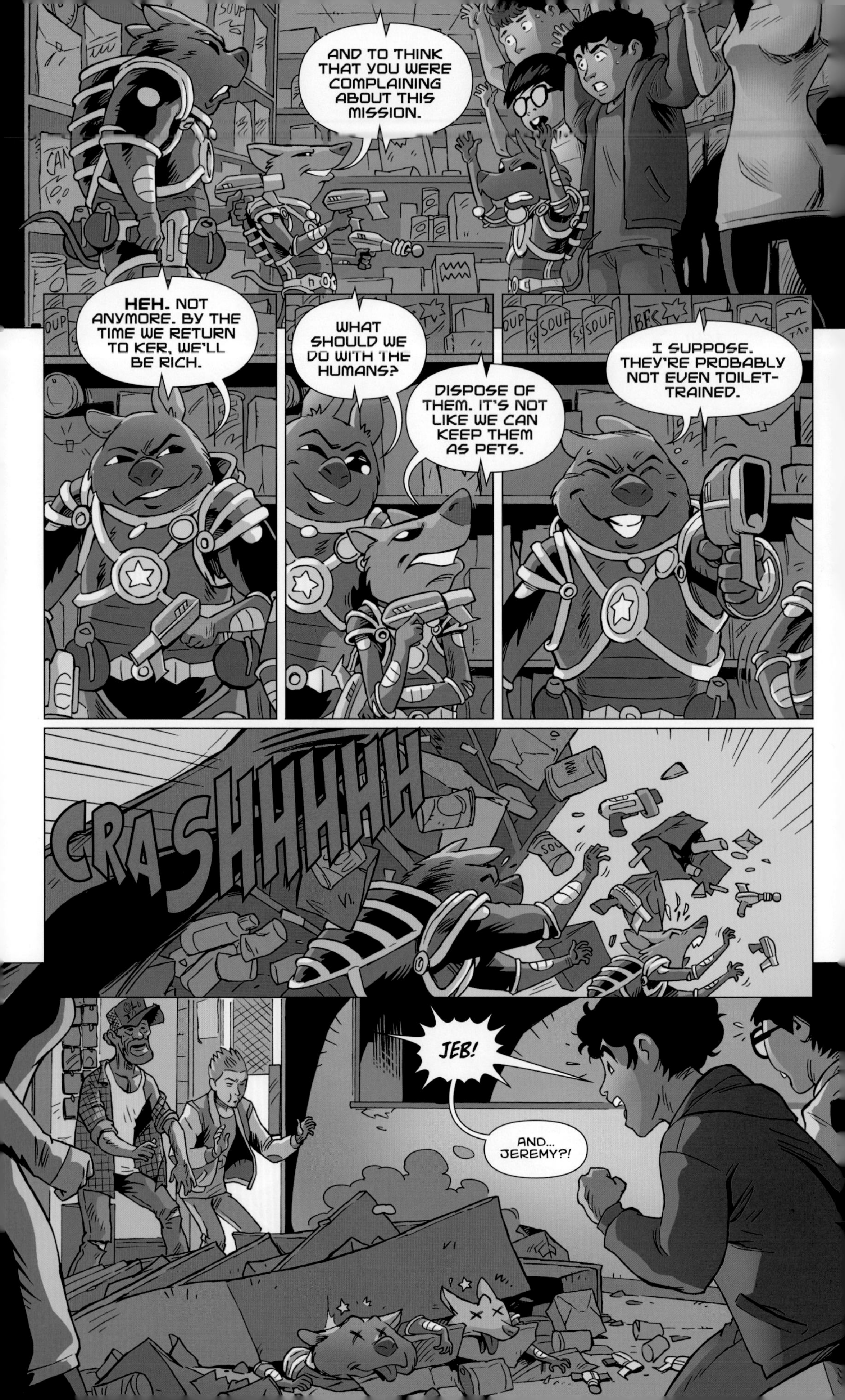
AND TO THINK THAT YOU WERE COMPLAINING ABOUT THIS MISSION.
HEH. NOT ANYMORE. BY THE TIME WE RETURN TO KER, WE'LL BE RICH.
WHAT SHOULD WE DO WITH THE HUMANS?
DISPOSE OF THEM. IT'S NOT LIKE WE CAN KEEP THEM AS PETS.
I SUPPOSE. THEY'RE PROBABLY NOT EVEN TOILET-TRAINED.
CRASHHHHH
JEB!
AND... JEREMY?!

I SAW ONE OF THEM SNEAKING IN ROUND THE BACK. THEY GOT TO CHAZ FIRST, BUT--

HE SAVED ME RIGHT BEFORE IT GOT ME. WE HID WHEN WE HEARD MORE COMING IN.

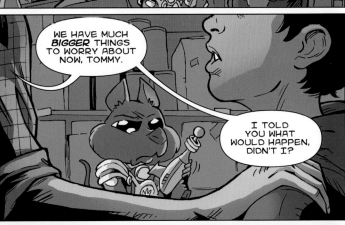

WOW... I NEVER THOUGHT I'D SEE YOU TWO WORKING TOGETHER.

WE'D BE DONE FOR IF YOU HADN'T HELPED US OUT. THANKS.

WHATEVER, MURPHY. YOU COVERED FOR ME WITH THE SHERIFF, THIS JUST MAKES US EVEN.

WE HAVE MUCH *BIGGER* THINGS TO WORRY ABOUT NOW, TOMMY.

I TOLD YOU WHAT WOULD HAPPEN, DIDN'T I?

I HAVEN'T FORGOTTEN.

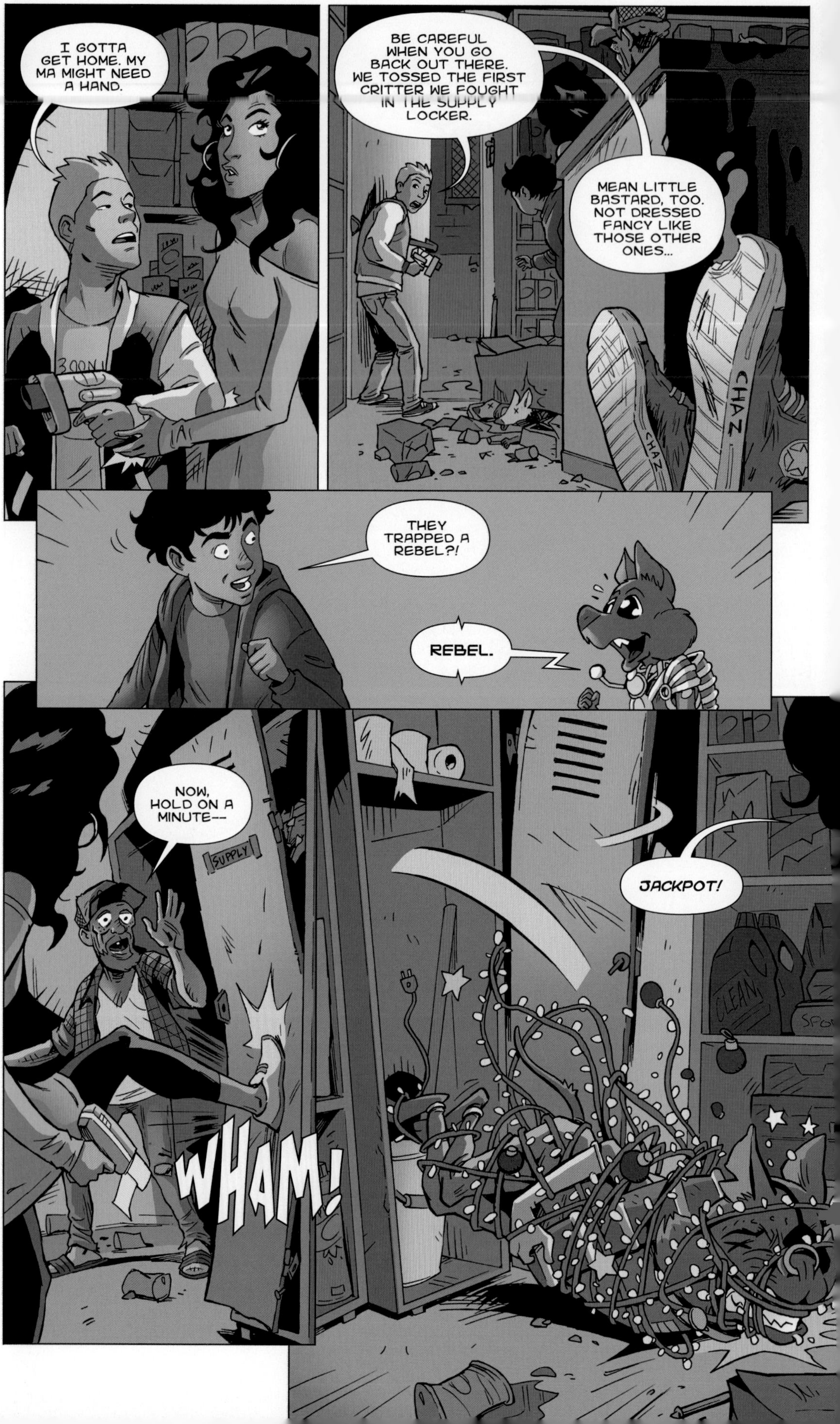
I GOTTA GET HOME. MY MA MIGHT NEED A HAND.
BE CAREFUL WHEN YOU GO BACK OUT THERE. WE TOSSED THE FIRST CRITTER WE FOUGHT IN THE SUPPLY LOCKER.
MEAN LITTLE BASTARD, TOO. NOT DRESSED FANCY LIKE THOSE OTHER ONES...
CHAZ
CHAZ
THEY TRAPPED A REBEL?!
REBEL.
NOW, HOLD ON A MINUTE--
SUPPLY
WHAM!
JACKPOT!
CLEAN

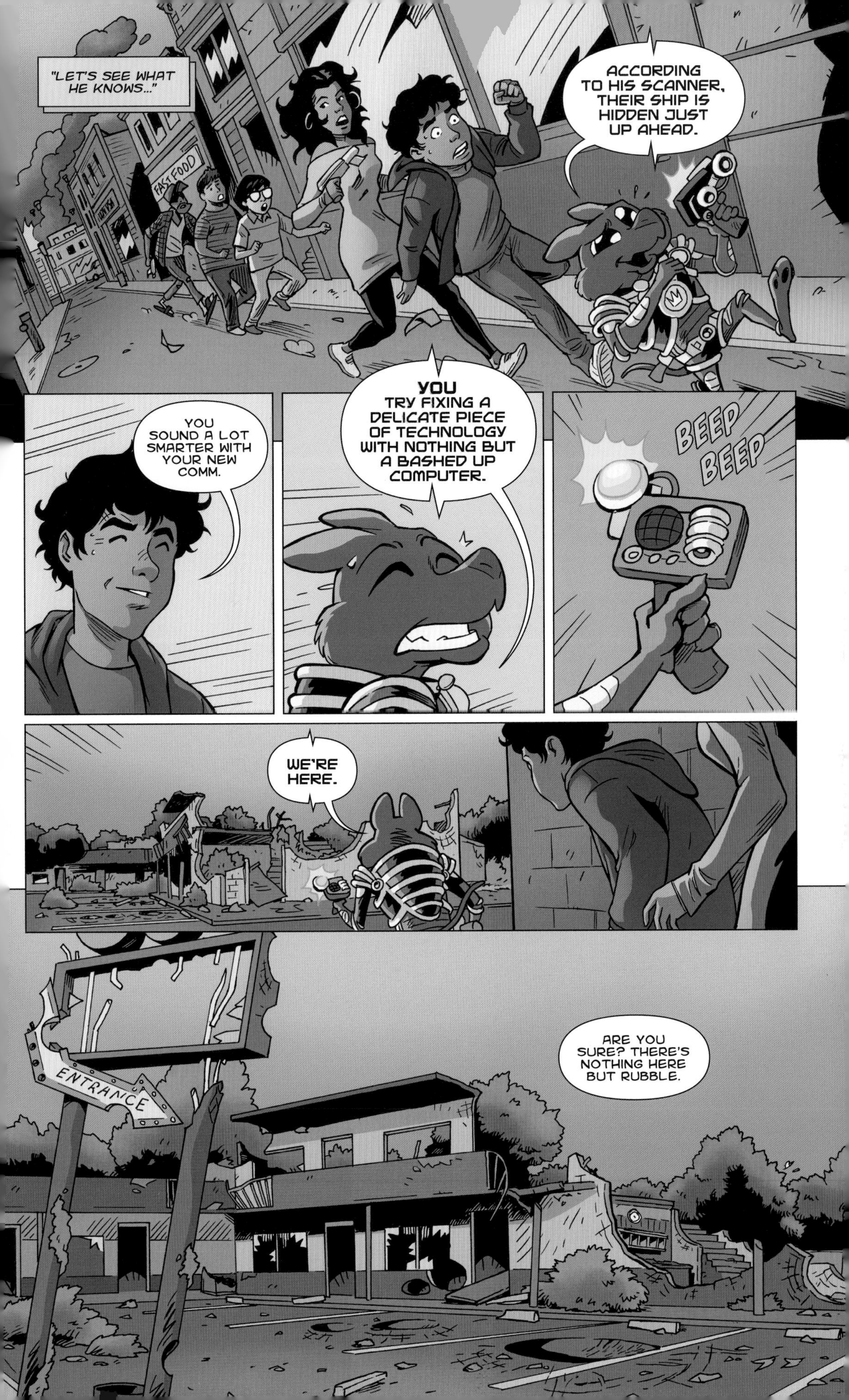
"LET'S SEE WHAT HE KNOWS..."
FAST FOOD
ACCORDING TO HIS SCANNER, THEIR SHIP IS HIDDEN JUST UP AHEAD.
YOU SOUND A LOT SMARTER WITH YOUR NEW COMM.
YOU TRY FIXING A DELICATE PIECE OF TECHNOLOGY WITH NOTHING BUT A BASHED UP COMPUTER.
BEEP BEEP
WE'RE HERE.
ENTRANCE
ARE YOU SURE? THERE'S NOTHING HERE BUT RUBBLE.

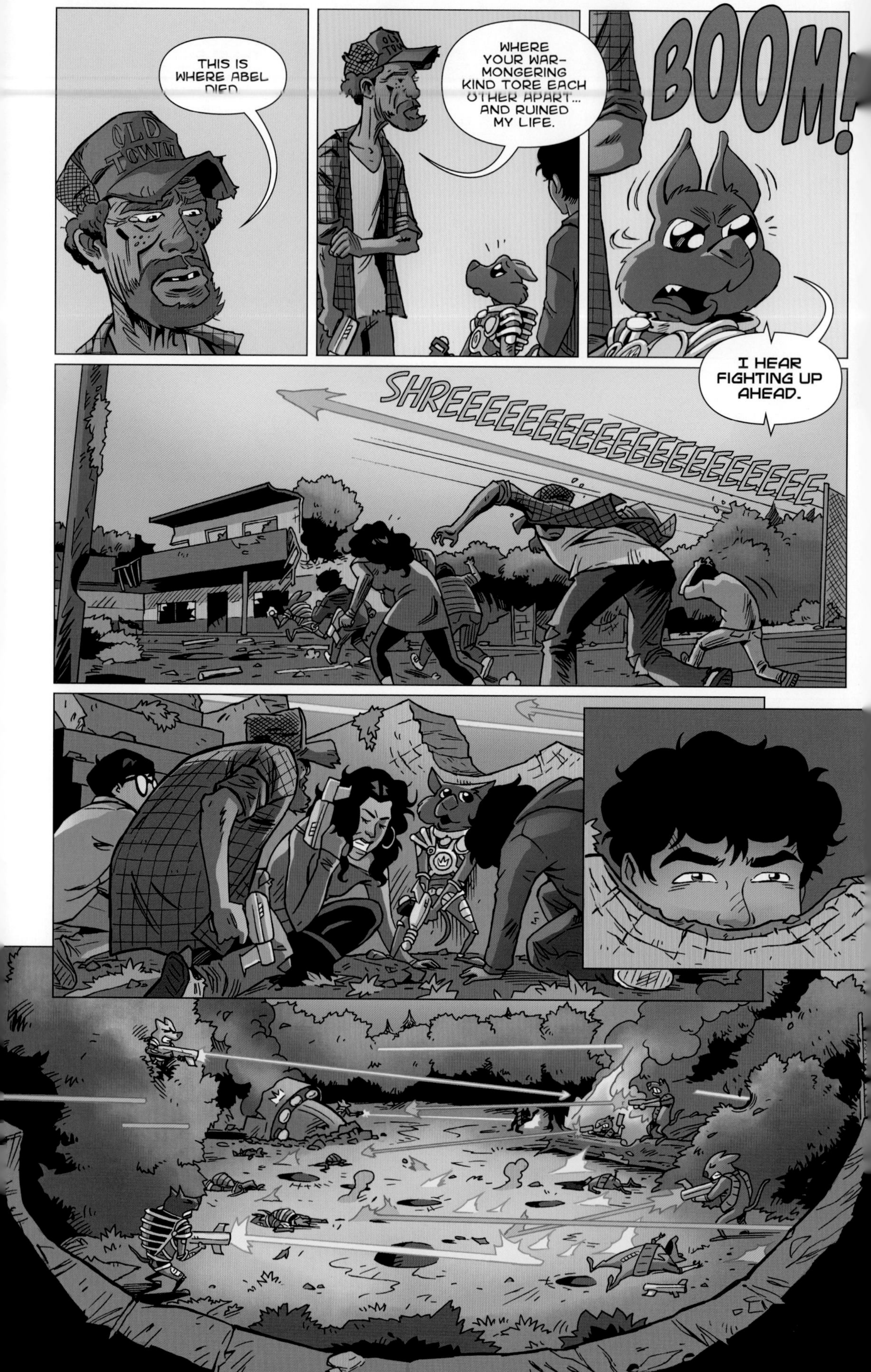
THIS IS WHERE ABEL DIED.
WHERE YOUR WAR-MONGERING KIND TORE EACH OTHER APART... AND RUINED MY LIFE.
BOOM!
I HEAR FIGHTING UP AHEAD.
SHREEEEEEEEEEEEEEEEEEEEEE

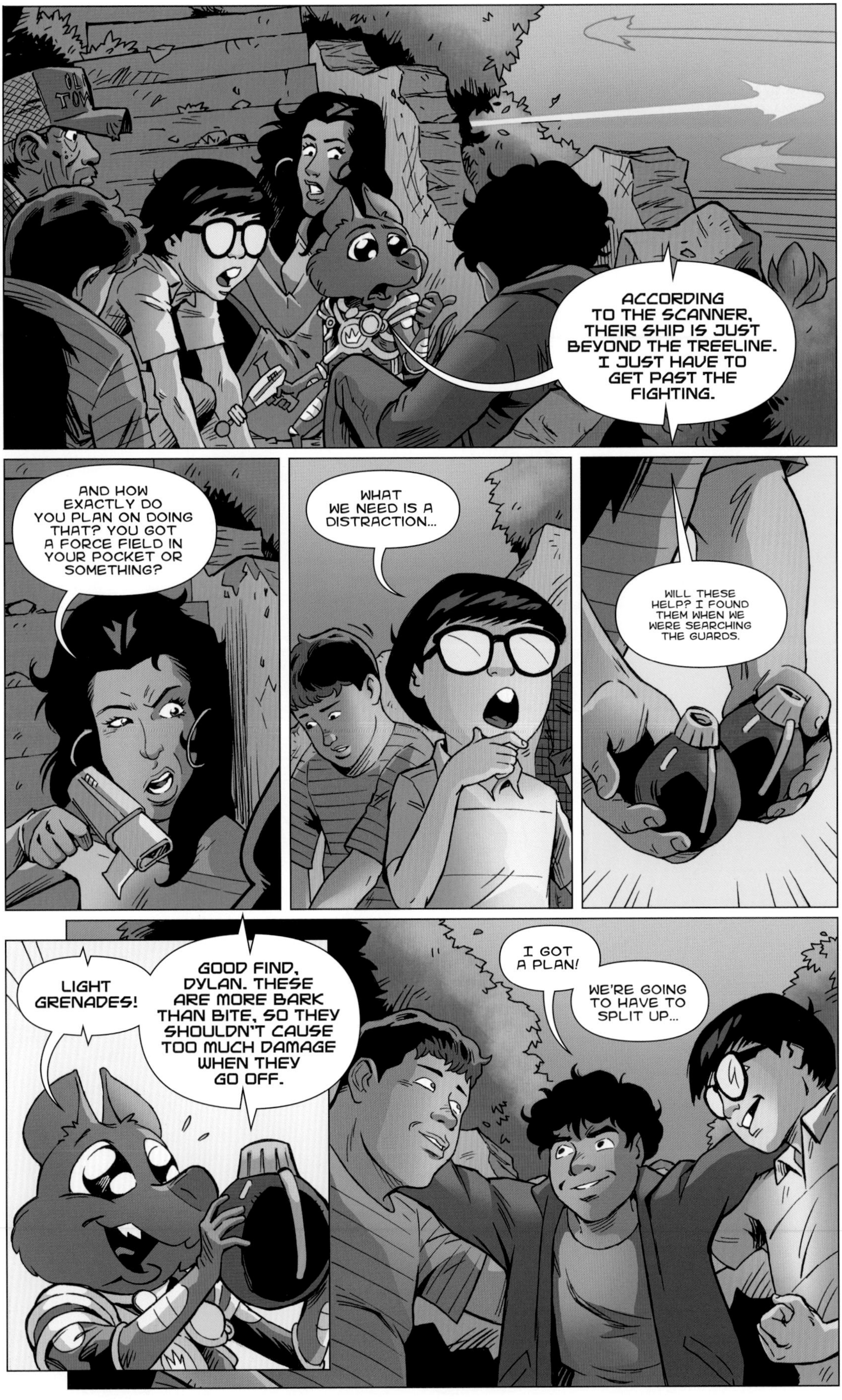
ACCORDING TO THE SCANNER, THEIR SHIP IS JUST BEYOND THE TREELINE. I JUST HAVE TO GET PAST THE FIGHTING.
AND HOW EXACTLY DO YOU PLAN ON DOING THAT? YOU GOT A FORCE FIELD IN YOUR POCKET OR SOMETHING?
WHAT WE NEED IS A DISTRACTION...
WILL THESE HELP? I FOUND THEM WHEN WE WERE SEARCHING THE GUARDS.
LIGHT GRENADES!
GOOD FIND, DYLAN. THESE ARE MORE BARK THAN BITE, SO THEY SHOULDN'T CAUSE TOO MUCH DAMAGE WHEN THEY GO OFF.
I GOT A PLAN!
WE'RE GOING TO HAVE TO SPLIT UP...

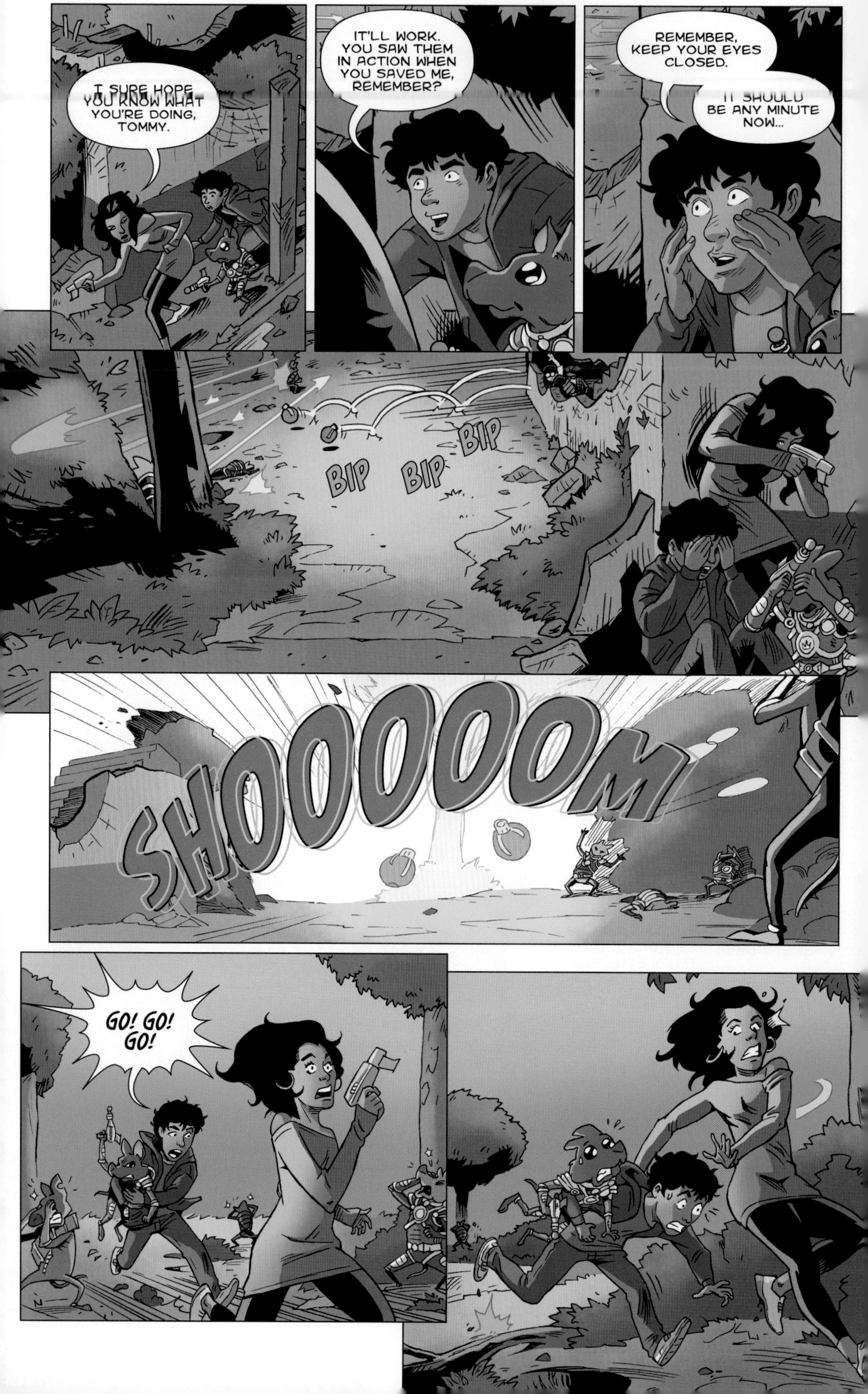
I SURE HOPE YOU KNOW WHAT YOU'RE DOING, TOMMY.
IT'LL WORK. YOU SAW THEM IN ACTION WHEN YOU SAVED ME, REMEMBER?
REMEMBER, KEEP YOUR EYES CLOSED.
IT SHOULD BE ANY MINUTE NOW...
BIP
BIP
BIP
SHOOOOOOM
GO! GO! GO!

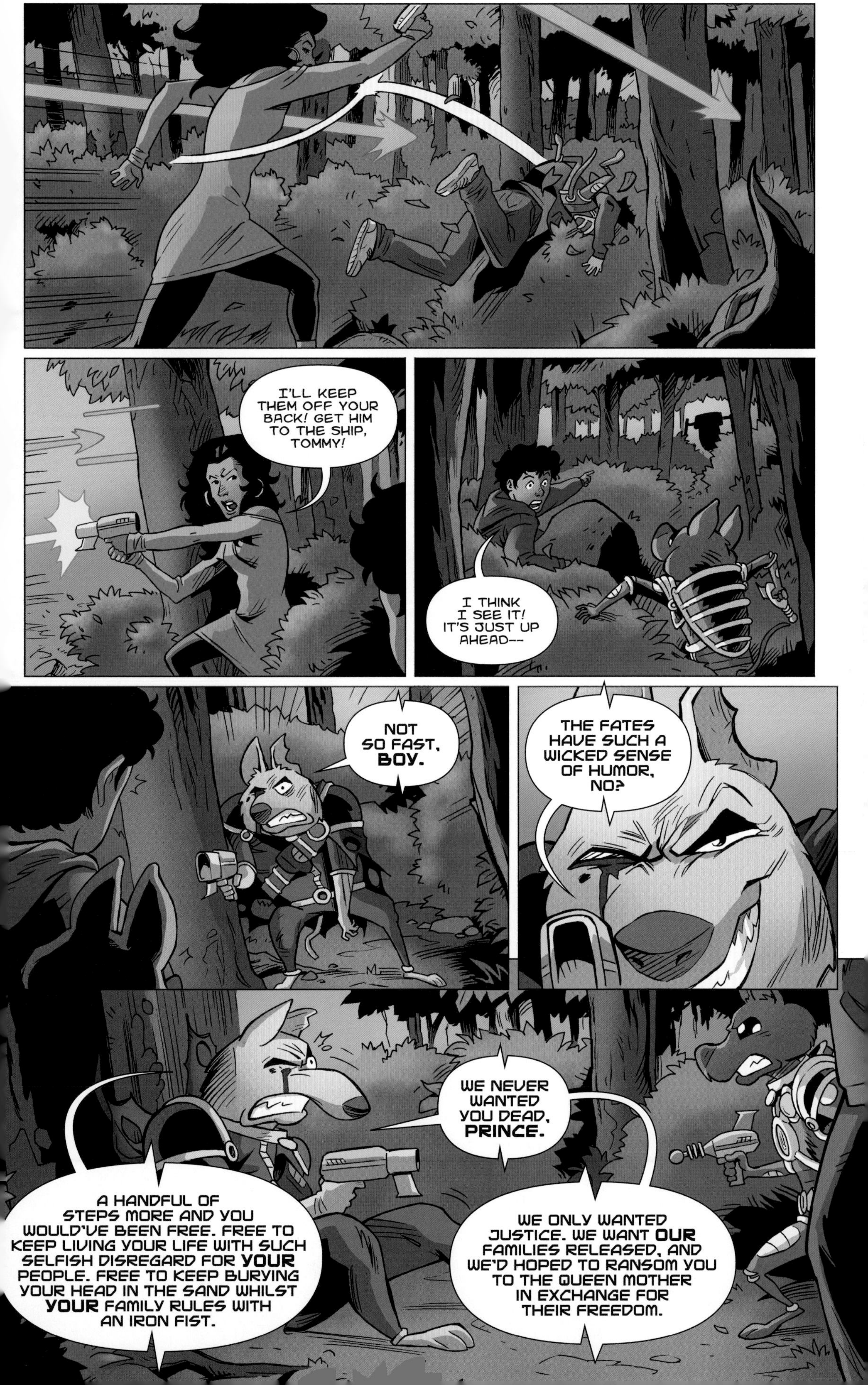
I'LL KEEP THEM OFF YOUR BACK! GET HIM TO THE SHIP, TOMMY!
I THINK I SEE IT! IT'S JUST UP AHEAD--
NOT SO FAST, **BOY.**
THE FATES HAVE SUCH A WICKED SENSE OF HUMOR, NO?
WE NEVER WANTED YOU DEAD, **PRINCE.**
A HANDFUL OF STEPS MORE AND YOU WOULD'VE BEEN FREE. FREE TO KEEP LIVING YOUR LIFE WITH SUCH SELFISH DISREGARD FOR **YOUR** PEOPLE. FREE TO KEEP BURYING YOUR HEAD IN THE SAND WHILST **YOUR** FAMILY RULES WITH AN IRON FIST.
WE ONLY WANTED JUSTICE. WE WANT **OUR** FAMILIES RELEASED, AND WE'D HOPED TO RANSOM YOU TO THE QUEEN MOTHER IN EXCHANGE FOR THEIR FREEDOM.

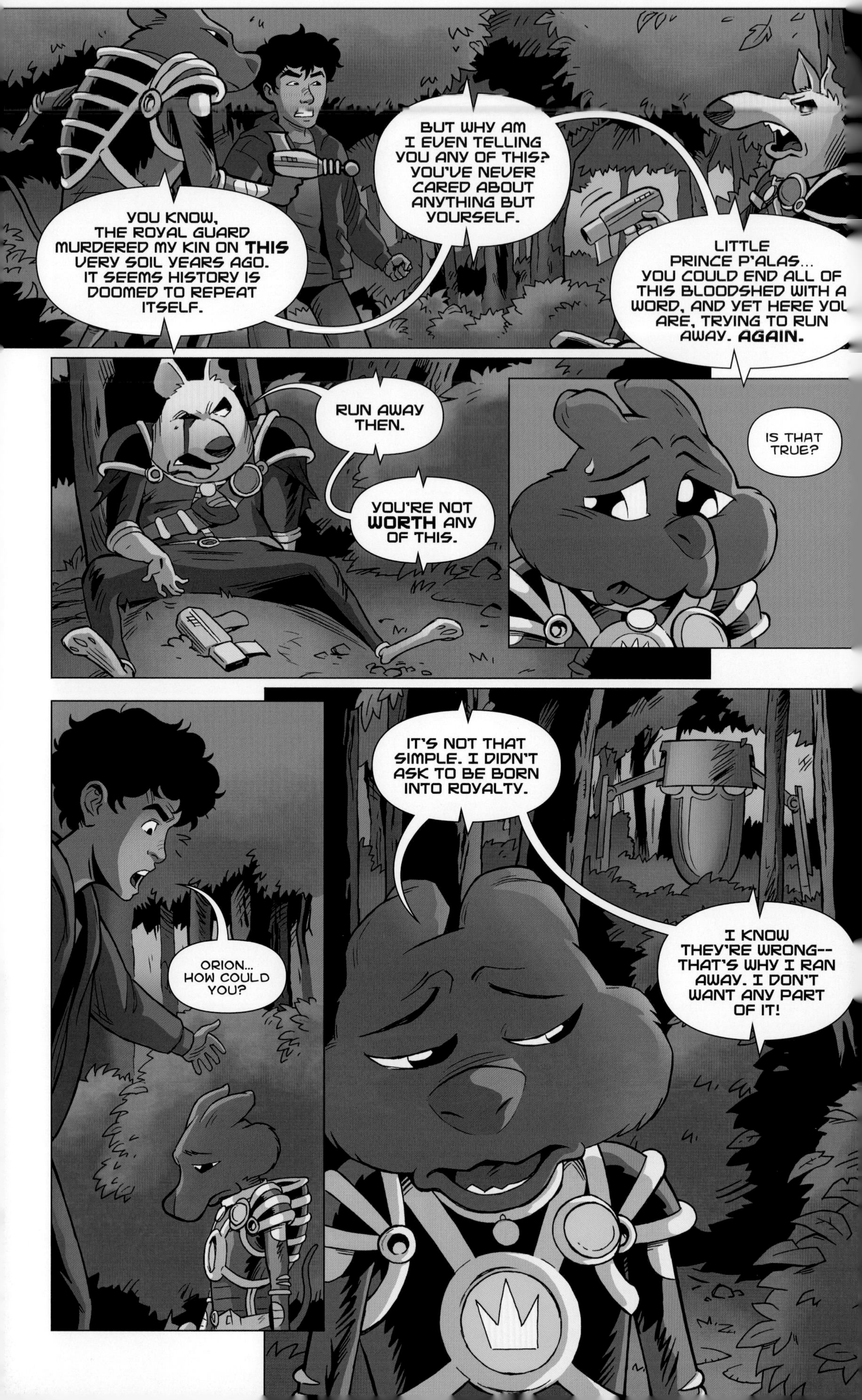
YOU KNOW, THE ROYAL GUARD MURDERED MY KIN ON **THIS** VERY SOIL YEARS AGO. IT SEEMS HISTORY IS DOOMED TO REPEAT ITSELF.
BUT WHY AM I EVEN TELLING YOU ANY OF THIS? YOU'VE NEVER CARED ABOUT ANYTHING BUT YOURSELF.
LITTLE PRINCE P'ALAS... YOU COULD END ALL OF THIS BLOODSHED WITH A WORD, AND YET HERE YOU ARE, TRYING TO RUN AWAY. **AGAIN.**
RUN AWAY THEN.
YOU'RE NOT **WORTH** ANY OF THIS.
IS THAT TRUE?
ORION... HOW COULD YOU?
IT'S NOT THAT SIMPLE. I DIDN'T ASK TO BE BORN INTO ROYALTY.
I KNOW THEY'RE WRONG-- THAT'S WHY I RAN AWAY. I DON'T WANT ANY PART OF IT!

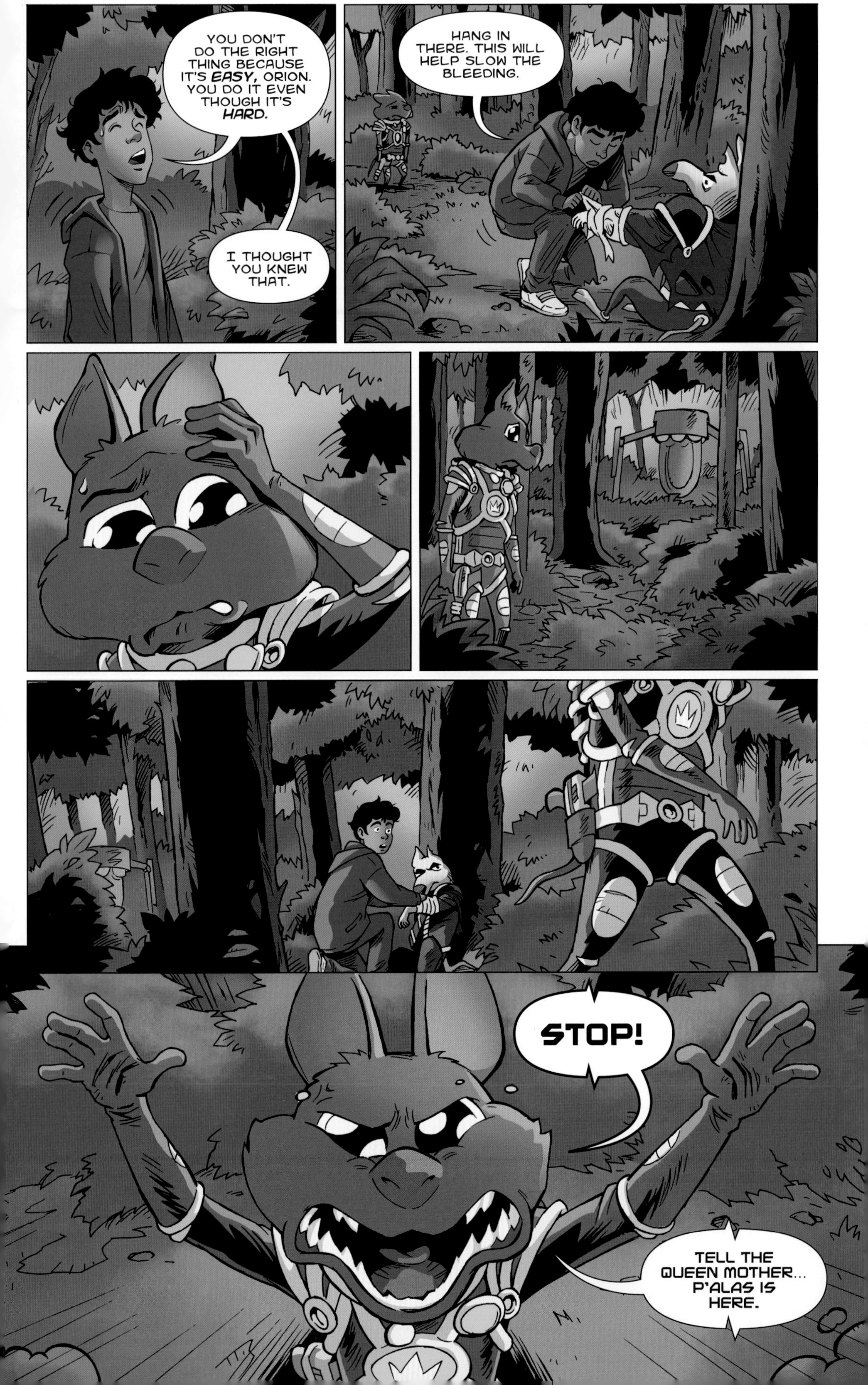
YOU DON'T DO THE RIGHT THING BECAUSE IT'S EASY, ORION. YOU DO IT EVEN THOUGH IT'S HARD.
I THOUGHT YOU KNEW THAT.
HANG IN THERE. THIS WILL HELP SLOW THE BLEEDING.
STOP!
TELL THE QUEEN MOTHER... P'ALAS IS HERE.

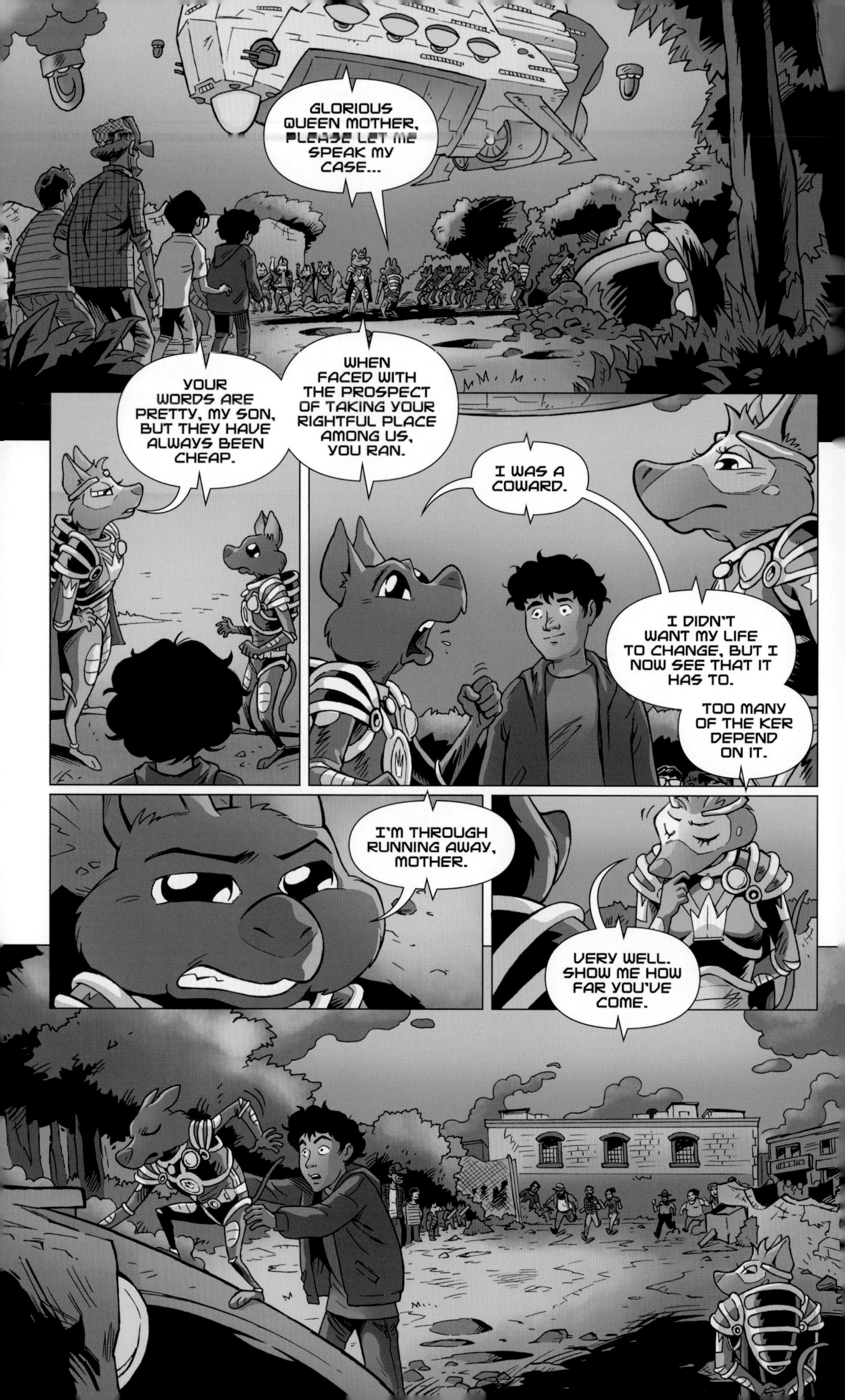
GLORIOUS QUEEN MOTHER, PLEASE LET ME SPEAK MY CASE...
YOUR WORDS ARE PRETTY, MY SON, BUT THEY HAVE ALWAYS BEEN CHEAP.
WHEN FACED WITH THE PROSPECT OF TAKING YOUR RIGHTFUL PLACE AMONG US, YOU RAN.
I WAS A COWARD.
I DIDN'T WANT MY LIFE TO CHANGE, BUT I NOW SEE THAT IT HAS TO.
TOO MANY OF THE KER DEPEND ON IT.
I'M THROUGH RUNNING AWAY, MOTHER.
VERY WELL. SHOW ME HOW FAR YOU'VE COME.

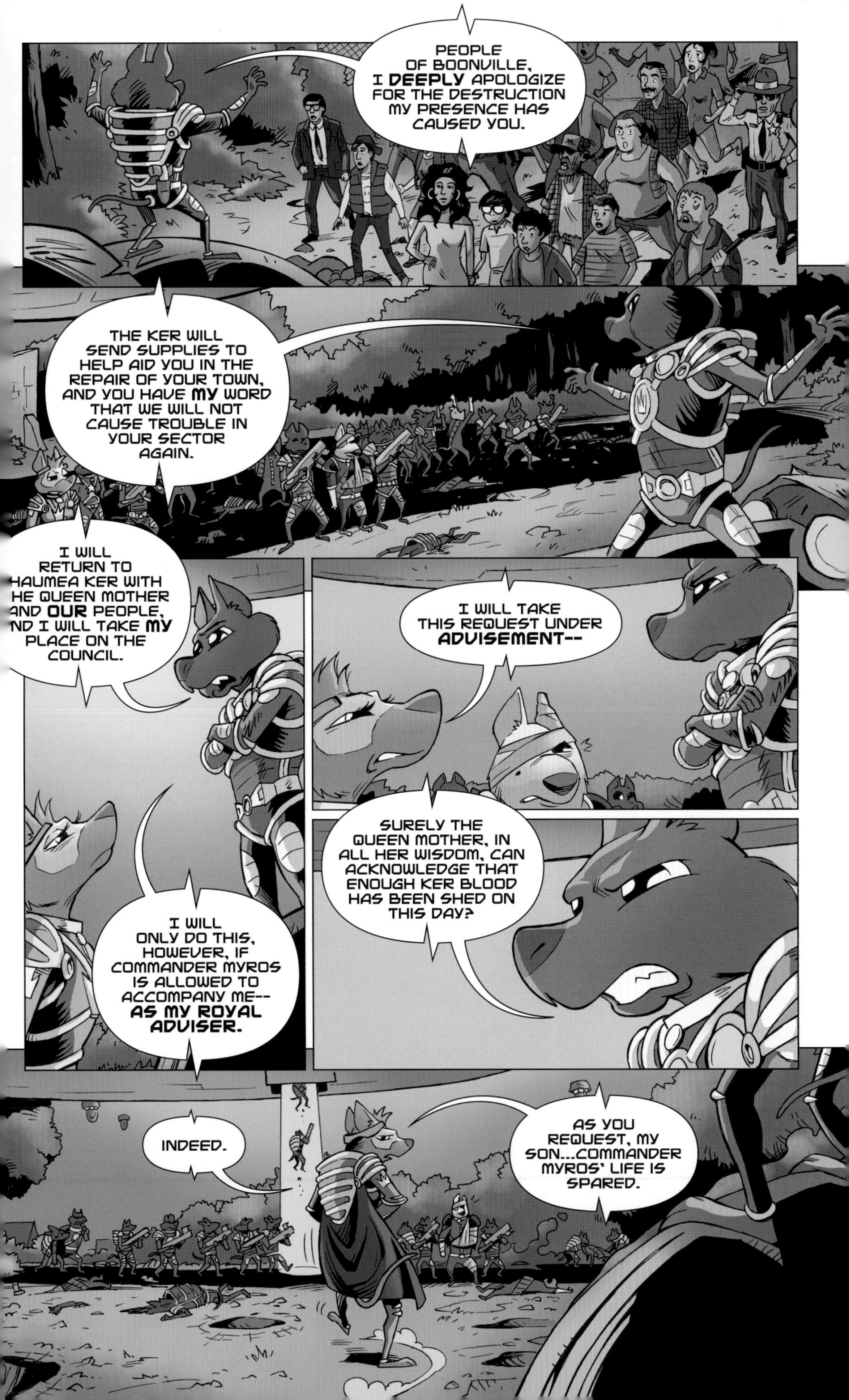
PEOPLE OF BOONVILLE, I **DEEPLY** APOLOGIZE FOR THE DESTRUCTION MY PRESENCE HAS CAUSED YOU.
THE KER WILL SEND SUPPLIES TO HELP AID YOU IN THE REPAIR OF YOUR TOWN, AND YOU HAVE **MY** WORD THAT WE WILL NOT CAUSE TROUBLE IN YOUR SECTOR AGAIN.
I WILL RETURN TO HAUMEA KER WITH HE QUEEN MOTHER AND **OUR** PEOPLE, ND I WILL TAKE **MY** PLACE ON THE COUNCIL.
I WILL ONLY DO THIS, HOWEVER, IF COMMANDER MYROS IS ALLOWED TO ACCOMPANY ME-- **AS MY ROYAL ADVISER.**
I WILL TAKE THIS REQUEST UNDER **ADVISEMENT--**
SURELY THE QUEEN MOTHER, IN ALL HER WISDOM, CAN ACKNOWLEDGE THAT ENOUGH KER BLOOD HAS BEEN SHED ON THIS DAY?
INDEED.
AS YOU REQUEST, MY SON...COMMANDER MYROS' LIFE IS SPARED.

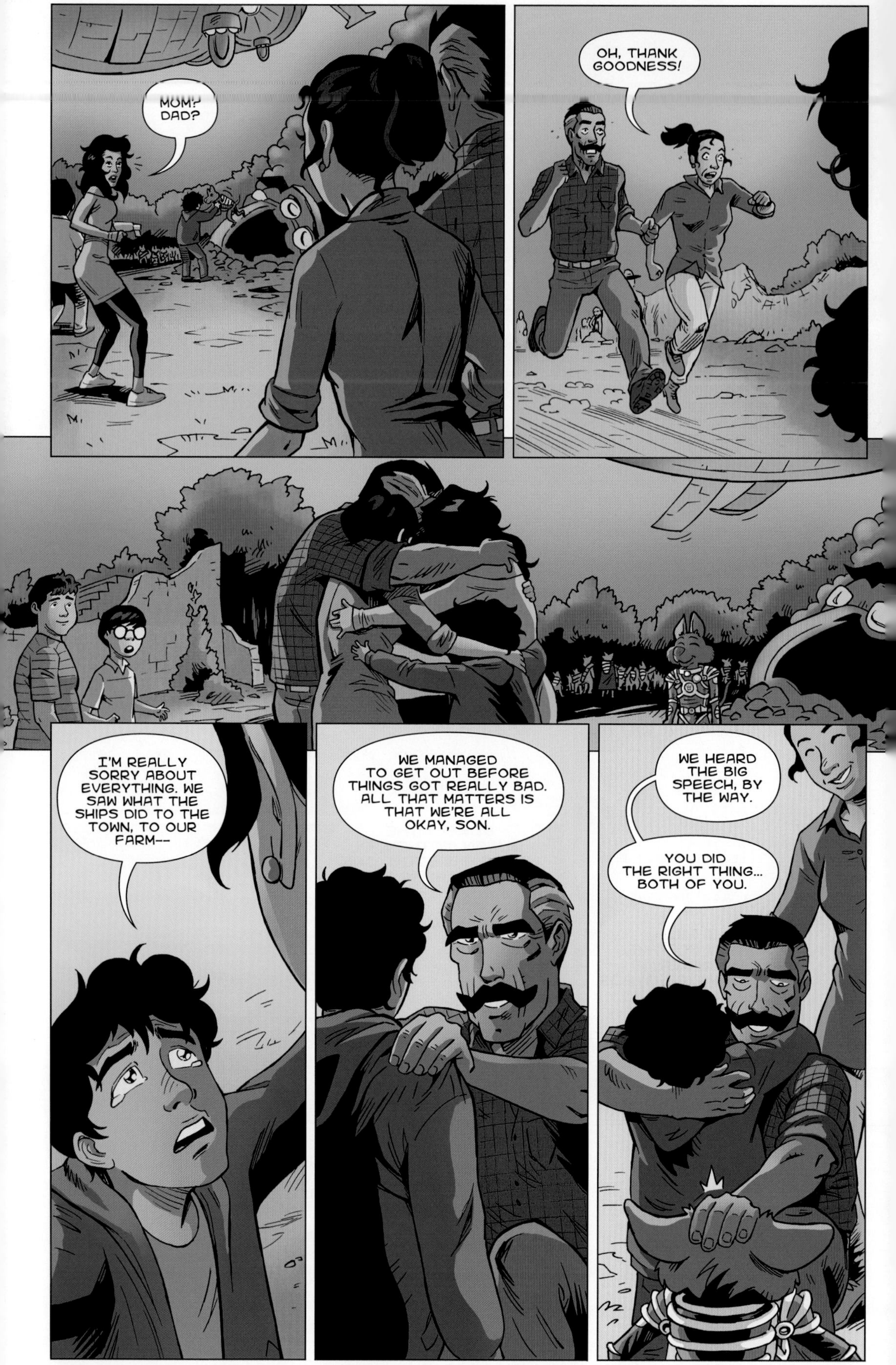
MOM? DAD?
OH, THANK GOODNESS!
I'M REALLY SORRY ABOUT EVERYTHING. WE SAW WHAT THE SHIPS DID TO THE TOWN, TO OUR FARM--
WE MANAGED TO GET OUT BEFORE THINGS GOT REALLY BAD. ALL THAT MATTERS IS THAT WE'RE ALL OKAY, SON.
WE HEARD THE BIG SPEECH, BY THE WAY.
YOU DID THE RIGHT THING... BOTH OF YOU.

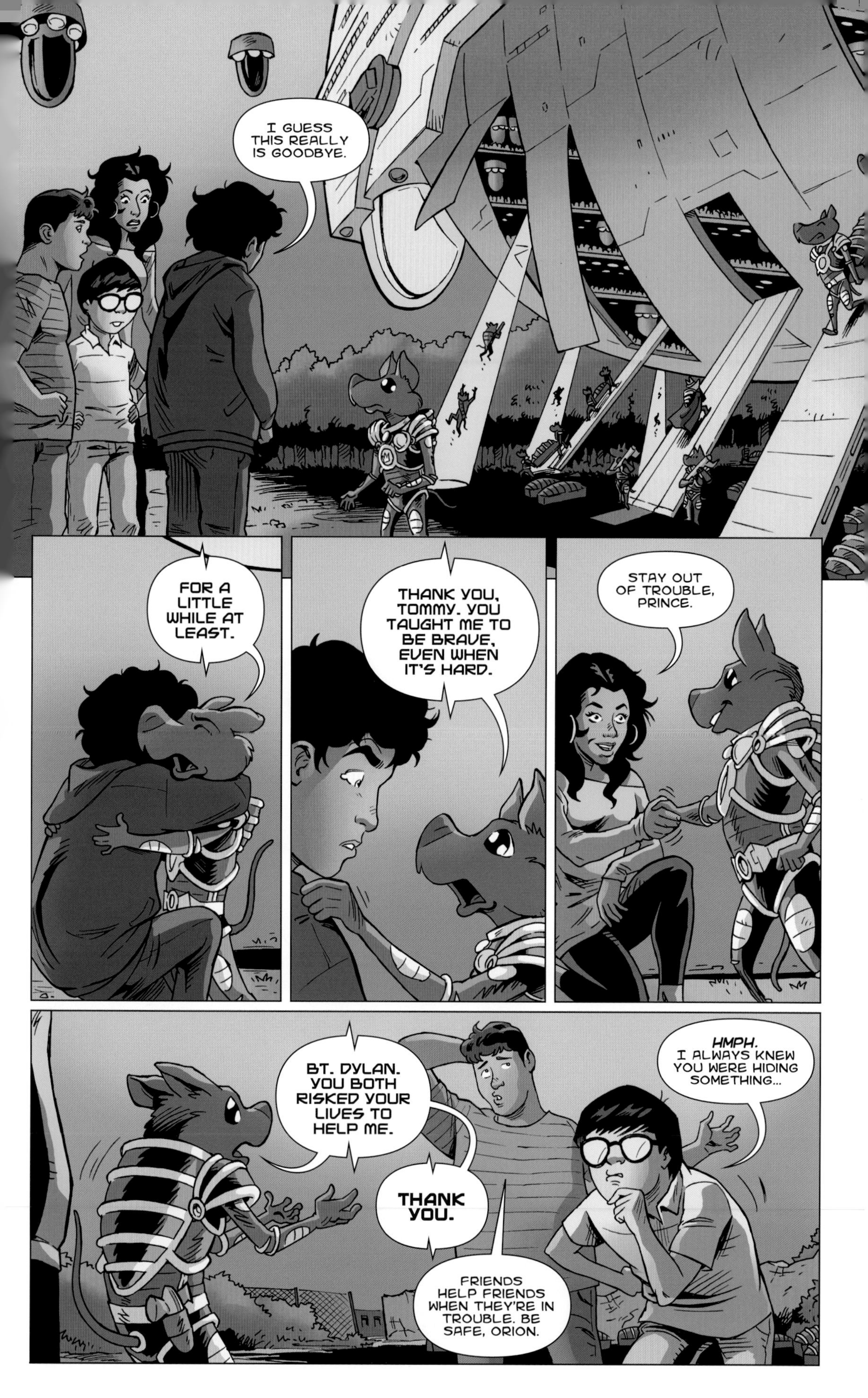
I GUESS THIS REALLY IS GOODBYE.
FOR A LITTLE WHILE AT LEAST.
THANK YOU, TOMMY. YOU TAUGHT ME TO BE BRAVE, EVEN WHEN IT'S HARD.
STAY OUT OF TROUBLE, PRINCE.
BT. DYLAN. YOU BOTH RISKED YOUR LIVES TO HELP ME.
THANK YOU.
HMPH. I ALWAYS KNEW YOU WERE HIDING SOMETHING...
FRIENDS HELP FRIENDS WHEN THEY'RE IN TROUBLE. BE SAFE, ORION.

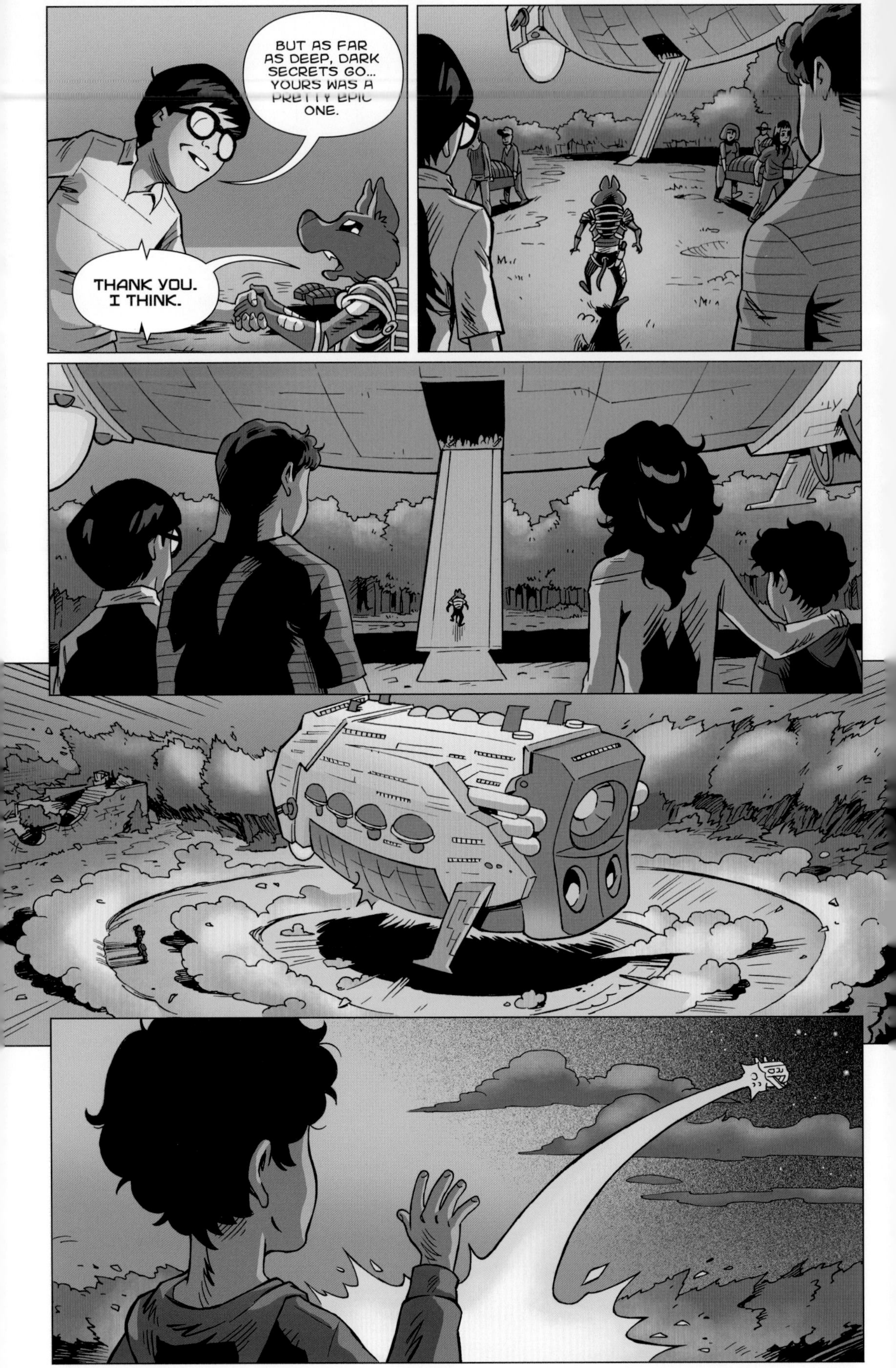
BUT AS FAR AS DEEP, DARK SECRETS GO... YOURS WAS A PRETTY EPIC ONE.
THANK YOU. I THINK.

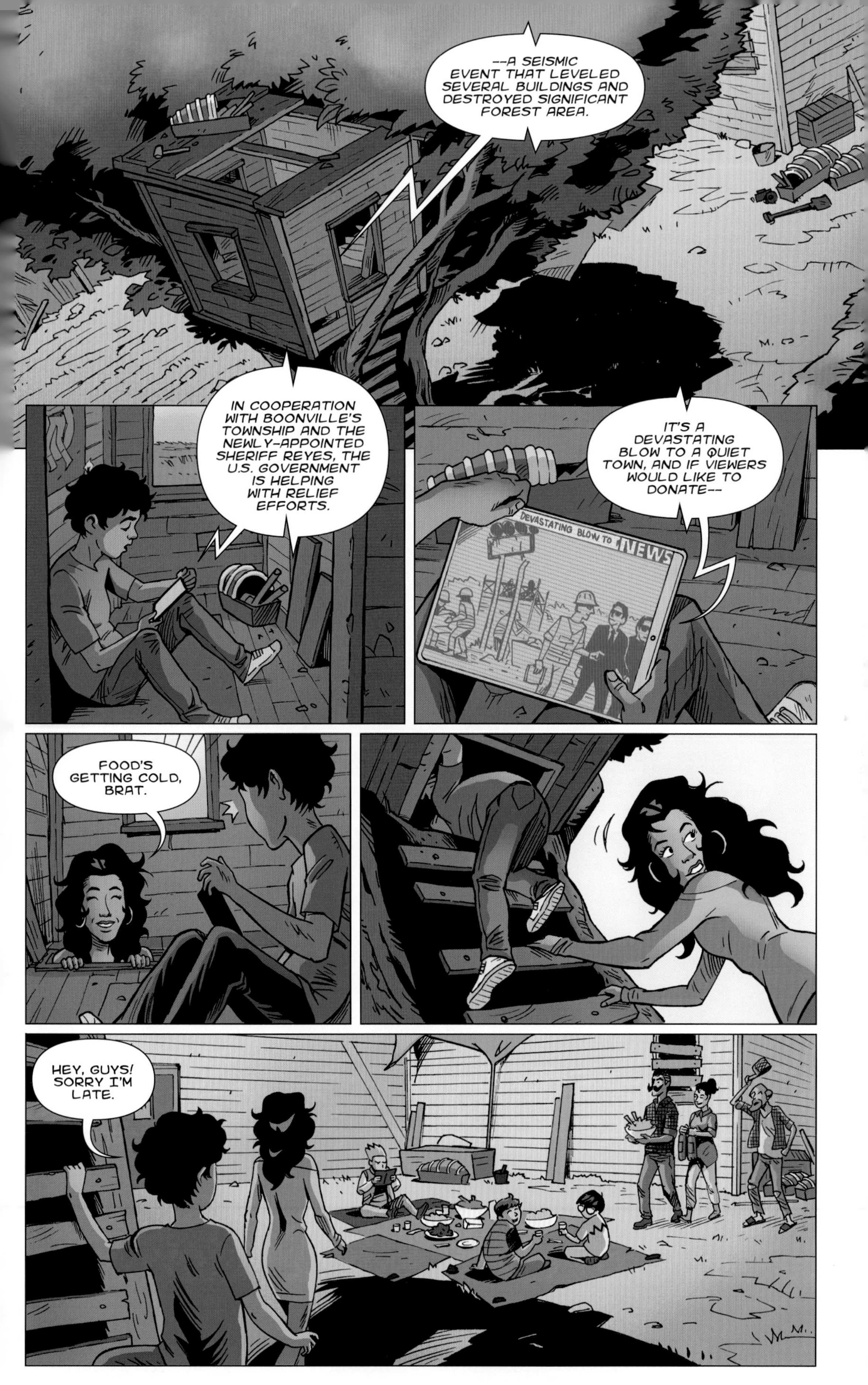
--A SEISMIC EVENT THAT LEVELED SEVERAL BUILDINGS AND DESTROYED SIGNIFICANT FOREST AREA.
IN COOPERATION WITH BOONVILLE'S TOWNSHIP AND THE NEWLY-APPOINTED SHERIFF REYES, THE U.S. GOVERNMENT IS HELPING WITH RELIEF EFFORTS.
IT'S A DEVASTATING BLOW TO A QUIET TOWN, AND IF VIEWERS WOULD LIKE TO DONATE--
DEVASTATING BLOW TO
NEWS
FOOD'S GETTING COLD, BRAT.
HEY, GUYS! SORRY I'M LATE.

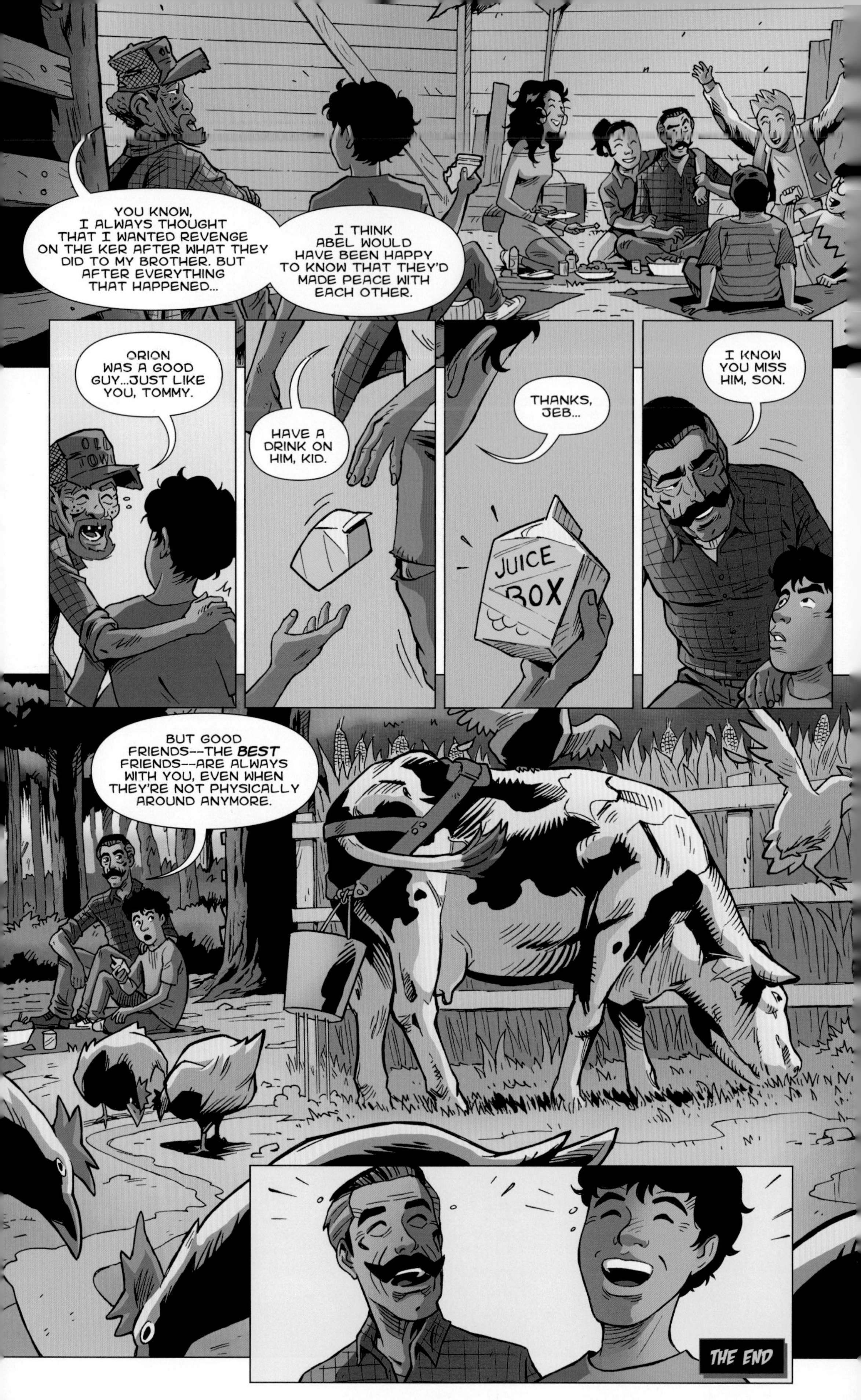
YOU KNOW, I ALWAYS THOUGHT THAT I WANTED REVENGE ON THE KER AFTER WHAT THEY DID TO MY BROTHER. BUT AFTER EVERYTHING THAT HAPPENED...
I THINK ABEL WOULD HAVE BEEN HAPPY TO KNOW THAT THEY'D MADE PEACE WITH EACH OTHER.
ORION WAS A GOOD GUY...JUST LIKE YOU, TOMMY.
HAVE A DRINK ON HIM, KID.
THANKS, JEB...
JUICE BOX
I KNOW YOU MISS HIM, SON.
BUT GOOD FRIENDS--THE **BEST** FRIENDS--ARE ALWAYS WITH YOU, EVEN WHEN THEY'RE NOT PHYSICALLY AROUND ANYMORE.
THE END

ADDITIONAL CONTENT

ORION

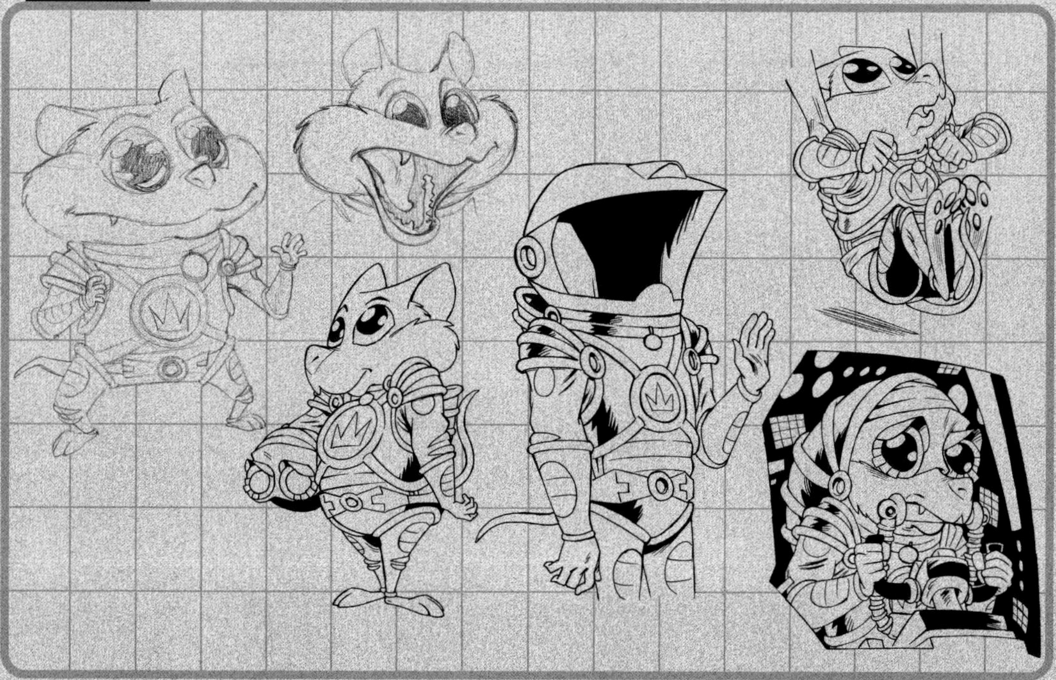

TOMMY MURPHY

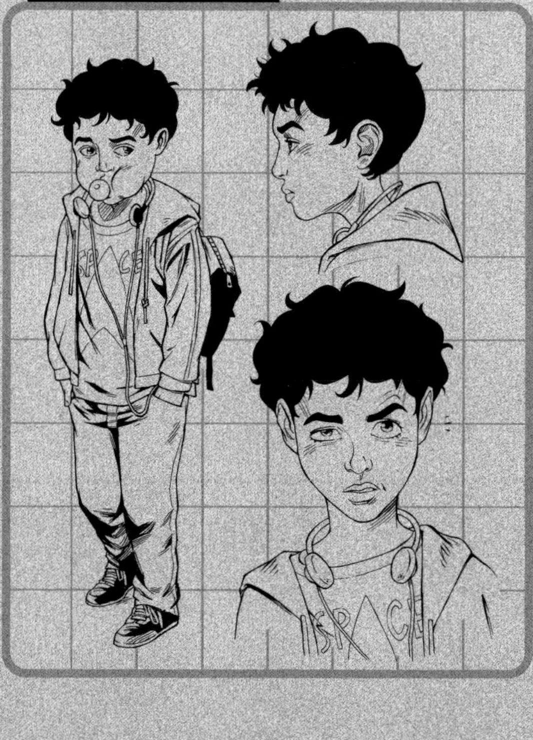

KATHERINE MURPHY

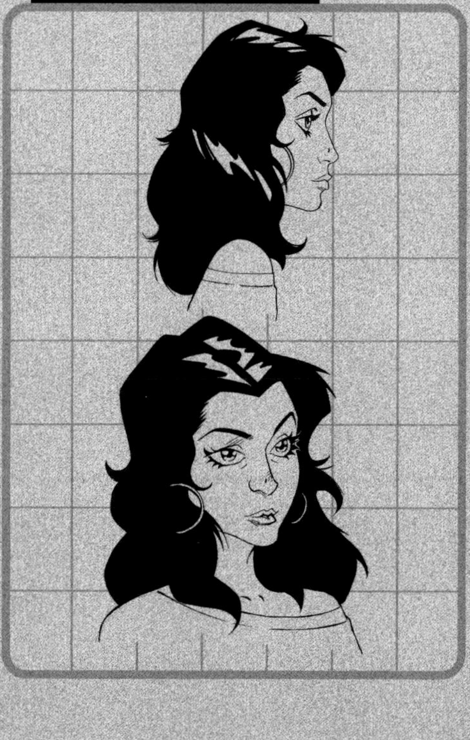

NICK MURPHY

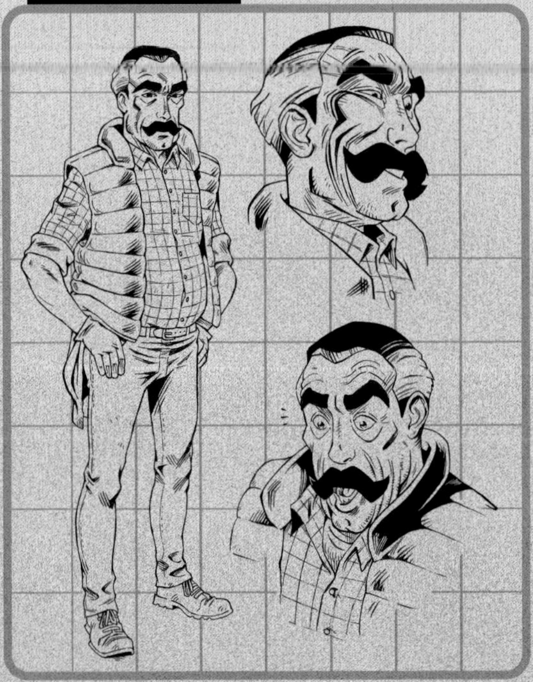

CHUCK DUNHAVY

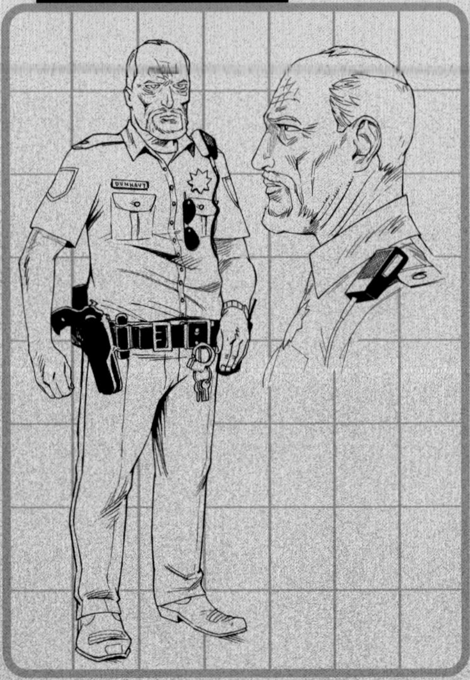

MARTHA MURPHY

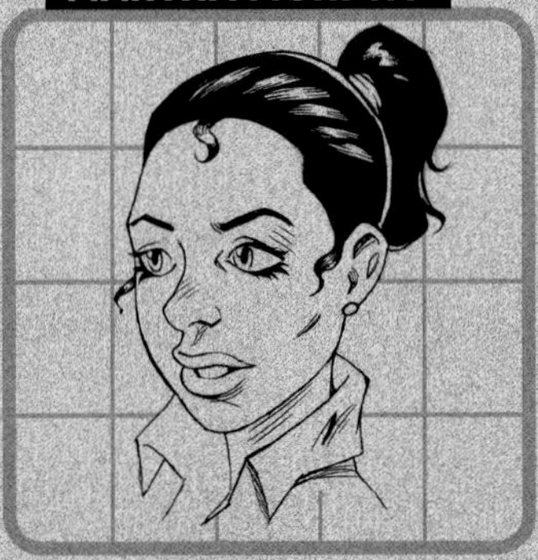

DYLAN HARKAVY

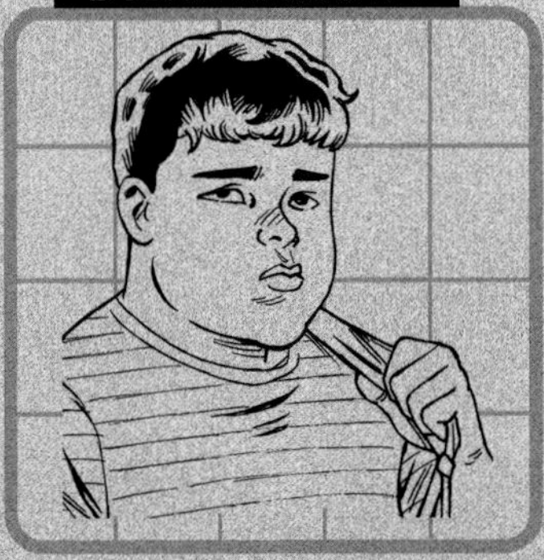

BRIAN THEODORE

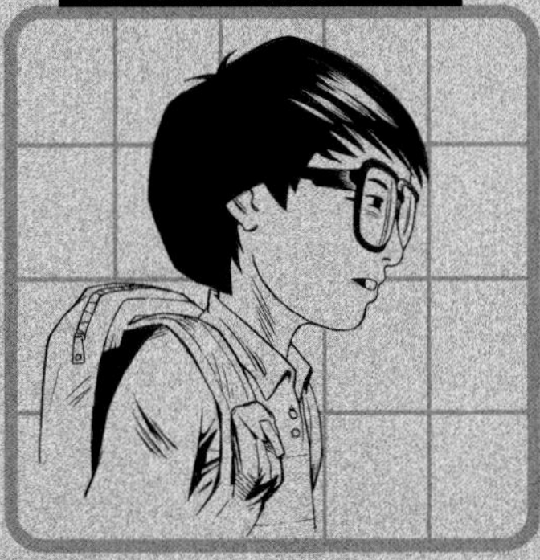

JEB DEAN

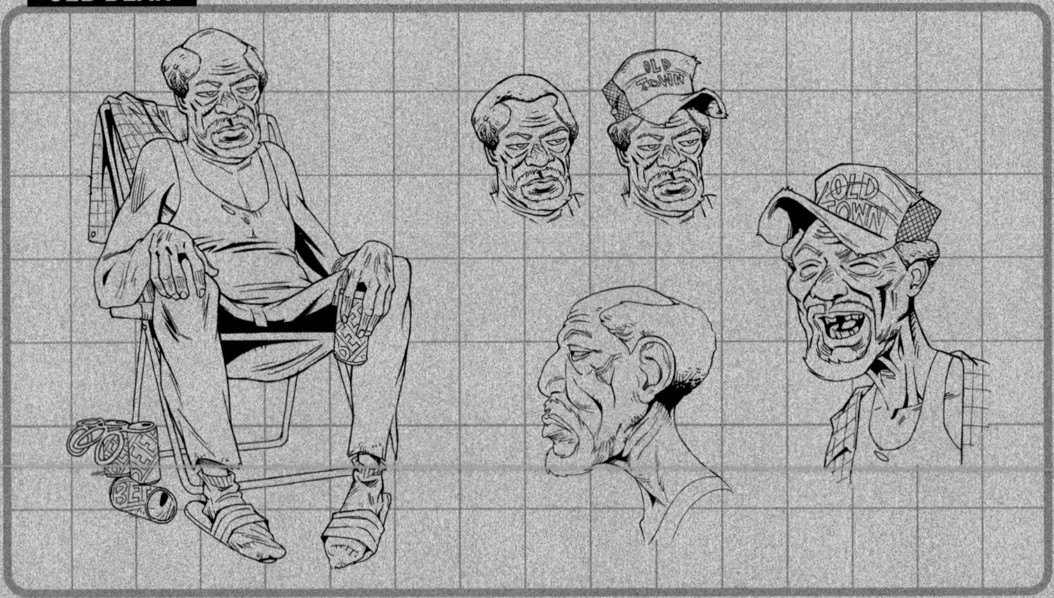
OLD TOWN
OLD TOWN

DISCOVER MAD CAVE
COLLECTED EDITIONS

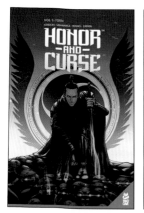

Honor and Curse Vol. 1: Torn
ISBN: 978-0-9981215-5-0

Wolvenheart Vol. 1: Legendary Slayer
ISBN: 978-0-9981215-8-1

Knights of the Golden Sun Vol. 1:
Providence Lost
ISBN: 978-0-9981215-4-3

Battlecats Vol. 2: Fallen Legacy
ISBN: 978-0-9981215-6-7

Stargazer Vol. 1
ISBN: 978-1-952303-04-3

They Fell From the Sky Vol. 1
ISBN: 978-1-952303-13-5

Pantomime Vol. 1
ISBN: 978-1-952303-09-8

Nottingham Vol. 1
ISBN: 978-1-952303-14-2

DISCOVER OTHER TITLES

Battlecats Vol. 1: Hunt for the Dire Beast
ISBN: 978-0-9981215-1-2

Battlecats: Tales of Valderia Vol. 1
ISBN: 978-1-952303-01-2

Midnight Task Force Vol. 1: Hidden
Voices
ISBN: 978-0-9981215-2-9

RV9 Trade Paperback
ISBN: 978-0-9981215-9-8

Over the Ropes Trade Paperback
ISBN: 978-1-952303-00-5

Savage Bastards Trade Paperback
ISBN: 978-1-952303-02-9

Hellfighter Quin Trade Paperback
ISBN: 978-1-952303-03-6

Dry Foot Trade Paperback
ISBN: 978-1-952303-05-0

Terminal Punks Trade Paperback
ISBN: 978-1-952303-07-4

Hollywood Trash Trade Paperback
ISBN: 978-1-952303-08-1

Villainous Trade Paperback
ISBN: 978-1-952303-06-7

SCAN ME

THEY FELL™ FROM THE SKY

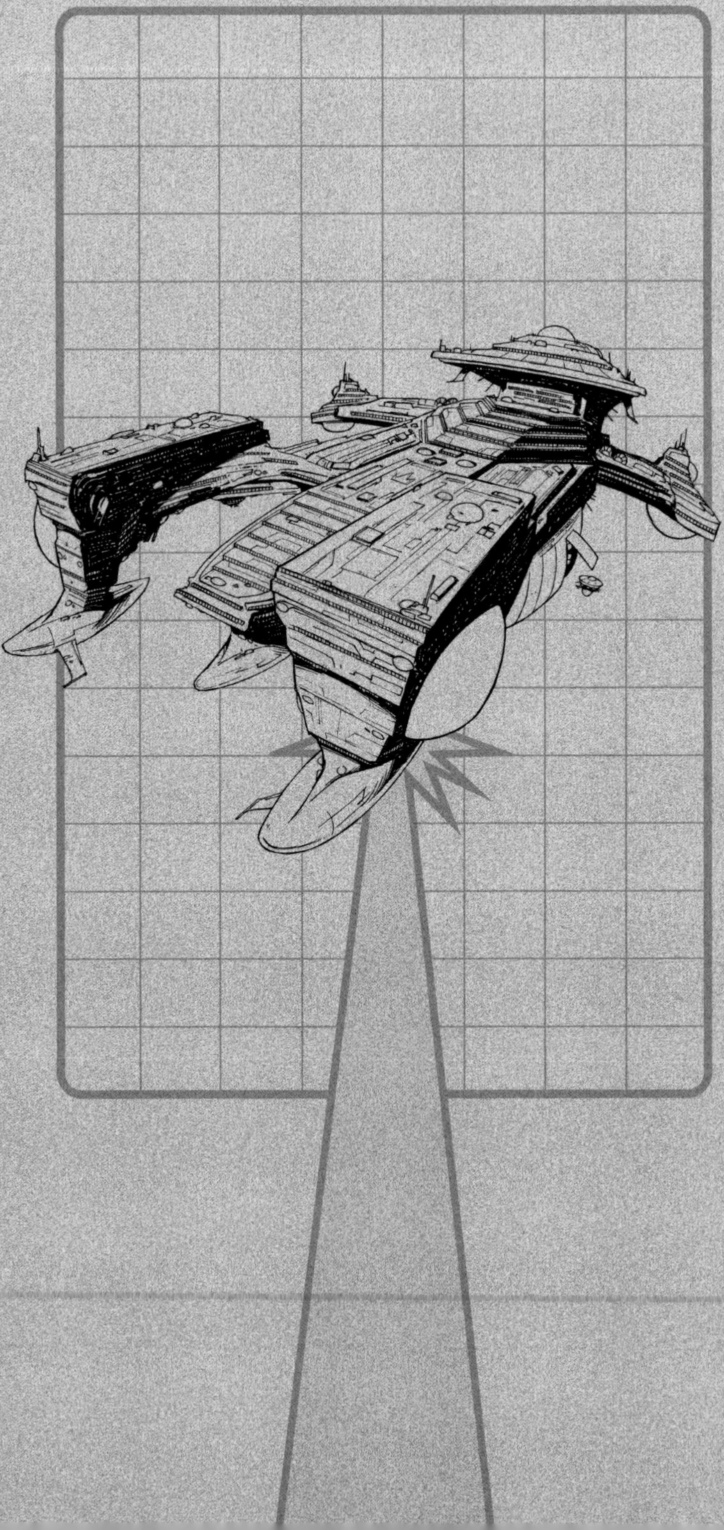